BLUE DRAGON

THE ROY VERNON STORY

BLUE DRAGON
THE ROY VERNON STORY

ROB SAWYER AND DAVID FRANCE

deCoubertin
B O O K S

First published as a hardback by deCoubertin Books Ltd in 2019.

First Edition

deCoubertin Books, 46B Jamaica Street, Baltic Triangle, Liverpool, L1 0AF.

www.decoubertin.co.uk

ISBN: 978-1-9162784-0-0

A CIP catalogue record for this book is available from the British Library.

Cover design by Thomas Regan at Milkyone Creative.

Typeset by Leslie Priestley.

Printed and bound by Jellyfish

Every effort has been made to contact copyright holders for photographs used in this book. If we have overlooked you in any way, please get in touch so that we can rectify this in future editions.

For Joan Sawyer,
who has spent many years
fretting about
both Blackburn Rovers
and Everton.

In memory of
father Ken and sister Louise,
both greatly missed.

People say that football is not as good as it was before the war. Nonsense. If I were to name the four forwards I would most like to have played with, they would be Sammy Chedgzoy, Alex Young, Roy Vernon and Alex Troup.

Dixie Dean

Contents

My advice to the young boys as well as the old pros who made their Goodson debuts in the early 60s? Enjoy yourselves, it'll be an unforgettable experience. But don't shower next to Taffy or you'll get fag ash between your toes.

Alex Young

FOREWORD BY
Bill Kenwright

LIKE MANY SCOUSERS, LIKE MANY KIDS OF THE 1950S, LIKE MANY Evertonians, my world is full of memories. Dave Hickson will always be the greatest centre-forward of them all; Alan Ladd's *Shane* will always be the greatest Western of them all; Elvis will always be in a different stratosphere. All three, plus a small elite few, will live with me until the day I say goodbye to this world and its memories. Royston will always be amongst that hallowed group.

I was just into my teens when he signed for us, in that wonderful period from the late 50s to the early 60s when we seemed to add another gem every other month. Roy was a part of the first group, alongside Tommy Ring and 'Angel' Gabriel, that earned Everton the nickname 'The Mersey Millionaires', thanks to the inestimable John Moores. It's difficult to fully convey the feelings of a lad in the Boys' Pen as he and the other new Everton greats took us up the table after what seemed like an eternity in the wrong half.

The inside-left wasn't a typical striker – to be honest he wasn't a typical footballer – but he enjoyed five wonderful years at Goodison during which he scored in over 50 percent of the games he played. Can you imagine what would be his value, and in his wage packet, if he had a ratio like that these days? But maybe it wasn't just the goals that made him a legend. He undoubtedly had a huge belief in his abilities – an arrogance, even. Along with his skills and his slight frame, there was toughness, a courage that made him stand out from the rest. I will never forget that little lift of the heel as he set off on one of his forays into the opponents' defence – a run that was nearly always followed by a strike of the ball that few could equal.

And I will always remember that moment when Alex 'Chico' Scott took a penalty in an FA Cup tie against Leeds, presumably because he had converted from the spot in the previous home game against Ipswich when Roy didn't play. Scott's spot kick was saved, but the referee blew for an infringement. All of us in the away end breathed a massive sigh of relief. There are few things worse than losing at Elland Road. As Alex picked up the ball to retake the penalty, Roy walked up to him and gently pushed him aside, as if to say: 'I gave you one, but you're not going to have another go'. He literally smashed the ball into the net to equalise and we won the replay at home, where he scored again. In that season, and indeed all the seasons that he wore the beautiful blue, he was a goalscoring machine. In each season that he made thirty appearances or more for the club – which happened on four occasions – he found the net over twenty times.

And then there was Royston and Alex. What Evertonian wouldn't think he'd died and gone to blue heaven when he watched those two? So different, yet so special. The Electric and the Magnifico. Memories that will live forever.

Roy was Everton's top scorer in each of his four full seasons at Goodison Park. He was one of the greatest footballers I've ever seen in an Everton shirt. Taffy was, and is, an Everton legend.

Thank you, Royston.

Bill Kenwright
Chairman
Everton Football Club

Principal References

THE MOST COMMONLY USED REFERENCE MATERIAL IS CREDITED IN superscript wherever possible.

1. Unpublished memoir notes by Roy Vernon
2. Interviews conducted by David France for *Gwladys Street's Blue Book, Alex Young – The Golden Vision,* and other titles
3. Interviews by Becky Tallentire for *Real Footballers Wives', Talking Blue* and *Still Talking Blue*
4. Interviews by Rogan Taylor, Andrew Ward and John Williams for *Three Sides of the Mersey*
5. *Liverpool Daily Post*
6. *Liverpool Echo/Liverpool Echo and Evening Express*
7. *Lancashire Evening Post/Lancashire Post*
8. *The Sentinel*
9. Everton Football Club matchday programme and Evertonian magazine
10. ToffeeWeb

Quotations not attributed are principally from interviews conducted by Rob Sawyer and David France for this book.

Authors' Footnote – Welsh names
Roy Vernon's birthplace, Ffynnongroyw (pronounced fur-non-groi-you) can also be spelt as Ffynnongroew. Both versions have appeared in the publications referenced in this biography. For consistency, the Ffynnongroyw version has been used throughout.

PREFACE BY
Roy Vernon

IN THE SUMMER OF 1972, FRESHLY RETIRED FROM PLAYING AFTER A spell at Great Harwood Football Club, Roy Vernon sat down to commit his football life story to paper. Over several exercise books he documented the highs and lows of his spells playing for Blackburn Rovers, Everton, Stoke City and the Wales team. Honest and forthright, the memoir gave an insight into the man behind the sports headlines. As Roy's wife Norma confessed, her husband was 'an all or nothing personality'. Sadly, he abandoned interest in the project before it came to fruition and the notes lay unseen by all but his wife for nearly five decades. We are grateful to Norma for sharing them. There is no better starting place for this biography than the words of the great man himself.

Well, here we are again: the start of another season. But this time I will be missing it. Missing that first day when suntanned, healthy-looking athletes report back to start yet another gruelling grind through, what will inevitably be, an even harder campaign – both mentally and physically – than the one that has just finished. For, make no mistake, football is getting brutal: not only on a Saturday – which is probably the only knowledge of the game that the average football supporter has – but also in its preparation and training. Quite soon these suntanned heroes will be reduced to vomiting exhaustion, their legs will turn to rubber, their hearts will be thumping, their lungs bursting. Without the physical condi tion that training gives them, they won't be able to earn the salaries they receive.

Mr Average Fan would say: 'I'd do it for their money, they like what they're doing.' Well, let's be honest, I'd do it too, but Father Time has slowed me down.

Last year I played in the Northern Premier League for my local club, Great Harwood. I vividly remember one remark made by a youngster as we left the pitch one afternoon. 'You're a has-been' he said. 'Yes son,' I replied, 'but it's great to have been. I doubt whether you'll ever go.'

Looking back, I still think that I have been lucky to have enjoyed so many moments that make up so many memories for me. So, let's start at the beginning ...

Roy Vernon
1972

INTRODUCTION

IT'S OCTOBER 1962 AND EVERTON FOOTBALL CLUB SITS PROUDLY atop the First Division. Inside a deserted Goodison Park, the club captain stands in his royal blue and white kit, shod in gleaming Puma football boots. With the famous Gwladys Street Stand as his backdrop, he repeatedly volleys the orange Slazenger Zig-Zag ball for the benefit of the photographer. When published on the cover of *World Sports* magazine, this iconic image captured the mercurial North Walian at the height of his powers. One of the most prolific forwards in the country at that time, he was not one for false modesty, demonstrated by a quote – perhaps allegorical – which has regularly been attributed to him over time. When asked about the best strikers in the land, Vernon's response went: 'There's Jimmy Greaves, Denis Law ... and then there's me.'

Come the final match of the 1962/63 league season, a campaign blighted by the harshest winter in living memory, Roy led out his teammates at a sun-bathed Goodison knowing that victory would clinch the title. The stage was set for 'Taffy' to give the most memorable display of his life. At the final whistle he was the hat-trick hero, Fulham had been swept away 4-1 and Everton's first post-war crown had been secured. A lap of honour and a champagne toast from the directors' box followed. This would be the zenith of the Flintshire-born inside-forward's fifteen-year career with Blackburn Rovers, Everton, Stoke City and Wales.

Roy was not your typical athlete; he was stick-thin in build – or as his Stoke City teammate Terry Conroy eloquently put it: 'If he turned sideways you would mark him as absent.' Yet his frame belied immense power and toughness which, when blended with his confidence – bordering on cockiness – and innate football intelligence, made him unstoppable on his day.

As a teenager, he had slipped through Everton's grasp to blossom at Ewood Park under the tutelage of ex-Manchester United and Ireland star, Johnny Carey.

On the international stage he helped Wales to reach the 1958 World Cup Finals, staged in Sweden. He had followed Carey to Merseyside in 1960 – one of the first big-money purchases made by the Toffees with the financial backing of John Moores, the Littlewoods magnate.

Leaving Blackburn with something of a reputation as a loose cannon, Roy's comment upon joining Everton was illustrative of his sardonic sense of humour: 'I am greatly looking forward to playing in front of that wonderful crowd. Some folk say the Goodison crowd are bad lads. Some have said I'm a bad lad. We should get on well together.'

With a strike rate of better than a goal every other game, the sinewy number ten went on to become Everton's leading scorer in each of his four full seasons there and remains one of only six men to have scored 100 or more league goals for the club. With devastating acceleration, balance, breathtaking body swerves, a keen sense of anticipation, rapier-like shooting and more than a bit of the devil, he dovetailed beautifully with the artisanal Alex Young. Those that saw them in action insist that they were the most intuitive striking partnership ever to have graced Goodison.

A chain smoker, a night owl, a gambler, a joker and no respecter of authority, Roy would test the mettle of all his club managers. He felt closest to Carey, yet the uncompromising Harry Catterick was able to channel his energies positively, for a period at least. Awarded the club captaincy, his infectious personality and match-winning goals drove the team to glory. Yet within two years, he was out of form and favour, with manager Catterick less inclined to overlook the transgressions that he might have turned a blind eye to previously. A parting of the ways suited both parties, if not the Goodison faithful.

At Stoke City, Roy enjoyed a fresh lease of life, thriving in the laissez-fare atmosphere engendered by Tony Waddington. After this Indian summer, however, injury and disciplinary issues saw him become a peripheral figure and he left the Victoria Ground, almost unnoticed, upon expiry of his contract in 1970. After a dalliance with South African and non-league football, he walked away from football in 1972, never to return. His love for the game had dissipated as the maverick element was overtaken by regimentation and onerous tactics. Instead he helped in the family business back in his wife's home town of Blackburn. A lifetime affiliation with Senior Service cigarettes took its toll and he succumbed to lung cancer in 1993, aged just 56.

To those that saw him in his pomp for clubs and country, Roy Vernon is one of the most exhilarating players they have had the pleasure to behold. However, at his three clubs he has, in retrospect, been somewhat overlooked. At Rovers he departed before he could be elevated to the status of Bryan Douglas and Ronnie Clayton. At Goodison, the sublimely skilled Young stole the limelight. Had he still been alive to be lauded at the famous Gwladys Street Hall of Fame dinners, maybe things would have been different. Stoke City fans rarely saw the best of the forward and had Gordon Banks, George Eastham and Jimmy Greenhoff to idolise. On the international front, it was his misfortune to be competing with the legendary Ivor Allchurch for the number ten shirt, hence his relatively meagre haul of 32 international caps.

While neither of the authors interviewed the man from Ffynnongroyw, the older wordsmith attended the vast majority of the matches he played for Everton and did meet him fleetingly: 'It was on the Wednesday afternoon before a game against Bolton in 1964 when a school pal and I travelled to Goodison early to collect our tickets for the European Cup game scheduled for the following week. With our Inter Milan tickets in hand, we were killing time waiting for the turnstiles to open when we spotted two stars leaving the massive wooden doors at the club's reception. Roy Vernon was dressed immaculately in a grey Italian suit, whereas Sandy Brown resembled an underpaid school teacher.

'Instantly, I sprinted across the road into the path of a Hillman Imp. While the vehicle was undamaged, I was bloodied and flattened. Sandy ran to assist me, while Roy confronted the driver as if he had disallowed his goal against the Reds. The club captain – with fag dangling from his mouth – berated him and appeared to disagree with the consensus that it had been my fault. Sandy got me onto my feet and helped me into the club's foyer where he watched a commissionaire in a military uniform clean me up and massage my ego. For his part, Roy reminded me of basic curb drill for pedestrians. Before going on their way, both stars put a smile on my face by autographing my ticket. Little did I realise that I would have to surrender it to attend the match against the champions of Italy. It was my only interaction with Roy. However, I was fortunate to befriend Sandy after his playing days were over and was delighted to reciprocate and help get him back onto his feet in his hour of need.'

We believe it is time to put right the omission of Roy Vernon from footballing folklore and bring his considerable achievements and colourful story to a wider audience. We have adopted a novel approach and drawn on first-hand recollections elicited from around 120 teammates and supporters, painstaking research of archive material and access to the Welshman's own unpublished memoir notes to chronicle the life of a unique talent and a true football giant. We hope to do him justice.

Rob Sawyer and David France
September 2019

Authors' Footnote:

It should be noted that the title of this book, *Blue Dragon,* has no connection with the popular purveyor of delicious fish and chips and mouthwatering Chinese takeaway meals, of the same name, located on Goodison Road.

CHAPTER 1

Ffynnongroyw

POINT OF AYR, THE MOST NORTHERLY POINT OF MAINLAND WALES, was for many decades home to one of the largest and advanced collieries in the land. It drew workers from surrounding villages in this predominantly rural area of Flintshire. One such small settlement, Ffynnongroyw, was home to Thomas and Phyllis Vernon who resided in a two-up, two-down terrace house in the deceptively luxurious-sounding Williamson Square. Thomas, a quiet man who enjoyed visiting the bookmakers for a flutter every Saturday, was employed as the colliery pilot – helping coal boats to navigate the so-called 'gutter' from Liverpool Bay.

The couple had five children, four daughters – Vivienne, Sylvia, Ethel and Janet – and one son – Thomas Royston, who was born at home on 14 April 1937. He attended the village primary school along with his friend Ray Jones who was aware that, even at a tender age, his pal had a strong personality and sporting skill to compensate for a lack of inches: 'I was ten months older and a school year ahead of him. We went to the village school down by the church. He was a real character and had he had an answer for everything. There was no football team in the village, so we played in the schoolyard with a little tennis ball. It became crowded once you had seven or eight-a-side but that's when you knew Roy was gifted. He could dribble – you needed two players to tackle him. After we got a proper football, we played in a farmer's field. If there was an odd number of us, the opposing team to Roy's always claimed the extra player as he was so good. We used our coats for goalposts and the goalie at the end that Roy was attacking would narrow them a bit to handicap him. We mostly played football and a bit of cricket. He also liked a game of snooker in a local shop which had a table and table tennis at the church youth club. When a miners' club opened in the village, we could get away with nipping in there in the afternoon.'

Mel Jones was another local boy impressed by his pal's natural talent: 'He could run, twist, turn and do everything – I think that you are born with that gift. Roy used to make a fool of us – he would start at one end of the pitch and dribble all the way to the other end and we would be trying to kick him. He just laughed at us. I always thought that he would have been a good politician as he was a 'Cheeky Charlie' – quick-witted and not afraid to talk to anybody.'

His sisters thought that their football-obsessed brother spent too much of his childhood kicking a ball outside – or inside the house if he was feeling lucky. 'He was very good and easy-going as a brother, he was happy as long as he had a football,' elder sibling Sylvia confirmed. 'As a young teenager he had a part-time delivery job for a grocery store, but such was his passion for football that he paid another lad to do his round whilst he went off to play football.'

Roy's talents were not confined to sport – he was an intelligent and capable student and possessed a decent singing voice. Along with Ray Jones, he was co-opted into the All Saints parish choir: 'We were in the church choir together – I think the vicar only put us in to make up the numbers. I couldn't sing but Roy didn't have a bad voice.' His sister, Ethel, remembers that Roy, ever the deal-maker, was 'bribed' by the vicar to sing in return for the gift of a new football. The angelic voice would be compromised by the lifelong smoking habit for which he would become infamous. Ray Jones called to mind how it came about: 'He was smoking when he was twelve or thirteen. You could buy packets containing five Woodbines and some shops would sell single cigarettes to the less affluent schoolboys.' By adulthood Roy was a fully-paid up member of the chain smokers' club.

Being the only boy in the family, Roy enjoyed his special status and was, according to his sisters, the apple of his mother's eye. It helped that Phyllis, like her son, enjoyed football. Wherever his career took him she followed to watch, be it in Cardiff, East Lancashire, Merseyside or Staffordshire. With no major Football League team in the vicinity, the schoolboy – like many other young North Walians – had been seduced by the soccer giants of Lancashire. If he had any football allegiance it was to Everton Football Club although, in truth, he was far more interested in playing than following the fortunes of the Toffees.

Young Vernon was very capable academically when he put his mind to it. Having passed his Eleven-Plus examination, he attended Rhyl Grammar School, and he soon made his mark on the football pitch at outside-right. A fellow pupil in Rhyl, two academic years his senior, was Billy Russell, who would go on to combine teaching with a successful career at Sheffield United: 'I was football-mad. At school there was a junior team plus a first team for the older boys. I was in the juniors when Roy arrived. He was a little shrimp, the tiniest lad you had ever seen. Seriously, you would never have pictured him as a football player, but he was brilliant right from the start. When you saw him I action, it was a case of "Wow". Of course, he joined the junior team straight away. Obviously, he wasn't slow but his skill factor – the control that he had over the ball at such an early age – was the important thing.'

Loyalties to his school were tested when he enlisted with local team, Mostyn YMCA. After a year with its junior XI, he progressed to the senior side which competed against the likes of Denbigh YMCA and Rhyl YMCA in the Dyserth League. Roy represented the club for two seasons, generally at inside-right forward or on the wing. Others associated with the club included Elfed Ellis (the future FAW President) and the father of Mike England (the future Blackburn, Tottenham and Wales star). Russell outlined his schoolmate's dilemma: 'There was a bit of a conflict because our headmaster wanted him to play for the school team whilst he had established an association with Mostyn YMCA. I understood completely that he wanted to play for his local team. There were many occasions that he turned out for Mostyn rather than the school team, so he ran into a bit of trouble.'

Independent, spirited and distrustful of authority, Roy stuck to his guns and continued to represent Mostyn. He was rewarded with selection for a representative Welsh YMCA team, and in a game against Irish YMCA opponents he netted twice, with Ray Jones also on the scoresheet in a 4-4 draw. Soon Roy was picked to play for Flintshire Schoolboys and, at the age of fourteen, received his first press write-up following the game against Wrexham Schoolboys: 'Some brilliant touches by Flint's inside-right, Royston Vernon of Rhyl Grammar, held the crowd's attention,' reported the *Liverpool Echo*. These performances drew scouts from professional clubs.

Freddie Bennett from Bagillt, who did a spot of scouting for Everton, was impressed and recommended Roy for a trial. A short while after that recommendation, Cliff Britton – the former Everton and England half-back who had assumed the club's managerial position in 1948 – wrote to Thomas and Phyllis Vernon in May 1952, proposing that he and club director Tom Nuttall visit Ffynnongroyw to discuss the possibility of their son joining the club. Subsequently, Roy was invited for a trial along with his pal Ray Jones and John Clayton, a youngster from St. Asaph who played with Roy in the Flintshire Schoolboys side.

Driven by Bennett, who also worked for a local taxi firm, and escorted by Bert Mothersole, the headmaster of Queensferry School and coach of Flintshire Schoolboys, the trial took place at Bellefield. All three boys impressed. Roy and Clayton were invited to take part in further sessions but only the latter, who was twelve months older and attended Rhyl Glyndwr Secondary Modern School, was signed. In subsequent years, Roy suggested that he was not offered terms by Everton Football Club on account of his diminutive frame, a claim that led to some ridicule of the club's judgement. The facts are slightly less clear-cut. Although Roy was keen to join a club, Phyllis Vernon had other ideas about her son's immediate destiny. A move to Merseyside – or anywhere else – was vetoed as she was insistent that her son, who was worldly, mentally mature but never in trouble, remain at home until he had completed his studies at school.

His grammar school reports give testimony that, as time progressed, Roy lost interest in his bookwork and did the minimum required to get by. In academic subjects, a typical assessment read: 'Fair – greater effort needed.' Though he excelled at football, his sports master's comments make amusing reading. The one dated Autumn 1953 stated: 'He is too one-sided and biased for soccer in his approach to physical education. He must develop other skills if he wishes to improve.' The following term, the sports master was similarly scathing: 'There is more to a game than the actual skill required to play. He would do well to remember this.'

The failure to persuade Mrs Vernon that her son's immediate future lay at Goodison Park would, in time, prove costly. Although Everton kept tabs on the youngster in anticipation of the end of his studies, it seems that Cliff Britton's enthusiasm waned. In 1962, Leslie Edwards of the *Liverpool Echo* quoted a letter, from 1953 or early 1954, attributed to Britton, which read: 'Vernon is frail, tires quickly. We are of the opinion that he is not up to the standard required. We judge Vernon by the standards of our other players which are quite high. We did not think the lad measured up in this respect.'6

If indeed Britton had passed on the opportunity, another former international player was not going to make the same mistake. In 1954 Johnny Carey, the ex-Ireland and Manchester United star and 1949 Footballer of the Year, was making his way in football management at Blackburn Rovers. Keen to expand the club's scouting net beyond East Lancashire, he had been tipped-off by an acquaintance to the Ffynnongroyw teenager's potential. A trial was duly arranged. However, when the youngster saw Carey walk away from the touchline after just twenty minutes, he feared that he had blown his chance. Far from it. Indeed, the opposite was true: Carey had seen enough and told the elated trialist that he would be contacting his parents immediately.

In spite of the lack of encouragement from his sports master, Roy was selected to represent Wales Youth against Ireland at the home of Flint Town in 1954. While the visitors were worthy winners, Roy was the star of the game. A perceptive *Flintshire County Herald* observed: 'The game's outstanding player was Royston Vernon, who plays for Mostyn YMCA. Vernon was the life and soul and brains of the Welsh forward line. His play was a pleasure to watch. Assuredly, Vernon is destined for stardom in the highest class.'

As promised, the Blackburn manager kept in touch with the Vernon family and as soon as the schoolboy notified him that his examinations were over, he sought parental permission to bring him to East Lancashire for two weeks of training. Subsequently, the Irishman used all of his charm to convince Thomas and Phyllis that the move would be in their son's best interests.

In early July 1954, the manager wrote:

Dear Mr and Mrs Vernon,

I have just received a letter from Roy telling me that his examinations are now over, but he has not yet received the results. Let us hope that they turn out well. But whatever way it turns out you can be certain that I will have the best interests of your son at heart, not just from a football point of view from but his whole future as well. That is why I am writing for your permission to allow Roy to come to Blackburn on Monday 9 August.

I feel that your son has the makings of a first-class player and, brought up in the right atmosphere of a good club, will surely make the grade. He will be placed in a good home and introduced to boys of excellent character. I shall personally keep an eye on his attention to studies and like the other lads will always be able to turn to me for encouragement and advice.

I look forward to hearing from you so that I can make the necessary arrangements for his accommodation.

Yours sincerely,

J. Carey

These were not to be empty words. Seven years later, Roy underlined the esteem in which he held the man who would become his footballing mentor. In his weekly column for the *Daily Post*, he wrote: 'I was very lucky for Mr Carey seemed to take a personal interest in me from the start. During those early years he was almost like a father figure to me. His door was always open. Mr Carey was never too busy to drop what he was doing and discuss a player's problems as though they were the only things that mattered in the world. It is a marvellous feeling for a lad to realise that someone is willing to work things out for him. If I was worried about my play, I could always go in and discuss it knowing that, from his great experience, he would be able to iron out the self-created mountains.'

It would appear that Everton's loss had been Blackburn's gain – at least for several years.

Rhyl Grammar School already boasted a football starlet in Billy Russell, two years older than Vernon, who was to progress to play for Sheffield United in the Second Division, Bolton Wanderers in the First Division and represent England as an amateur international. Russell was aware of the potential of the boy from Ffynnongroyw: 'Roy was a brilliant footballer. Despite being slight, he had so much speed, terrific ball control plus the physical strength and fiery personality to play against and get the better of much bigger lads.'

CHAPTER 2

Roy of the Rovers

'Roy Vernon was a bloody good footballer. If he had stayed a little longer at Rovers, we may have beaten Wolves in the 1960 FA Cup Final.'

Bryan Douglas

IN THE SUMMER OF 1954, ROY ATTAINED HIS SCHOOL LEAVING Certificate and joined Blackburn Rovers, then a Second Division club. Along with a couple of other hopefuls, the seventeen-year-old was placed into digs in Darwen. True to his word, manager Johnny Carey saw to it that the youngster studied part-time at Blackburn College with a view to gaining an accountancy qualification, should his football career stall.

In no time Roy made an impression on fellow youth players at Blackburn, amongst them Dave Whelan, and gained a nickname which would stick. Whelan, who became a successful entrepreneur and chairman of Wigan Athletic after injury curtailed his playing career, reminisced: 'I was seventeen when we signed Roy. When he arrived at Feniscowles, Rovers' training ground, he said, "I'm from Wales," and we all responded, "Oh, you're a Taffy," and it stuck for the whole length of his career – he was always Taffy. From the start he exhibited significant confidence, more than we were used to seeing. I remember playing against Manchester United's Under-17 team when we got a penalty near the end with the score at 0-0. It was his first game, but he just picked up the ball and declared: "I'm the penalty taker – I'll score." He was so confident. I was the captain and got a ten-bob bonus for a win, so I did not want him to take it. I looked across at the trainer and he said: "Oh, let him take it." So, he put the ball on the spot, looked at the goalkeeper, pointed to the keeper's right-hand side and said: "It's going in that corner." He then stepped and planted it straight in the right-hand corner. Then he said to the keeper: "I told you." That was Taffy – from the very start he had such belief in himself, it was extraordinary. Also, what he did have was ability.'

Roy's speciality was the spot kick – that test of nerves between nominated taker and goalkeeper. He was perfectly suited to it, possessing the confidence and the clean ball-striking required to beat the keeper practically every time. Even in his Mostyn YMCA days he had an enviable record. It was reported that prior to his arrival, the team has missed from the spot in fifteen consecutive attempts. Upon taking on the duties he scored fifteen in sixteen – his one miss being in a 13-0 win.

Initially signed on amateur terms and employed as an office boy before transferring to the ground staff, he was no great lover of menial tasks. It was a time when footballers had to work as part of their apprenticeship before they became fully-fledged professionals and, in the post-war era, also had to do their National Service. Bryan Douglas, three years Vernon's senior, was undertaking his when the Welsh youngster arrived at Ewood but was still eligible to play for Blackburn. Soon enough, he became unwittingly instrumental in an off-the-cuff positional switch with Roy which shaped both of their careers.

'As part of Roy joining Rovers, Johnny Carey had arranged for a Blackburn Rovers XI to play an end-of-season game against a Rhyl and District representative team,' said Douglas. 'Roy was on the right-wing and I was at inside-forward. He wasn't doing much in front of his local crowd, and neither was I. As I had played on the wing for Blackburn Schoolboys, I said: "If you want to get more in the game, go inside and I will play on the wing." It was only a friendly, after all. He went on to have a good game and I enjoyed the afternoon. I am convinced this planted the seed in Johnny Carey's mind. Afterwards our careers ran in parallel, with Roy at inside-left and me at the outside-right.'

Driven by a burning desire to become a professional footballer and well aware of his slight frame and physical limitations, Roy strove to enhance his inherent abilities to look after himself against bigger and more robust opponents. Bryan Douglas recalled that his new pal was unphased by mixing – and mixing it – with senior professionals: 'Right from the word go, from when I first played with him, he was very confident – all the time. Even playing in training matches against experienced people like Bill Eckersley, he didn't shy away from any confrontation. With that confidence it was only a matter of time before he became a regular in the first team.'

This view was shared by Harry Berry, then a young Rovers supporter: 'I remember him in the Rovers youth team, you could tell that he could play. They didn't advance him very fast, perhaps because they thought he was a bit fragile. He did look frail and you thought that he would not like the physical side of the game, but he could dish it back if he got hit. The Flintshire youngster didn't back down to anybody. He had everything that you could care to mention as a footballer and was one of those players who could do everything. He was quick and once he was away from the defender there was no way he would be caught. He could tackle, pass, shoot, pick out a man and also avoid markers to find space for himself. If he'd have looked after himself, Roy Vernon could have become one of the world's greats.'

Taffy made his debut for the reserves, as an amateur, in the Central League in November 1954. He displayed significant promise. An unattributed report in the *Blackburn Times* noted: 'Royston Vernon, the seventeen-year-old Welsh inside-left of the Rovers' youth side, who is considered to have exceptional promise, had his first outing in the reserve team at Stoke City as a stand-in on the right-wing. He gave a most encouraging display in atrocious ground conditions.' The writer also noted that Vernon had been chosen to play for an FA of Wales XI against the Welsh Universities in Wrexham the following month.

Following a brilliant display for Wales Youth against Scotland at Cardiff, the forward was selected to play at outside-right in an amateur international - a notable achievement in that era. That hankered-after appearance came on 5th March 1955 at Bangor City's Farrar Road ground – Wales lost 5-0 to Scotland. In addition to men named Williams, Evans, Griffiths and Owens, the Wales side included Phil Woosnam, then of the 55th Heavy Anti-Aircraft Regiment of the Royal Artillery and Idwal Robling of Lovell's Athletic. Woosnam, a graduate of Bangor University, progressed to earn seventeen full international caps and later served as Commissioner of the North American Soccer League. Robling would go on to make his name as a football commentator at BBC Wales for almost forty years.

The scrubbing and painting of the Ewood stadium ceased when Roy, having achieved his ambition of being capped at amateur level, turned professional. The terms of his first contract were £8 per week and, in due course, he made his professional debut for Blackburn Rovers reserves at Goodison in a 2-2 draw with an Everton side featuring John Clayton, his one-time Flintshire Schoolboys teammate.

The future looked bright. Johnny Carey was committed to easing out his veterans and replacing them with the hungry, talented teenagers who would come to be dubbed 'Carey's Chicks' by the press, a nod to the Busby Babes. The likes of Tommy Briggs, Eddie Crossan and Eddie Quigley were gradually eased out, and in came Ronnie Clayton, Bryan Douglas, Mick McGrath and others. Roy's big break came in September 1955. It was one of his happiest memories in football: 'Johnny Carey called me into his office and said, quite calmly: "You're in the first team tomorrow against Liverpool." He whispered something about having confidence in me, the other players having the same confidence in me and that all I had to do was play in the way I had in training and the reserves and I would claim the outside-right position for my own. I came out of his office somewhat stunned and yet so delighted that I ran to tell Jack Weddle, the trainer, and Jock Wightman, his assistant, that I was in the first team. Of course, they knew already, it seems that everyone had known but me, and they all wished me good luck. In my debut I got rave write-ups. After all, how could I have played badly with the other four forwards being Crossan, Briggs, Quigley and [Bobby] Langton?'[1]

Roy enjoyed a very encouraging debut in a Second Division clash with Billy Liddell and Liverpool at Ewood Park. William Westall of the *Blackburn Times* reported: 'An interesting feature was the debut of eighteen-year-old Royston Vernon who last season gained youth and amateur international honours for Wales and became a professional in March.' Though Liverpool scored two goals and had another disallowed in the opening ten minutes, Blackburn fought back. The journalist marvelled at the youngster's maturity: 'Vernon, who was showing excellent control and craft, cut in dangerously to be stopped by John Molyneux, another debutant, in a desperate tackle. The right-winger also went close with a cross-shot.' Rovers persisted and reduced the arrears after 32 minutes following more splendid work on the right by Vernon. Westall continued: 'From a corner won and taken by the Welsh debutant, Tommy Briggs got in a shot which was beaten out to Bobby Langton, whom with his back to goal hooked the ball over his head and into the net.' Clearly enjoying his senior debut, Vernon was also involved in the goal to make it 2-2: 'Vernon cut in from the wing and chipped the ball into the middle where Tommy Briggs's rather tame effort was blocked for Eddie Crossan to follow up and slam home. After falling behind again, Blackburn piled on the pressure. The equaliser came in the 75th minute: 'Vernon made ground on the right and won a thrown-in. Ronnie Clayton's long throw resulted in a melee in the goal-mouth from which Crossan scored.' It had been an impressive baptism. Vernon had been involved in all three goals.

The *Lancashire Evening Telegraph* also acclaimed Vernon's performance: 'He was the boy behind the comeback. His fast runs were a constant source of trouble to Lambert. The eighteen-year-old debutant right-winger showed that manager Johnny Carey has a 'find'.'[7]

That momentous day marked another milestone in the debutant's life as he started dating Norma Tierney, who worked as a shorthand typist at the local Gas Board. Norma recounts that the couple were, in fact, already acquainted: 'I didn't know it at the time, but he used to see me on the bus on his way home from technical college. Then we met at the Easter Fair. I was with my friend Marion and he was with Derek Hughes, a player from the Rovers B team. They paid for us to go on one of the rides and we made a date for the following week. He didn't turn up! I didn't see him again before he went home to Wales for the summer. After he played in the first team against Liverpool, he went to the dance at King George's Hall and came over to me. I thought to myself: "I'll dance with him and then stand him up like he did to me". Roy apologised, saying: "I am awfully sorry – I didn't have two ha'pennies to rub together – that's why I didn't turn up." Then he kept hold of my hand, as if to say, "I've told you and that's that." Norma didn't stand him up and they were soon going steady.

What was life like for Norma with her sometimes hot-headed future husband? She told the Everton matchday programme: 'He could be a bit fiery! He had his Welsh temper and used to drive me mad sometimes. But it would blow over in two minutes and we did get on well. He didn't wallow, he didn't sulk. He'd shout and bawl and the next minute he'd be smiling at me, especially when he was in the wrong!'

Just weeks after his auspicious debut, a buff-coloured envelope dropped onto his doormat. It told him that he was to report for National Service. 'I took the letter to show Mr Carey who told me that everyone had to do National Service, but if I kept up my training, I would be able to travel at weekends to play. He always gave me sound advice and I've always had the greatest admiration and respect for him. He along with Jack Weddle and Jock Wightman gave me my chance in football. To these men I will always be grateful.'[1]

Roy was lucky in comparison to other young pros who were posted much further afield and was assigned a desk job upon joining the Royal Welsh Fusiliers.

This convenient posting enabled him to get back to Blackburn for weekend matches. He would move to digs two doors down from the Tierney household on Infirmary Road and was treated as almost a surrogate son by Norma's family.

Graham Lewis, who served alongside him, recalled: 'He was a Lance Corporal Company Clerk at Hightown Barracks. This involved a bit of typing and issuing rail passes, etc. Mr Carey, his manager, used to ring Company Sergeant Major Davies to ask for Roy to be allowed time off to play at weekends. Sometimes he paid other clerks a few bob to do his weekend duties so that he could play. The Army was very good to him. The only physical activities he undertook were morning muster parades and occasional guard duties.' Lewis disclosed that even in a military setting, his friend's cheeky personality shone through: 'He was what you would call in Army terms "a cocky little bastard".'

Gareth Pritchard also encountered Roy on National Service in Wrexham: 'He was a bit of a character. The Royal Welsh had a Second Lieutenant there – the son of Lord Trevor. He had come down from Sandhurst and was on his first job. He used to ride a horse and Roy would say mischievously: "That's a nice horse you've got there, sir." Perhaps missing his wit, the son of Lord Trevor replied: "Oh thank you, Corporal Vernon."' Another benefit was that the military regime helped build up his physique. Although Roy was a reasonable 5ft 9in or even 5ft 10in stature, there was – to coin the phrase – more meat on a butcher's pencil. While his excessive nicotine intake may have contributed, he didn't have a great appetite for food, preferring small portions and playing with what was on his plate rather than eating it. 'I eat to live, not live to eat,' was the explanation he would give to his girlfriend. Nonetheless, through his military regime at Wrexham and training at Blackburn he developed a deceptively strong, wiry frame which gave him the ability to take a buffeting but also accelerate and swerve past opponents. Latterly, he would state that his modest frame never held him back: 'The only way to play is the hard way, full out all the time.'[1]

'I was in the Army Medical Corps in Wrexham,' Gareth Pritchard remembered. 'At the time, Roy was playing for Blackburn Rovers and we treated him at the medical room on Mondays. There were cuts and bruises from top to bottom. He would say: "And they reckon I'm a dirty player!" On the playing field at the back of the barracks, he had a forty-gallon oil drum filled with sand – he would practice kicking the ball at it and for ages. Nine times out of ten, he would be there to meet the rebound. Roy would practice on his own or with a couple of lads passing to him. I recall that he turned out for the Royal Welsh football team once or twice. During the Ambulance Cup competition at Rhos, he came on for ten minutes in the second-half and scored three goals.'

The Welshman would reap the benefit of that practice, hitting double figures for the Blackburn first team during the 1956/57 season. Whilst on desk in Wrexham Barracks in April 1957, he took a call from The *Daily Post* sports desk advising him that he had been called up to the Wales senior squad for an international fixture against Northern Ireland in Belfast. On the Sunday before the midweek match, Roy joined the rest of the squad at the Adelphi Hotel in Liverpool and penned a touching letter to his parents:

Monday

Dear Mum and Dad,

Just a few lines checking you are all ok at home. I arrived here ok on Sunday and we were training on Liverpool's ground this morning. We sail across to Ireland tonight.

If you decide to go, Mum, Norma and I will pay for you, seeing as this is my first game for Wales. I'll be looking out for whoever goes with tickets for them. Hoping you can make it.

As ever, lots of love.

Roy xxx

Four days short of his twentieth birthday Roy Vernon ran out at Windsor Park proudly wearing the red shirt of his country. Prior to kick-off, he received numerous telegrams of congratulation from family and friends, including Mostyn YMCA, Flintshire Schoolboys and his parish priest. His family would not make the crossing to Belfast but never missed future international appearances on home soil. The game, which finished goalless, was exciting with many missed chances. A couple of newspapers suggested that 'young Vernon showed many good touches'.

Nevertheless, Roy's Army-enforced absence from Ewood Park presented openings to Bryan Douglas, his friend but competitor: 'For the twelve weeks I was square-bashing, Dougie turned it on and when he did that no words can express the brilliance of his performance,' Roy lamented. 'So that was that – no more football for me whilst the Rovers went on their winning way, yet again they just missed promotion [finishing in fourth in the 1956/57 campaign, two points behind promoted Nottingham Forest in second].' Then another sensation shook Blackburn: most of the older players were transferred and when I came out of the Army, I was a Welsh international and a regular first-team player.'[1]

When his two-year stint of National Service concluded in November 1957, his Commanding Officer rated his behaviour as 'very good' and commented: 'Vernon will be a great asset to any soccer club or sporting organisation as a sportsman and as a leader in physical recreation in Wales or England.'

Back on civvy street, Roy could focus on Blackburn's push for promotion to the First Division. Johnny Carey had blended an attacking team of youth and experience that was a joy to watch. Along with promoting talent from within, Carey made astute signings, none more so than Ally MacLeod, St Mirren's outside-left, and Matt Woods, Everton's imposing reserve team centre-half. Fred Cumpstey was a young supporter who retains fond memories of 'Carey's Chicks', especially Vernon and Douglas: 'It was a golden era – probably even more so than when Rovers won the Premiership in 1995. Vernon was a delight to watch. It helped that he played in a very good team with a very good forward line with Bryan Douglas, Peter Dobing, Tommy Johnston (then later Derek Dougan) and Ally MacLeod. For me, he is just behind Douglas as the greatest player I have seen in a blue and white-halved shirt – even above Alan Shearer. Shearer was a prolific goalscorer but couldn't do things with the ball that Vernon and Douglas could do. The Welshman was a very creative footballer with an advanced football brain. He could pick a pass and see things happening that other players couldn't, and he had a terrific shot on him. He could hammer a ball and could also spray forty-yard and fifty-yard passes just like Eddie Quigley, his predecessor. He was paper thin yet very powerful and sinewy – it took a lot to knock him off the ball.'

Cumpstey also mentioned the fire that many of the greatest players possess: 'He had a mean streak – he didn't take any prisoners. If there was a bad tackle on Douglas, the right-winger would get up and walk away and shake it off – like Finney and Matthews – but Vernon would always tend to react and be quite vicious in those situations.'

In the FA Cup, Roy made a lasting impression on the 75,000 supporters present for the fourth round tie at Goodison between Everton and Blackburn in January 1958. The visitors were not flattered by the 2-1 scoreline. The local journalist Ranger wrote: 'Well that's that. Rosy dreams of Everton making a splash in the cup this year have gone west. They were demolished almost without trace by an infinitely better footballing side. Blackburn looked like the First Division side whereas Everton struggled and struggled – lacking co-ordination in attack and bewitched and bewildered in defence by the speedy and talented Rovers forwards. Blackburn were well ahead individually and collectively and might have won by a bigger margin had the home goal not enjoyed some miraculous escapes.'[6]

Fellow reporter Leslie Edwards concurred: 'The man of the match was Douglas. He is in the Matthews mould and has copied some of the maestro's tricks – which coming in such confined space look so spectacular. Towards the end, he came in for some tough treatment from Donovan and on one occasion after injury was carried from the field like a babe-in-arms by the trainers. Vernon began to tire after his great work in the first half, but this Rhyl boy showed what a great potential he has. The Blackburn line, with MacLeod threatening to do as much on the left as Douglas and with the hard-working Dobing and Stephenson to commend it, was far ahead of Everton's, which failed to move together despite the prompting of Meagan and Birch. Blackburn's other great personality was Clayton at half-back. When in doubt they let the right-half have it. This seemed to be Blackburn's main tactic, and rarely did he fail defensively or as a constructing force.'[5]

Off the pitch, Roy was developing a new racing passion to complement his love of having a flutter on the horses. Herbert Smith, a Blackburn-based dealer in war salvage, owned several racing greyhounds and introduced the footballer to the sport. In the late 1920s and 1930s, dog racing was an extremely popular spectator sport and tracks sprung up all over the country, particularly in the North West. There was, therefore, no shortage of venues for the Blue Dragon and his pals to visit with weekly meetings held in Blackpool, Chester, Ellesmere Port, Liverpool (Seaforth and White City), Preston, Salford, St Helens, Westhoughton and Wigan. Nowadays very few of these venues survive. One of his favourites was the Raikes Park Stadium near Bolton's Burnden Park. With a main stand containing three bars, it was considered the leading independent track in the land. Inconveniently for Roy, the meetings were held on Wednesday and Saturday nights.

It meant that during the winter he patronised the Hill Street Stadium in Blackburn. Located just one mile from the town centre, it boasted a two-tier grandstand which stretched the length of the start and finish straight and a single-tiered covered stand on the back straight. Slightly further from home, he enjoyed the luxurious facilities at the Belle Vue Stadium in Gorton, Manchester. The first purpose-built greyhound stadium had a capacity of 25,000 and was popular with professional footballers from across the North West. Both of its main stands and restaurants were packed on Saturday evenings. Nowadays, the venue is shared with stock car racing and motorcycle speedway. Less luxurious but more convenient was Manchester's White City Stadium, located near United's Old Trafford ground. Long gone, it provided a grandstand with 9,000 seats and additional covered accommodation for 40,000 other spectators.

His interest in greyhound racing was shared with Bryan Douglas: 'We enjoyed going to the dogs. There was a race meeting in Blackburn on Mondays and Fridays and one in Bolton too. A couple of our friends owned dogs and we went along to support them and have a few bets. When Rovers were playing in London, Roy and I would go to Harringay Stadium. There, we'd meet some of the lads from Tottenham and Chelsea. So, we'd be outside at the dog track on a Friday night whilst the rest of the team was at the Palladium.'

More important matters were pressing, however, with his pending nuptials, and the couple tied the knot at St Mary's Catholic Church on 17 February 1958. Norma revealed that Roy had not proposed in the traditional manner: 'He did not get down on one knee, he just more-or-less said: "We'll get engaged." That was Roy; no such thing as proposing. He was so confident. I think that he asked my dad if it was okay though.' Roy had been raised as an Anglican so, in preparation for the wedding, took Catholic instruction from the parish priest. With Father Wilkinson being a devout Rovers supporter, the conversation soon turned to soccer rather than scripture. At the point at which the instruction was supposed to have been completed, the priest asked: 'Are you converting because you want to become a Catholic or just because you want to get married to Norma in church?' When he intimated that it was the latter, the priest was clear: 'As long as you bring up any children Catholic just remain a good man in your own religion.' And that was that, he didn't convert to Catholicism.

The best man was Norma's brother, David. The bridesmaids were his sisters, Ethel and Janet, alongside Norma's sister, Liz. Johnny Carey and a few Rovers players attended the wedding. The bride recalled that the honeymoon plans were compromised by the demands of football: 'Rovers had played in the FA Cup on the Saturday and drew. We got married on the Monday and Roy had to train on the Tuesday in preparation for the replay on the Thursday night. So, after the reception we went back to my parents' home for a buffet. Whilst the party carried on, we left for one night at the Metropole Hotel in Blackpool and returned by the train during the next morning to our nice house on Ramsgreave Drive.' Roy duly turned out in the replay against Cardiff – a 2-1 victory.

The FA Cup run continued with a sixth-round tie against Liverpool at Ewood on 1 March. Trailing 1-0 with about fifteen minutes left on the clock, things looked bleak when Ronnie Clayton was forced off the field following a clash with Billy Liddell. However, the right-half returned to head home Roy's precise free-kick and level the scores, and the magnificent comeback was completed soon after when Ally MacLeod volleyed home a Bryan Douglas cross. Three weeks on, Roy and his teammates stepped out against neighbours Bolton Wanderers in the semi-final at Maine Road. Wembley appeared to be on the horizon with Rovers leading through a headed goal by Peter Dobing, but two goals in a minute – the first suspiciously offside – from Ralph Gubbins, Nat Lofthouse's stand-in, broke Blackburn hearts.

There would be a happier ending to the league campaign. With Roy ever-present at inside-left, Blackburn picked up points in all but two fixtures after Boxing Day. Although integral to the team's push for promotion, he was not prolific until the season approached its climax. The acquisition of experienced Scottish centre-forward Tommy Johnston, from Leyton Orient, was a fillip but when the directors baulked at the asking price, Johnny Carey issued the telling ultimatum that his signing was essential if the club was serious about reaching the top flight. Mick McGrath was impressed by the new recruit: 'He looked like an old man compared with some of us kids but he knew his job - if you supplied him in the box he'd get the goals.'

With three matches remaining, Roy benefited from the space created by the new number nine – who played with a bandaged withered arm, the result of a coal mining injury. He went on to net a memorable hat-trick in an emphatic 4-1 victory over Johnston's former team. In the opening minute, Vernon side-footed home a pass from Roy Stephenson. His second came in the 47th minute. It was far more dramatic. Centurion in the *Blackburn Times* reported: 'Harry Leyland's punt was headed on by Johnston to Vernon. The Welsh international had the ball under control in a flash, ran with it and then let loose a terrific drive which went over Frank George's outstretched hands into the net – a brilliant goal.' Shortly after Ally MacLeod had added another, Roy completed his hat-trick in the 61st minute. Centurion continued: 'Goal hungry, the Rovers hit Leyton with everything bar the trainer's bucket and Johnston's back-header left Vernon with a clear path to goal. He took the ball on and from an acute angle belted in a terrific drive which George could only touch on its way into the net.'

The campaign concluded with two more matches in the nation's capital, with Rovers requiring three points against close rivals Fulham and Charlton to seal promotion. At Craven Cottage, the home team led until the last minute when Tony Macedo made a great save from Ally MacLeod to deny an equaliser. Almost immediately, under a challenge from Mick McGrath, the goalkeeper dropped the ball and MacLeod poked the ball home via the post. It was the last kick of the game. The goal prompted amazing scenes as Fulham players – claiming a foul had been committed on Macedo – refused to kick off. Referee R.E. Smith, under the direction of PFA Chairman Jimmy Hill, was virtually frog-marched to consult the linesman. After the Newport-based official stuck to his guns, Fulham's Johnny Haynes was booked for delaying the restart by sitting on the ball.

Earlier that afternoon the referee had missed another display of petulance. Dave Whelan recalls: 'It both ended up on the floor. He scraped up a load of mud, rolled over and whumped it straight into Haynes's face – unbelievable! I can't tell you the language used. I had never seen anything like it in my life.' At the final whistle there was a chorus of boos for the match officials and, with many irate supporters loitering outside, a police escort was enlisted to enable the referee to exit the stadium.

If there was anxiety at Craven Cottage, the experience at The Valley was positively nerve-jangling. The mathematics were simple: Charlton needed a draw to guarantee promotion whereas Rovers needed a win. Minutes into the game and shortly after the hosts had taken the lead, Charlton's Stuart Leary missed a gilt-edged chance to double the advantage. The mistake would prove costly. In the 25th minute, Roy flighted a free-kick onto the head of Peter Dobing to level the scores. There was better to come from the blonde forward, who collected Bill Eckersley's pass down the left flank and fired past the keeper Sam Bartram as he came out to narrow the angle. Not to be outshone, Roy made it 3-1 with a 25-yard left-footed screamer and Bryan Douglas converted a spot kick midway through the second half. To Charlton's credit, they hit back with two goals. As a result, the final five minutes were agony for the visiting supporters and, as Mick McGrath recalls, the Rovers players on the pitch: 'Once Charlton had pulled it back to 4-3 our knees were knocking. The Valley had a huge bank like the Kop and it was packed with supporters who were urging their team on.' The visitors held on to the slender lead and the relief at the final whistle was palpable. Rovers ended the season with 56 points, just a single point behind champions West Ham United. Back home the team was invited for a civic reception which Mick McGrath looks back on fondly: 'It was marvellous – we went on the town hall balcony and the captain said a few words to the people assembled in the square.'

With promotion secured, the Blue Dragon was selected in the Wales squad to compete at the 1958 World Cup to be held in Sweden. It remains the only time that all four home nations have qualified for the finals. Vernon had set Wales on course for Scandinavia by scoring the decisive goal in the first qualifying match at home to Czechoslovakia in May 1957. It was a proud moment for him: 'A red jersey and Ninian Park, a truly wonderful setting for an international game – is a dream come true for a boy from Ffynnongroyw. When I was chosen for Wales against Czechoslovakia at Cardiff, I could have jumped through the ceiling. There was still no score with eight minutes left when Cliff Jones pushed the ball over to Terry Medwin, who headed it down in my direction. I hit it on the volley and it fairly screamed into the net. It was my lucky day, that shot might have gone anywhere.'[5]

With both Ivor Allchurch and John Charles unavailable through injury, Roy retained his place at inside-left for the remaining matches in the qualifying rounds. Although the campaign was rounded off with a 4-1 victory over East Germany in Cardiff, away defeats in Prague and Leipzig appeared to consign the Welshmen to second place, with only the team in first progressing to Sweden.

However, geopolitics offered a most unlikely reprieve. First, Turkey refused to compete in the Asian group so Israel, their opponents, advanced to the second round. Then Indonesia withdrew after FIFA rejected their request to play Israel on a neutral ground, so Israel advanced to the final round. At the final stage of Asian qualifying, Sudan refused to play Israel because of the Arab League boycott. FIFA had ruled that no team, except for the defending champions and the hosts, could qualify for the finals without playing at least one match. Therefore, a special play-off was hastily organised between Israel and a runner-up of one of the UEFA Groups. After Belgium refused, Wales was chosen to represent UEFA. Although Roy was overlooked in favour of fit-again Ivor Allchurch, Wales defeated Israel with ease in both the away and home legs. The second fixture coincided with Manchester United's fateful European Cup tie in Belgrade, meaning that manager Jimmy Murphy – who juggled commitments for club and country – avoided the fate of many of his club colleagues in the Munich Air Disaster.

The arrangements made for the build-up to departure for Sweden, which bordered on farce, have been detailed in Mario Risoli's insightful account of the World Cup campaign, *When Pelé Broke Our Hearts*. Apparently, the FA of Wales instructed the eighteen selected players to rest – preferably by the sea – before assembling in London for five days of preparation before flying to Scandinavia. The players – who were almost outnumbered by selectors and FAW officials – booked into the Lancaster Court Hotel in Paddington, which was also the base for the England squad, for the duration of the five-day stay. Finchley Football Club had agreed for the Wales squad to train on its pitch but, unfortunately, had failed to notify their groundsman. Oblivious to the pending arrival of the squad, he had covered the pitch with topsoil and reseeded it, making it unsuitable for use. A desperate search for alternative facilities proved fruitless so the players resorted to training across the road from their hotel in Hyde Park, literally using jumpers for goalposts. As ball games were officially banned, the practice matches and drill sessions were conducted furtively, until Jimmy Murphy was able to secure the tacit blessing of the park keepers. The only time spent on a bona fide football pitch was a behind-closed-doors match against England at their well-appointed training base in Roehampton.

The ill-prepared squad – decked out in their new black blazers embroidered with FAW crests – touched down at Stockholm's Bromma Airport in glorious sunshine on 2 June. Met by a welcoming FIFA delegation, they made the hour's drive to the luxurious Grand Hotel in Saltsjöbaden overlooking the Baltic Sea. Each player had been permitted to bring 200 cigarettes but no alcoholic spirits. No doubt Roy would have exhausted his supply of Senior Service – his preferred brand of cigarettes – in no time and smuggled a few extra cartons in his luggage. Perhaps in light of his inexperience – or reputation – he was assigned to share a room with squad captain Dave Bowen. Team talisman John Charles's arrival at the Grand Hotel was delayed by two days due to a club versus country stand-off between the FAW and Juventus.

With Allchurch given the nod at inside-left, Roy watched his countrymen from the sidelines as they drew their first two matches against Hungary – the World Cup runners-up in 1954 – and Mexico. The latter was an underwhelming performance. Jimmy Murphy shuffled the pack for the third match against the host country. Out went the right-side pairing of Colin Webster and Medwin, with Roy being drafted in on the wing. At the age of 21 years and 42 days, it makes him the youngest player to have represented Wales at the final stages of a World Cup. The match was a hard-fought but dour spectacle. Even though Sweden had already qualified and fielded a weakened team, they still exerted pressure on the Wales goal. Wearing the number eighteen shirt, Roy did come close to scoring, narrowly failing to connect on the volley after a cross from Ivor Allchurch. The result necessitated a play-off with Hungary to decide who would progress to the knockout stages.

Roy was required to give way once again to the recalled Terry Medwin, as less than 3,000 watched Wales edge the match by 2-1. Victory came at a cost though, and the rough treatment of John Charles by the Hungarian players meant that the Cambrian colossus was unfit to face Brazil in the quarter-final. Still, Roy was an onlooker as a goal by Pelé propelled the South Americans towards the final and the seventeen-year-old Brazilian towards worldwide fame. Although rarely playing to their highest standards, the Welsh players came away with great credit. Their advancement to the final stages of a major competition would not be emulated by any of their predecessors until 2016, when Chris Coleman's side reached the semi-finals of the European Championships in France. To this day Wales have still competed just once in the World Cup. In the matchday programme for World Cup qualifier between Wales and Scotland in October 1977, Roy Vernon reflected on the 1958 clash with Brazil and Pelé's winner: 'Yes, we did well in Sweden,' before adding, with a typical flash of Vernon wit: 'I was a spectator for that match. It was Brazil who played their young ace!'

Though selected for the annual encounter with Scotland in October 1958 – which Wales lost 3-0 in Cardiff – and despite having made nine appearances for the Wales senior side, Roy was demoted to the Under-23 team for the match against Scotland in December 1958. He was subsequently left out of the senior international side for sixteen months and only returned to represent the senior team against Northern Ireland in April 1960, shortly after his big money move to Everton. Back in the United Kingdom, Blackburn's return to the top flight after an absence of a decade could not have started better. The newcomers hit five goals in each of the opening three games, with Roy netting in every fixture. The campaign kicked off with the 5-1 thumping of Newcastle at St James' Park.

Johnny Carey had selected the promotion-winning line-up, who in their previous seven games together had dropped only one point. His side took the lead after ninety seconds courtesy of a Vernon strike. William Westall described the goal in the *Blackburn Times*: 'Rovers kicked off and a first-class Douglas-Dobing move brought a clipped shot from Vernon which, however, was too high. In the second Blackburn raid, Douglas cut inside and had McMichael moving the wrong way with a clever feint before he slipped the ball out to Dobing, whose backward centre from the byline was coolly flicked inside the near post by Vernon.'

For Bryan Douglas, his pal's contribution to the match remains fresh in the memory, albeit for an altercation with veteran half-back Jimmy Scoular rather than his goal: 'Newcastle had Jimmy Scoular, a bit of hard man at right-half. So, when Roy held the ball a little bit too long in the first five or ten minutes, Scoular clobbered him. While they were lying on the floor, Roy, aged 21 but respected as a bit of a firebrand, said to Scoular, who was about 33: "Listen here old man, if you try that again I'll make you look such a pillock that you'll have a job getting in Newcastle's reserves." He snarled back: "You little Welsh bastard." A few months later, we played them at Ewood and the same thing happened. Roy dallied on the ball and Scoular flattened him. As Roy got up, he said: "You might be old but there's bugger-all wrong with your memory," and they were pals after that. He was a cocky bugger full of that sort of thing. Roy had a lot to say on the pitch. He'd say to me: "How does this fella get in the bloody Blackpool side?" He'd do it so that they could hear; just winding them up. That's how he was, confident in everything he did.'

Despite Blackburn being back in the top flight, just a month into the 1958/59 season came the shocking news that Johnny Carey had been lured to Merseyside. After Cliff Britton had walked away from Goodison in 1956, the Everton directors, flying in the face of emerging trends, decided to grab back some power for themselves and appointed Ian Buchan, an inexperienced head coach, rather than a proven manager. Belatedly acknowledging that power should in fact rest with the manager, the board appointed Carey on 22 September 1958. He signed a five-year contract with a salary of £3,000 per annum, plus a mandate to have full control of first team and scouting affairs. Out of respect to Blackburn, the Dubliner served a month's notice to give his employers time to recruit a successor.

Reflecting on Carey's departure some fifteen years earlier, his one-time protégé was still bitter about the circumstances, which he perceived to be a result of the parsimony of the Rovers directorate: 'First of all, let me lay the blame for the failure of the Rovers squarely where it belongs, and that is at the boardroom of surely the blindest, most narrow-minded and short-sighted board of directors ever to attempt to run a football club. How the hell could they let the team disintegrate when they were only kids, just learning this trade? I will never know. Here they had a team of boys who came into the First Division and won their first three games by five goals. Here they had a manager who had unearthed most of the youngsters who now represented the Rovers. Who had, in his youth team, players like Mike England, Fred Pickering and Keith Newton to compete for places and stimulate his first team. So, they allowed this man to leave. I don't think it was any inducement that made Mr Carey accept Everton's offer, it was the realisation of what a pathetic board he was representing at Rovers that swayed him'.[1]

He continued: 'Our young Rovers had everything; as kids we went to the semi-final of the FA Cup and won promotion to the First Division. Naturally, professional players expected some reward – let's face it, if a man does something special for his boss, he expects a bonus. Well we got one. What a fantastic, even-handed gesture. The directors ruined everything from the start. A bonus gladly offered is a pleasure to receive but when the players must make their feelings known about the club's lack of appreciation it takes all the gloss off it. Mind you, the gloss on our eventual bonus was so slight that it didn't take much knocking off. After a few requests we received a silver plate cigarette box. Now wait for it, and I do know a bit about this subject, they would only fit the cheapest brands of cigarettes. How's that for a bonus? I think that Mr Carey was aware that his players wouldn't be content for long, so he departed to greener fields, as most of the Rovers were destined to do. Here and now I indict that board of directors for the plight today. The team I was so honoured to play in was doomed by stupidity and ignorance. Blackburn Rovers could, and should, have reaped a boardroom full of trophies – the only people to leave should have been those who could not make the grade. Where, oh where was the one man to keep together such great footballers, such great friends? There was only one man, Johnny Carey, and he was away to Everton.'[1]

To replace Carey, Rovers turned to Dally Duncan, the former Scotland outside-left who was managing Luton Town. Predictably, Roy was underwhelmed and unsettled by the appointment and set about making life difficult for the incoming manager and the directors: 'They selected Dally Duncan, mainly – I think – because of his ability to get the best out of what he had without spending too much money – the last five words underlined. I had no trouble with Dally, but was determined, by this time, to leave the Rovers, so I was deliberately awkward with the trainers and discourteous to the directors.'[1]

Never backwards in coming forwards when it came to voicing his opinion, Roy found himself as the spokesperson for other discontented players who lacked the bottle to air their grievances directly. Many assumed wrongly that he was the source of all agitation: 'I was blamed for many things that I had no knowledge of. I didn't deny anything; I was willing to be the scapegoat for all the breaches of discipline, leaks to the press etc, just as long as they would let me go.'[1]

Johnny Carey would soon be reminded of the ability of his former star when Rovers visited Goodison Park for a league match on 1 November. It ended all square, 2-2, but it was Douglas and Vernon who caught the eye, the latter having drawn Blackburn level with a stunning free-kick described by the *Daily Post* as 'a rocket-like drive into the top corner of the net'. Leslie Edwards, reporting for the *Liverpool Echo*, was smitten by the Rovers pair: 'If Douglas was outstanding, Vernon's contribution was little less satisfying. His method of strolling with the ball, making his pass and moving at great speed to pick up the return stamped him as one of the finest inside-forwards in the game.'[6]

Many of his teammates at Ewood Park would agree. In 2018, when asked for his opinion on the man from Ffynnongroyw, left-half Mick McGrath said: 'Roy was a man you wanted on your side rather than play against. He was tough – if you hit him, he would bide his time and get you back. He was a top-class player who wanted to do things his way. With free-kicks it was always: "Me. Me. Me. I'll take it." Of course, he was very good at taking them.' Full-back Dave Whelan, the former owner of Wigan Athletic, elaborated: 'His self-confidence was unbelievable. Roy used to do exactly what he wanted to do. When Blackburn lost him, it was a tragedy for the club. He was a character in the dressing room and on the pitch – a great player.'

Away from troubling football developments, Roy and Norma became parents for the first time with the birth of Mark on 31 January 1959. Rovers were playing away at Wolverhampton and, in anticipation of forecasted fog, stayed over in the Midlands on the Friday night. With the baby already overdue, Norma went into labour on the Saturday morning and was taken to hospital. Mindful not to distract her other half from his focus on the game, she left instructions that, should her husband call, he was to be told the white lie that she was out shopping. Norma's attempts to keep her husband's mind at rest were all for nothing as Rovers slumped to a 5-0 defeat. Roy was dropped off at his sister-in-law's home at 11:00pm, expecting his wife to be there, only to discover that she was in hospital and that he had become a father. The arrival of fatherhood did not quell his quick temper, and despite the obvious happiness he was also annoyed that his wife had not pre-warned him of the imminent birth.

Despite the loss of Carey early on, the season ended with Blackburn in a comfortable tenth position, with Roy contributing sixteen goals in 36 appearances. As preparations for the 1959/60 season got underway, the star striker notified the non-plussed manager and the Rovers chairman, Norman Forbes, that he was submitting a formal transfer request. He told local journalist Harry Peterson: 'I'm not happy with certain recent happenings and feel that the tension and petty squabbles are upsetting my play.' Rovers did not entertain the request, and shortly after the season got underway with a 4-0 win over Fulham, Duncan publicly voiced his suspicion that his star was being tapped-up: 'We think it's definite that some club's getting at him. It's difficult to obtain clear-cut evidence; if we do the league will be brought in. I've told Vernon that he has not got an earthly chance of leaving Blackburn. Someone's got to be the boss, someone's got to be firm otherwise we'll have every player wanting to go.' Duncan was particularly frustrated by the fall-out from the 'Vernon Affair' as he has high hopes for the season ahead: 'This young forward line can go places. Vernon is the schemer, the distributor who can be deadly on his day, but the sort of thing I suspect is happening behind our backs is upsetting in the dressing room and I want it stopped.'

Despite the distractions, Rovers started in a vein of fine form which continued into the autumn. For Roy, however, things were not going so smoothly. A bout of appendicitis necessitated an operation, leading to a five-week lay-off. A subsequent thigh-injury and the onset of tonsillitis, which required hospitalisation, also affected his form and availability. Some members of the press, unaware of the ailments, surmised that the Welsh star had downed tools: 'It did not take my critics long to decide: "He wants away and is playing for it." They were as wrong as it was possible to be, but all this did not help me.'[1]

To add to the discord, rumours circulated of a schism between captain Ronnie Clayton and his younger teammates. Rovers supporter Harry Berry explains the circumstances: 'Ronnie wasn't your typical player of that time. There were some big drinkers in the team, but he and his big mate Ken Taylor didn't drink or smoke. He had a paper shop in Darwen, so he was up early in the morning looking after it and if he was a bit late in to training nobody did much about it. The big revolt occurred when they were required to stay in a hotel in December and suddenly discovered that Clayton wasn't staying there, so of course Roy was asking: "What's happening about this?" The directors did not handle it well and it split the Rovers. Roy was the instigator of the revolt but, in all honesty, a lot of the team was happy to go along with him. They liked to pretend that they didn't, but they did. I find it hard to believe that Derek Dougan didn't have anything to do with it, but Roy got pushed to the front and I don't think he minded.'

In the *Blackburn Times* on 16 December, William Westall revealed the mutiny in the Blackburn ranks and the accusations by some of Clayton's teammates that their captain was neglecting his duties: 'Dally Duncan said that Clayton had his newspaper business to look after and had to be up at 5:00 in the morning, therefore he did not hang about the dressing rooms after training and liked to get home after the matches. He added that Clayton had not wanted to go to Blackpool for special training before the trip to Fulham and had to stay behind for treatment to his ankle and knee injuries. Had he been fit, however, he would have had to come along.' He added: 'One player remarked to me that since he became England's captain, he is more aloof than ever.'

In his autobiographical notes Roy mentioned the affair but sought to play down his role: 'Some of the lads complained – and I thought along similar lines – that Clayton was not as sociable with the boys as he should have been for the good of team spirit. A further complaint was that, as captain, he did not spend as much time with us as he might. I was singled out as being the spokesman, but I can assure you that many of the things that I was supposed to have said didn't cross my lips. We had a players' meeting at which the whole thing was thrashed out. We found out the true facts and you can take it from me that there was no ill feeling rankling against Ronnie. The whole thing was grossly exaggerated.'[5]

When fit and selected, Roy Vernon took his place in a forward line blessed with the talents of Douglas, Dobing, Dougan and MacLeod, the future Scotland manager. Roy would eulogise Douglas, who had taken Tom Finney's place in the England team, and the diminutive wingman's mastery of the ball at his feet: 'As a ball-player he is brilliant. It takes a near-genius to take the ball right up to a player as Douglas does and still be able to work it to his liking, almost as one is able to mould soft clay.'[5]

Having defeated Blackpool on Christmas Day, Blackburn were fourth in the standings. Nonetheless, the situation regarding the Welshman's future remained unresolved. Although the matter over Ronnie Clayton's relationship with his teammates had been smoothed over, there is little doubt that it helped convince the club's directors that Roy should be moved on if the right offer came in. The issue would soon dominate the newspapers. Football enthusiasts nationwide wondered how long he would remain Roy of the Rovers.

CHAPTER 3

Taffy the Toffee

*'Anyone who ever met him was aware that Taffy retained a strong affinity
for the Rovers. But, like any good pro, he was committed to defeating his old mates
by as many goals as possible. I think that he appeared eight times for Everton
against Blackburn – of which he won three and drew three others. I remember him
scoring twice in these contests and celebrating as if he'd won the Grand National.
Back then, there was none of the nonsense about not celebrating after scoring
against your former club. Taffy liked to win and be seen as a winner.'*

Tommy E. Jones

THE DAWN OF THE 1960S SAW THE REAWAKENING OF EVERTON
Football Club. Since winning the league title in 1939, the Merseysiders had yet to
recover from the seven-season hiatus in the competition brought about by global
conflict. By 1946, when domestic league fixtures resumed, top players such as
Tommy Lawton and Torry Gillick had left and Joe Mercer was soon to follow,
whilst others were in the twilight of their careers. The ignominy of only the second
relegation in the club's history, in 1951, had resulted in three disheartening years
in the second tier. Having finally regained a place at the top table, a clash with
overbearing directors saw manager Cliff Britton walk away in 1956. As mentioned
previously, the board reclaimed control of team affairs with the appointment of
Ian Buchan to head up the coaching team. The former Physical Education lecturer
tried to overhaul and improve the fitness of the ageing squad. However, it was only
towards the end of his two-year tenure that the club began to attract first-class
talent. Right-back Alex Parker and forward Eddie O'Hara arrived from Falkirk,

followed by Bobby Collins from Celtic and, equally importantly, moves were afoot to recruit an experienced manager who could turn the club round whilst playing in the club's cultured tradition. Johnny Carey was duly identified as that man and, with the permission of Blackburn, an approach was made. He took charge at Goodison in October 1958.

The visionary responsible for reviving the fortunes of the Merseyside club was John Moores. Active as a shareholder in both Everton and Liverpool for some years, the head of the Littlewoods Pools, department stores and mail order empire had stealthily increased his influence at Goodison. In the late 50s, he began to up his involvement in Everton, providing interest-free loans to facilitate ground improvements and player recruitment. However, little in the way of further reinforcements occurred during the 1958/59 season, Carey's first at the helm, in which Bobby Collins almost single-handedly kept relegation fears at bay with some inspirational performances.

As Moores grew impatient for signs of progression – exacerbated by an FA Cup embarrassment at Bradford City – a bid of £40,000 to entice Huddersfield Town to part with Denis Law failed in November 1959. Another negative response was received from Hibernian after a £45,000 offer was made for Anglo-Scot Joe Baker. Maurice Setters of West Bromwich Albion then rejected Everton and joined Manchester United.

However, the recruits finally started to arrive at the start of the new year – Clyde's Scottish international left-winger Tommy Ring, was followed in quick succession by Mickey Lill from Wolves and Dundee's wing-half Jimmy Gabriel, tipped to follow in the footsteps of his compatriot Dave Mackay. Another target, however, was proving more difficult. When Carey had left Blackburn, he had counselled the board to retain Roy Vernon's services at all costs but now he, backed by cash-rich Moores, was determined to test that resolve. On 4 January, the Goodison board sanctioned an offer of up to £35,000 having been discreetly advised by Rovers that the club would be open to considering realistic offers. An agreement was swiftly reached between the clubs.

This came as a surprise to the man Everton had targeted: 'Out of the blue, the secretary asked me to call into the boardroom. I thought: "They're going to ask me why I'm carrying on like this and ask me to apologise". The incident on this occasion had been in Blackpool. We had a good school of poker players and had retired early to one of the bedrooms to play cards. Well, what started as a friendly game developed into a hot one with plenty of money changing hands. I'm sure that every professional footballer can visualise the scene: a smoky bedroom, many on the bed, 2:30am and in walks the trainer and the manager. I remember that Dally had green pyjamas on, but they were nothing on the shade of green their faces went when we told them what they could do. As Dally said, "Make it the last hand," I exploded: "Make it the last hand? It's the first good hand I've had all night!" and it really was. After ten minutes of abuse, they retired to bed and so did we, for the mood was gone and the game was dead. Now I stood waiting to go into the boardroom, thinking: "If I have a go at them, they may let me go. After all, they must be sick of me by now". So imagine my surprise when I was told that Mr Carey was waiting to interview me.'[1]

Such was Roy's determination to force a move that many would have expected a deal to be finalised quickly. Nothing could be further from the truth. Everton, despite their new-found wealth and raft of high-quality signings, were not in the higher echelons of the First Division. Keen to maximise his financial gain, Roy described the chain of events candidly: 'Johnny Carey came straight to the point and said he'd agreed a deal with the Rovers and it was up to me. He told me of his plans to make Everton great again. I believed him and said that I'd think it over. "Okay," he said, "I'll pick up you and Norma tomorrow and show you some houses." That night I discussed the move with my wife. I had been as green as grass when I had first gone to Blackburn, but I'd learnt quite quickly. She went to bed early and I sat looking into the dying embers of the fire. It seemed that all my grievances passed before me. How, when I was in the Army, they paid me £1 per week and a £6 fee when I appeared in the first team, when I knew other Army lads were getting their full £5 plus expenses. How they made me pay £7 towards the cost of the fireplace I was staring into. How we sat outside Goodison after beating Everton 2-1 in an FA Cup tie, in front of a capacity crowd, and received Mint Imperials for our troubles. "Well played lads," this director said as he put a closed hand on the table. There were no fivers in that fist, just the Mint Imperials. "I know we've played well," I said, "but to get these we must have been brilliant." Well the fire was out, time for bed. I wondered was it true that players could pick up as much as £2,000 under the counter? Tomorrow would tell. As I tucked my son up in his cot I vowed: "If there's a few quid in it for me, I'm moving."

'The next morning Mr Carey showed us some nice houses, including the one occupied previously by Dave Hickson, who had been sold to Liverpool. But when

I asked about a backhander, Mr Carey said that it was out of the question. When we returned to Goodison, a club director was waiting. He said we could pick any of the houses and he would personally pay for any carpets etc. that we wanted, but I insisted on £1,500 in my hand, tax free. It was deadlock and then we returned to Blackburn.'

Although Roy had promised to sleep on his decision, the moment he got home he phoned the Everton manager to confirm that the deal was off: 'Mr Carey was bitterly disappointed and so was I. That night I decided to play my heart out for the Rovers and for the next few weeks I did just that.'[1]

The Goodison hierarchy had not lost all hope of signing their target, and an incident occurred soon afterwards which bore all the hallmarks of John Moores's modus operandi. The footballer's oblique reference in his memoir to his visitor was, no doubt, intended to maintain anonymity: 'My form must have impressed the great Evertonian who called at my house one night and asked if I was still interested in coming. "Not to Everton," I replied. "They could have signed me a few weeks ago but we could not agree on terms." He replied, quite calmly, that he wanted to make the Toffees great again and that if I was prepared to wait for my money he would see if it could be arranged amongst some of his friends. When this stranger left, I recognised that he was a man of substance for he drove off in a Rolls Royce.'

Roy continued: 'I didn't think that anything would happen. Dally said that he was going to fashion his team around me. I felt good again but the incident that was to end everything between the Rovers and me was only a few days away. We had been drawn away against Sunderland in the FA Cup and were behind 1-0 and battling for the equaliser. We were pounding them with a brand of football rarely seen at Roker Park but couldn't equalise. Then Alan O'Neill and I crashed together in a hard, vicious tackle. I felt his legs cross over my left leg. I thought in a flash: "He'll break my leg", and I lashed out with my right boot. It was an instinctive action, but O'Neill collapsed in a heap and I was ordered off. Hot tears of temper burned my cheeks and I made that long walk. Jack Weddell, the trainer, said: "Bad luck son," as he put an arm around my shoulder, "but he's coming off as well." And, sure enough, O'Neill, now recovered, was also marching.

'The match ended in a 1-1 draw and I set off for the railway station. I was sat on a luggage trolley, still a bit dejected at being sent off, but determined to hammer Sunderland in the replay on the following Wednesday, when up came the Mint

Imperial Man. "I knew that Welsh temper of yours would get you into trouble, sooner or later," he said. I blew my top. "**** off," I said, "before I smack you between the eyes and throw you on those lines." Ronnie Clayton and one or two others restrained me. I was so mad that when Dally came up, I told him straight: "I've had enough off this bloody shower. I run my arse off for this club but that's the end. You can sell me to anyone, I'm finished here." I cooled off over the weekend and when the replay came up on the Wednesday, I was ready to penalise Sunderland on my own.'

Significantly, Johnny Carey was in the Ewood Park's Nuttall Street stand to witness one of the finest displays of Roy's career. The Welshman channelled his pent-up frustration to deliver a virtuoso performance, destroying the Wearsiders almost single-handedly. The *Blackburn Times* eulogised about his role – including two smartly-taken goals – in the 4-1 victory: 'Johnny Carey was at Ewood on Wednesday night to see the greatest display yet by Roy Vernon, the Welsh football genius he developed but failed to persuade to follow him to Goodison Park. It was a superb display of cultured yet challenging inside-forward craft which carried the Rovers safely through their tie. Vernon played as if his very football life depended on it. His intelligent foraging, probing, passing, picking up loose balls by dint of a hundred percent endeavour and quick-thinking reminded one of the great inside-forwards of the past.'

'How foolish the Rovers would be to denude themselves of such all-round soccer genius,' the *Blackburn Times* reporter concluded, and yet this would turn out to be the Welshman's swansong in front of the adoring Ewood faithful.

Roy described what happened in the days that followed: 'The headlines on Thursday proclaimed: "Vernon's Super Dividend" and "Roy's The Boy". I was quite chuffed with everything. My teammates had known the disappointment of a semi-final defeat but were confident as early as this that they were Wembley bound. And so they were – but not me. Not long after, the mystery man in the Rolls Royce called to tell me that Everton were to bid again and they would agree to my terms.

'I was instructed to be at Ewood Park by 9:30am. There, I was told sharply that Everton had made another bid and the best thing for both the Rovers and me was to sign. The secretary drove me halfway to Liverpool where we met Mr Carey and Eddie Thomas, who was joining Rovers in part-exchange. This time everything went smoothly and after about ten minutes I was an Everton player.' To get the deal over the line, his suitors had put forward a creative solution to the signing-on fee impasse. As part of the agreement Norma was given part-time secretarial work with the Littlewoods Organisation – with hours to sit her childcare duties.

While Roy Vernon's career at Blackburn had been a roller coaster ride, his scoring record of 49 games in 131 league appearances had been decent for such a young forward. The local reaction to his transfer was summarised in 12 February edition of the *Blackburn Times*: 'Rovers have voluntarily and with aforethought deprived themselves of one of the few top-class scheming-type inside-forwards left in football: 22-year-old Roy Vernon, who on Wednesday was transferred to Everton in a big exchange transaction that brought inside man Eddie Thomas to Ewood plus the biggest fee that the club has ever received. They have parted with the brains of their attack at a time when the club are in the last sixteen of the FA Cup, while declining rapidly in the league. On the face of it, it is an amazing move. But the Ewood board and management, having weighed up all the consequences, cannot have taken the step without good reason. Indeed, the reason is well known. The club value harmony in the camp more than mercurial performances interspersed by regular blow-ups. Attempts to make up differences between the club and player have not worked out. It has apparently been impossible to "tame" this fiery character, after further incidents and carpetings.'

In the absence of their star striker, Blackburn's form went downhill, and relegation seemed a distinct possibility. The season was salvaged when Dally Duncan's team reached Wembley. With Bryan Douglas taking over at inside-left and Liverpool's Louis Bimpson recruited as a right-winger, they defeated Sheffield Wednesday 2-1 in the semi-final at Maine Road and progressed to the FA Cup final against Wolverhampton Wanderers. Nothing went to plan at Wembley. On the eve of the big game, Derek Dougan submitted a transfer request and did little to further endear himself to supporters and teammates by hobbling after just fifteen minutes, despite declaring that he had shaken-off an injury and was fit to play. Then Dave Whelan broke his leg. In the sweltering heat, the remaining fit players wilted with the exception of Ally MacLeod, who performed heroics down the left flank as the Midlands team ran out comfortable winners by 3-0. It was a bitter pill for Blackburn followers, including Fred Cumpstey: 'For Rovers supporters the game was a farrago of missed opportunity. The showpiece wasn't a spectacle and it was described by some in the press as "The Dustbin Final". I'd like to believe that if Roy Vernon had still been at the club we would have won the cup, but we'll never know.'

The loss at Wembley signalled the end of Duncan's career in football – he went on to manage a guesthouse on the south coast. In the subsequent seasons there was some success under new manager Jack Marshall, with Keith Newton, Mike England and Fred Pickering graduating from the 1959 Youth Cup-winning side to the first-team squad. However, the club could not continue to sell its best players like Roy and, in 1964, Pickering with impunity. Consequently, Rovers were relegated in 1966 and spent a quarter of a century in the second tier of the English game.

Though Roy got his wish to leave, his exit was tinged with some regret: 'When I returned to Blackburn, after signing for Everton, I went to the golf club where the lads were having their weekly session. I had mixed feelings as I prepared for the mammoth task Everton faced. Although I was leaving the worst club directors, I was surely leaving the embryo of what should have been the greatest team in Britain. I knew then that others were already planning to get away. Poor blind Rovers, they even got to Wembley that year and managed to lose most of their supporters because of the way they allocated their FA Cup final tickets.'

Bryan Douglas, although less outspoken, echoes some of the views of his former teammate: 'Looking back, I feel that we had board members who were shopkeepers and the like. They did not have a football grounding – they were all pals. With proper directors who would have invested a little bit on one or two more players, we might have won something. Instead we were a nearly team. That's why Roy left.'

The Vernons, with fourteen-month-old Mark, and a second child on the way (Neil was born in October 1960), moved into a three-bed semi-detached house on Ridgeway Drive in Lydiate to the north east of the city, a more salubrious area than the environs of Goodison Park where they had been offered accommodation previously. Liverpool players Ron Yeats and Bert Slater lived in proximity. In time Mark would acquire the nickname 'Fingers' for his inquiring mind and need to disassemble things. It's part of Vernon family folklore that on one occasion he deflated Ron Yeats's car tyres on a derby matchday, no doubt amusing his father. Roy and Norma were lucky to have good neighbours to share babysitting duties. Ken and Shirley Kidger, who ran a newsagent business, were one of the first couples to befriend them. They were responsible for planting an idea in Roy's mind which, in late 1961, resulted in him seeking the club's blessing to pursue a newspaper shop venture in parallel with his football career, mirroring his former teammate Ronnie Clayton. He received short shrift. The club minutes state: 'A request was considered from Vernon for permission to open a newsagent business. The board were against this.'

Shortly after his move across Lancashire, Roy gave an exclusive interview to Arnold Howe of *The Herald* in which he opened up on his reasons for leaving Rovers and his aspirations at Everton. Both his candour and humour shone through:

'I am leaving the Rovers with some regrets because it is the only club I've played for as a professional, and I've made a lot of friends in Blackburn. But I feel that in order to better myself in my football career Everton have more to offer. First, I shall be joining my old boss Johnny Carey whom I've always admired as a player and a manager. Also, I feel that Everton have more advanced facilities for training and a much greater atmosphere of the big time in their massive stadium. I am greatly looking forward to playing in front of that passionate crowd. 'Have I been a firebrand as some people have suggested? If sticking up for one's rights is being a firebrand, then I must be. But I've never ceased to do my stuff for the Rovers. After recent events, however, it has become plain that many have tried to blame me to cover up for themselves. It has become increasingly clear that if there was any more trouble at Ewood Park I would be blamed for causing it.

'The prospect of joining players like Bobby Collins, Alex Parker, Tommy Ring, Alan Shackleton and other players who have been bought in the club's determined bid to make Everton a great side again, is exciting. I am convinced the Toffees can be great again and hope to play some part in the revival of a club with such wonderful traditions. One final word, I want to wish all my old colleagues at the Rovers all the very best in the FA Cup.'

Before his arrival, Everton had suffered several defeats over the 1959/60 festive period and were sitting in the lower reaches of the table. The new man's debut came at on 13 February 1960 at Goodison. He lined up at inside-forward alongside Bobby Collins – with the Scotsman moved to number eight to allow the new man to wear his favourite number ten shirt – Tommy Ring, Alan Shackleton and Jimmy Harris. It was not a fairytale debut: 'My first game brought an early surprise. I had been acknowledged as a midfielder at Blackburn but was now to play the role of striker, with Bobby Collins grafting and scheming. I felt out of my depth; I played too deep to be an effective striker. I missed the speed of Dougan and Dobing, the subtlety and class of Bryan Douglas, the driving force of Clayton and McGrath. As I drove home, I realised that my new club was in a worse state than I had thought. Players would have to be signed and I would have to work harder at being a goalscorer rather than a creator. In my fourth game we drew 2-2 at West Ham. I got both goals and was satisfied that I could, indeed, be a striker.'[1]

Evertonian John McFarlane was a youngster in the crowd for that visit of Wolves and was underwhelmed by his first exposure to the big money signing: 'I didn't fancy him and thought: "What have we bought?" Then gradually he blossomed. Yes, he was an ugly duckling that turned into a swan.'

Writing for the *Daily Post*, Roy addressed the pressures of being a big-name player: 'I have been asked if Mr John Carey gave me a ribbing after the Wolves game. The answer could not be shorter: no. He saw that I was lost in a sea of new faces and ideas that were completely different from what I had been accustomed to. Jimmy Harris, for example, is completely different from Bryan Douglas. At Everton, we have any amount of ball practice and five-a-side games and these are invaluable for teaching positional play and moves. I'll have to modify my game to some extent to suit my new conditions. Already, when I look up in a match expecting a player to be in a certain position, and lo and behold he is more often than not.'[5]

Come Good Friday, Roy exhibited his talent and coolness against Blackpool. As reported by Leslie Edwards in the *Liverpool Echo*, he recovered from a leg injury that required treatment off the pitch to score a goal of jaw-dropping audacity: 'Vernon's goal was remarkable. When he received Ring's pass…he sped on with the ball, rounded the out-going Waiters, and then in a close dribble seemed to have delayed his shot fatally not once, but three or four times. Yet he maintained control, beat man after man in the space of a few feet and then cracked the ball home when the opening had been completed to his liking. Only Vernon could have scored this one.'[6]

Such was the brilliance of the goal that Derek Temple, watching from the stands due to injury, detailed the event as if it was yesterday: 'Taffy was on the six-yard line and went to push the ball into the corner. Seeing Tony Waiters dive to where he thought it was going, Roy stopped and put it in the other corner with the keeper on the floor. That was class – if he had been a continental player, they would have been writing about it for years.'

One by one, the new players bedded in and, bit by bit, progress was made:

'Slowly the team was to change. Slowly the results improved. The magic was returning and some of the poetry I had known at Ewood Park was being expressed at Goodison Park. Surely, with a little more devil in the defence, we could become a top team. Well, we have the money.'[1]

Jimmy Harris, who had come through the ranks at Everton, was impressed by the talents of the new challenger for his first-team spot but noted: 'Roy played for himself and would not play you back in after you had given it to him. Instead, he'd use you as a decoy – he'd make to give it back to you but then cut and go on his own – which is alright if it comes off!'

Another player who became reacquainted with Roy was Mick Meagan. The Irish international, who could be relied upon to play diligently at wing-half or full-back, had been invited over from Dublin for the same trials as Roy when they were both teenagers but, in contrast to the Welshman, had joined at that time and had become a first-team regular in 1957: 'Taffy had a reputation for doing his own thing on and off the pitch, but he was a very good fella. For a chap that didn't look after himself as perhaps he should have done, he was a very good player. When I was at left-back or left-half he said: "It's your job to get the ball up to me – it's not my job to be running back helping you." And looking back at it, he was 100 percent right. He made you aware that you were there to give it to him and he'd do the rest. He was a great finisher and could hit the ball. He didn't like heading balls – looking at him you'd say that he should have been a jockey. At half-time, all I wanted was to do was get a drink of water in the changing room, but Taffy, Tommy Ring and others would slope off to the toilets and puff on their cigarettes.'

Ring's wing-play was a boon. This was no better illustrated than on 10 September 1960 when Everton met Wolves at Goodison. Don McWhinnie, writing for the *Sunday Pictorial*, likened the performance by a 'classy, fight for every ball, Everton side' to that seen in the Dixie Dean era. Roy, described as 'sparkling and elusive' by McWhinnie, notched two goals against Stan Cullis's men after Jimmy Harris had opened the scoring. With the score at 1-1, the Blue Dragon – fed by Tommy Ring – unleashed a howitzer that crashed in off the underside of the bar. Straight away, he added a contrasting – but no less accomplished – second. McWhinnie captured the excitement: 'A brilliant individual effort in which he beat four men in a lethal burst down the middle. Then Ring dribbled around goalkeeper Sidebottom and tapped the ball home.' Only Geoff Sidebottom's acrobatics denied further goals.

In one of his weekly columns for the *Daily Post*, Roy referred to the ethos of fluid football instilled at the club by Johnny Carey, an approach readily accepted by his players: 'We have a new motto at Goodison Park these days. It is: nobody stops the ball in our team except the goalkeeper. Everybody else has to keep it going because our manager Mr Carey believes that to keep on playing football is the surest way to obtaining results.'[5]

In fact, a few veteran Evertonians believe that the five-man forward line of Lill, Collins, Harris, Vernon and Ring was one of the most exciting they had ever seen. Two weeks after the demolition of Wolverhampton Wanderers, West Ham United were humbled 4-1 at Goodison and the cameras were there to capture goals by Lill, Ring and two from Vernon. Both were textbook finishes – low and hard into the corner of the net. For the first, after being fed by Collins, Roy paused for a split-second, eyed the keeper and then hit the ball low past his right hand. The second was a brilliant first-time finish following exhilarating wing play and a low cross from Ring. Tragically, one week later Everton were shorn of the blossoming left-flank partnership when Ring broke his leg in a collision with goalkeeper Reg Matthews at Stamford Bridge. Roy was saddened the incident: 'I saw Tommy move on goal. The turf was slippery and as Matthews came out Tommy's feet shot from under him. I was running into position in case there was a rebound from his shot – it was a shot that was never made. I heard a sickening crack and, to the referee at my elbow, I said: "He's broken his leg sir." I dashed over to Tommy. He said: "Don't touch me, my leg is broken." I have not known a feeling like it. Everyone was unnerved and shocked.'[5]

It was a career-changing injury. The Scotland international winger failed to recapture the level of fitness required in top-flight football. Sadly, he made no further appearances for Everton and was sold to Third Division Barnsley. Without further ado, Everton moved to sign a highly experienced right-winger, namely Luton's Billy Bingham in a part-exchange deal involving inside-forward Alec Ashworth, full-back John Bramwell and no little cash. On his debut at Craven Cottage, Bingham marvelled at Roy at his goalscoring best: 'The goal came from my pass, flung so hard and high to Roy that he appeared to have no chance of doing anything save flick it on with a header. Instead, he drew himself up to his full height, breasted the ball down, took it forward past a surprised defence and then when appearing to lose possession had sufficient resource to side-step in gently past Hewkins.'[5]

Not long afterwards, the Welshman earned bragging rights over Jimmy Gabriel in an international match at Cardiff, scoring in the 2-0 victory for the home side. By now Roy had settled in at Goodison and was vying with Bobby Collins to be the club's most influential player. This was no better illustrated than a scintillating home win over of Manchester City in October in which Denis Law was eclipsed by both Vernon and Collins. Roy netted twice and Collins converted from the spot in a 4-2 victory. The *Daily Post's* Horace Yates proclaimed that the two inside-forwards provide rare quality: 'What's wrong with football? Nothing, absolutely nothing, just so long as it is played like it was last night. Call Everton what you will, the English Real Madrid, the English Barcelona or any other of the world's great teams, and they would not be flattered by the comparison. There was play and craft of the highest level, sportsmanship, speed, action and a spot of controversy thrown in as a makeweight. Nobody would attempt to deny Everton's entitlement on this showing to rank with the top names in sport. It was a night to remember.'5

His salutation continued: 'The interplay between Collins and Vernon beggars description. How wonderfully they run into position and how bewildering it must be for opponents who try to thwart them. Repeatedly, we saw the ball apparently pushed to nobody in particular and then almost with a touch of the miraculous Collins or Vernon would be found with it at his toe. Vernon was simply terrific. His control, his judgement, his feeding and his shooting were magnificent. Law, a highly talented player, seemed to be merely very good as he played in the reflection cast by two of the most successful inside-forwards in modern football. What a great pairing this is – tireless and relentless in its surge of energy that commands unstinted admiration. Why Blackburn did not go out of their way to make Vernon content at Ewood Park must remain a major mystery, for his release at whatever the fee strikes as being one of the blunders of recent history. Not only is he a golden link in any chain but he has the gift of a shot laden with dynamite dynamic and directed with an arrow's swiftness and accuracy.'5

Roy being Roy, it was almost inevitable that this high should be followed by an almost immediate aberration. A mistimed tackle from behind on Dick Le Flem of Nottingham Forest resulted in a sending off. Vernon was almost lost for words: 'When the referee pointed to the dressing room with the terse words "Get off" I could scarcely believe it was happening. Though I tried to obey the order my legs were like jelly. To say I was shocked would be a gross understatement. My world simply disintegrated. As long as I live, I'll never forget Nottingham at 4:21pm on 29 October 1960.'

Roy recounted the incident: 'I tried to take the ball from behind. As I shot out my foot, Le Flem parted with the ball as though in anticipation of the tackle. There was nothing I could do to halt the progress of my tackle. Now I am left wondering dare I try another tackle from behind?'[5]

After the two-week suspension was handed down, Leslie Edwards advised his readers that the tendency to overstep the line was part of Roy's footballing make-up: 'His rather fiery Welsh temperament, his artistry, his big shot for so light a man, and his ability to make the most telling passes are all facets of his football make-up.'[5]

In December 1960, Everton plundered Scottish football again to sign Alex Young and George Thomson from Heart of Midlothian, the reigning Scottish champions. Young recounted how Roy had previously left his mark, literally, on him whilst on international duty: 'Our paths crossed for the first time when he played against Scotland at Ninian Park in 1960. Indeed, Taffy contributed Wales's second goal in a 2-0 triumph. My first impression of him? He was scrawny – seriously so. Taffy reminded me of a malnourished Denis Law except that he was one-footed and impotent in the air. I like the fact that he shared Law's combative spirit and knew how to look after himself on the pitch. I bumped into him again during my first visit to the home dressing room at Goodison. I had yet to sign for the club, but Johnny Carey wanted me to savour the atmosphere under the massive floodlights. Only 20,000 attended the League Cup tie with Third Division Bury but I was impressed.'

Young added: 'The post-match dressing room was crammed with old pals from Scotland – Alex Parker, Bobby Collins, Jimmy Gabriel and Tommy Ring (on crutches) and a couple of other big money signings – Billy Bingham and Mickey Lill (also on crutches) along with a gang of Scousers in Albert Dunlop, Tommy Jones, Brian Harris and Derek Temple. But I was drawn towards an immaculately dressed man seated quietly by the door. Attired in a very expensive tailored suit, Roy Vernon knew how to look after himself off the pitch. Taffy confided that had been sent off a few weeks earlier and was serving his suspension on the naughty bench after his ultra-competitive spirit had got the better of him at the City Ground. While budding centre-forwards such as Jimmy Harris and Frank Wignall viewed my presence with no little suspicion, he greeted me like a long-lost brother and, in an almost religious ceremony, offered me a cigarette. This ritual of the sharing of tobacco was the start of a great friendship. That evening, my new teammate confessed that he was aware of my deeds north of the border and guaranteed that I would fall in love with Everton Football Club and its followers.'

Young was correct about Roy's taste in clothing. One perk of being a high-profile footballer and wife was that they could afford to frequent the Diana Warren designer clothing boutique in Blackpool. Whilst Roy treated Norma to outfits to suit her petite frame, he'd nip into the menswear department to get fitted out in the latest Italian fabrics. Sometime later, when Diana Warren opened a branch in Liverpool, Alex and Roy were there to cut the ribbon, in exchange for some complimentary threads.

Taffy continued to catch the eye, notably in a 3-2 setback at Highbury at the end of November. Horace Yates reported for the *Liverpool Echo*: 'Vernon could well have been a match-winner in the mud. He seemed to find it very little handicap. In the last minute, the speed of Vernon was phenomenal as he flicked the ball away from Kelsey's fingers, raced to catch it on the byline, brought it back infield and beat two defenders to drive the ball into the goal at the second attempt.'6

An injury to Alex Young meant that Goodison wouldn't see him, Vernon and Collins in harness until February 1961. Strangely, this coincided with an erratic run of results in which Everton suffered ten defeats and Roy managed only four goals in seventeen league and cup outings. Drastic action was required, and Roy was dropped for the home encounter with Aston Villa in late March 1961, a game Everton lost 2-1. He was replaced by eighteen-year-old Alan Tyrer. In his weekly column, he elaborated: 'It goes without saying that I don't like being dropped. Few ever do, but I am not so conceited not to grasp that better players than I have been dropped and have stayed on to win back their place. Some have said that I have not been the same since I was dismissed at Nottingham. That may be so, but if it be true then it is purely coincidental. If ever that worried me, I have got it right out of my system and my only concern has been doing my best to help the club out of a rut. I realise in these circumstances that changes are inevitable in an effort to bring about a change of fortune, but our formation had been left alone for so long that we rather thought we enjoyed the confidence of the board and manager in our ability to come through and, in my opinion, the climb out of the slump had started. It may not have been a spectacular beginning, but at least it was a start. Every player recognises that the time will come when his position is under challenge and if he cannot fight it off then the alternative is clear-cut. But I hadn't thought I had reached that stage yet. Naturally I hope to win back my place in the very near future, for I have enjoyed my football at Goodison Park.'

After an improved run, in which the Toffees won four times in seven games and Vernon had scored two goals, even more momentous action was taken – the employment of Johnny Carey was terminated in April 1961. Predictably, the Welshman was saddened: 'Mr Moores was undoubtedly the person to put Everton back on top. With his backing and determination, the self-made multi-millionaire demanded success. His influence was so great that it seems ironical that the players should call him "Little John". Of course, he was called many other things when, out of the blue, he sacked Mr Carey. The sensational "sacking in a taxi" shook us all. Certainly, we'd had a difficult time early on, but we were playing well and winning when the axe fell. When the boss met the players to say goodbye it was very emotional. I was choked, near to tears. I'm sure many others felt the same way for we went out and murdered Cardiff City. I still think that game was the players' tribute to Mr Carey. Mr Moores' famous quote on this occasion was, "The King is dead, long live the King!" Of course, the new sovereign turned out to by Harry Catterick and he was to rule with an iron fist.'[1]

Johnny Carey – hailed as 'Gentleman John' – left Everton in fifth place in the table but did not depart on friendly terms. He sued the club for wrongful dismissal. The case did not go to trial because his employers settled out of court, ten months after his ill-fated London taxi ride with the club chairman.

CHAPTER 4

Harry the Catt

'Nine stone odd and as athletic as Pinocchio, Taffy was deceptively tough and, as a son of the mines was no pushover. While he lacked the muscular physique of modern-day strikers, he possessed the qualities displayed by top finishers in all eras – technique, intelligence, composure and a glowing opinion of himself. He had the self-confidence – bordering on arrogance – of Ball and Kay combined.'
Brian Labone

HARRY CATTERICK WAS AT THE HELM FOR THE FINAL TWO FIXTURES of the 1960/61 league campaign. A swift return to Hillsborough was met with a hostile reception but Catterick had the satisfaction of coming away from the Steel City with a victory thanks to a brace from Frank Wignall. The season was rounded off in fine style with a thoroughly entertaining match which saw Everton defeat Arsenal 4-1. It marked Roy's first senior hat-trick, with Alex Young bagging the other. Michael Charters described the first two goals in the *Liverpool Echo*: 'Everton deservedly went ahead after 22 minutes with a goal from Vernon – one of the finest seen on the ground this season. It started with a powerful header from defence by Parker, which was picked up in midfield by Temple and pushed quickly through for Vernon to chase. He outstripped Groves, took the ball around keeper Kelsey and slotted it into the empty net. Vernon got a second after 25 minutes with another excellently worked effort. I give major honours here to Thomson who came forward to the outside-left position to take a pass from Fell, move it to Collins and the ball then passed via Young to Vernon whose shot from the edge of the penalty area hit Groves and deflected away from the diving Kelsey.'[6] Although the second half was tame by comparison, Roy completed his hat-trick by converting a final-minute spot kick after Young had been fouled.

Harry Catterick's style was a stark and less welcome contrast to that of Carey. Roy acknowledged the new manager's impact: 'He felt that the club had lacked discipline and control under his predecessor. Initially, the players were in awe of Mr Catterick. He had come to us with a reputation of being a disciplinarian but a fair one, although my first taste of his justice was bloody hard, but it wasn't fair.'[1] That taste would come from the other side of the Atlantic Ocean.

At the season's end and to the new manager's dismay, his first-team squad jetted off to participate in the North American International Soccer League. Everton's involvement was only confirmed hours before the first match against Montreal Concordia when John Moores telephoned Helmut Käser, general secretary of FIFA. The tournament had not been approved by the organisers with football's international governing body, raising concerns that participating clubs might face sanctions. Dr Käser assured Moores that the issues were not of Everton's making and that the club could take part as planned. It was the first prolonged period of time that the squad had spent with Harry Catterick and the arch disciplinarian put a marker down shortly after the arrival in Canada: 'After a gruelling flight, we arrived at the hotel and went to bed. Rested, we showered and shaved and made our way downstairs for dinner at 7:30pm. Punctual, properly dressed, a credit to our club. Quite casually I said to Jimmy Gabriel, my roommate, "Fancy a drink before dinner?" "Yes, why not?" replied Jim. We strolled into the bar where skipper Bobby Collins and Alex Parker were casually sampling the local brew. Soon Alex Young and George Thomson joined us. A harmless enough event really, a quiet aperitif before dinner, but not to Mr Catterick. The next day we were summoned to his room where he told us that on this occasion, he would overlook our behaviour but the next one out of line would be on his way home. We protested that a drink before dinner didn't harm anyone. He was adamant though – his word was law. We were flabbergasted but powerless to do anything about it. Now we knew that he meant to be absolute boss. I suppose inevitably I was to be made the next example of his power.'[1]

The tournament gave this ambitious and moneyed version of Everton the opportunity to make a statement on the international stage. In line with the club's Latin motto, only the best was good enough. Having defeated Kilmarnock in the second match staged in Montreal, the squad moved to a new base in New York. The hotel, which also served as the headquarters of the league, left Harry Catterick almost speechless: 'When we arrived into New York we booked into some third-rate hotel. Harry won his stripes back when he promptly moved us out into a far better hotel on Broadway. The players appreciated his actions not only on their own behalf but also the club's. The whole image of Everton was on the upgrade, on the field and off the field.'[1]

Having relocated to superior accommodation, the focus could turn to the fixtures to be played at the Polo Grounds, the home of the New York Giants. However, to Harry Catterick's alarm, many of the arrangements were amateurish. The team was expected to travel via the underground Subway system to training sessions on a baseball pitch at Central Park, and once there they had to use their own kits as makeshift goalposts. Improvements were made after the first outing: they switched to hiring taxis.

Days later, the sensational news broke in the national press that Roy had been expelled. Harry Catterick's opaque statement shed little light: 'Vernon has been sent home as a disciplinary measure. I felt it would be in the boy's best interests and the interests of the team.' With details so scant and murmurings of a curfew being broken, the rumour mill went into overdrive. The circumstances were more prosaic than the theories spreading rapidly on Merseyside.

Apparently, he had promised to meet a family friend whilst in Manhattan. Having met for coffee at the hotel, they wandered to the main street to say goodbye and hail her a cab. He described what happened next: 'I looked at my watch – it was about 10:50pm – just time to get some supper at the restaurant at the top of the street and return to the hotel before the 11:00pm curfew. It was, in fact, about 11:20pm when I got in and trainer Gordon Watson greeted me: "The boss will see you tomorrow." I wasn't worried, after all he had seen me in the hotel lounge, so he knew that I hadn't been out on the town. Imagine my dismay the next day when I went up to his room. "Pack your things. You're going home on the 4:30pm flight." "But ..." I said. "No buts," he said. "I saw you with a woman in the lounge and then you came in late." The implication was enough. It was just the chance Harry had wanted to impress on everyone that he was master. But I remember thinking, "There are two sides to everything – I'll tell mine when I get home".'[1]

Any thoughts that Roy may have had of going public with his discontent were quashed as he was driven to the airport with the manager, club director Fred Micklesfield, and loyal teammates Alex Young and Alex Parker. The latter would fly back with the Welshman, albeit not sat next to him. Harry Catterick's coup de grace was yet to come. On the way to the airport, the manager leaned over and said quietly in Roy's ear: 'This incident is now closed, but if you speak to the press you will be subjected to further disciplinary action. If you ask for a transfer it will be refused. However, if your wife is concerned at speculation, I will be glad to speak to her when I get home.'

Arriving back at Manchester's Ringway Airport, the jet-lagged player told journalist Horace Yates in a somewhat terse manner: 'I've absolutely no comment to make about that. Maybe the chairman, Mr Moores, will want to see me tomorrow. Only to him will I tell my story.' When pressed by the journalist as to whether his involuntary repatriation was an outcome of a personality clash with Catterick he replied: 'I refuse to say a single word about what happened.'[5]

As speculation – some of it salacious – continued to swirl around the circumstances of Roy's sudden return to England, he made further comments to the *Daily Post*: 'If only I could say what it was all about, I am sure there would not have been all this publicity. I suppose I must accept it as an occupational hazard. Some of the stories I have heard since I arrived home might have been originated by a New York scriptwriter and would have contained just about as much truth. Not until after the New York tournament will I even consider lifting the veil of secrecy. By that time, I hope people will have completely lost interest.' In fact, Roy never went public with the circumstances, only recording them in his unpublished memoirs. He did cable his teammates via Bobby Collins, most of whom he had not seen before he had been whisked to New York's Idlewild Airport: 'Good luck lads. Hope you win the competition,' was the sum of his message.

Down the line, Alex Young set the record straight: 'I was Taffy's roommate in New York and know nothing about prostitutes or wild parties. Such false allegations were absolute nonsense. Yes, my pal had been irresponsible in not complying with the club's curfew. He was angry because he should have known better. It was an unnecessarily harsh punishment act by an unnecessarily harsh disciplinarian. As intended, it got the message to the other lads.'

Without Roy, the team had shone against Montreal Concordia, Kilmarnock, Karlsruhe, Dinamo Bucharest, Bangu, Beşiktaş and New York Americans. Their impressive record of six wins from the seven games meant that they would advance to the final of the competition, to be staged in the summer. Back at home, many thought that the public dressing down would herald a transfer of the carpeted forward away from Merseyside. However, having made his point, Harry Catterick appeared to have remained true to his word. On the team's return from New York, the two main protagonists in the affair sat down to clear the air. The manager concluded: 'As far as I am concerned, and the board is concerned, the matter is closed. There will be no further action.' With the drama seemingly put to bed, Roy agreed to extend his stay at the club. And when Harry Catterick's side returned to the USA in late July for the culmination of the tournament – a two-legged final against Dukla Prague – the Welshman was included in the sixteen-man party. Unfortunately, Everton were thumped 9-2 on aggregate by the Czechoslovakian Army-backed side.

With preparations underway for the new season it appeared that peace had been restored. The 'sometimes-wayward' (as Catterick described him) striker, however, was blissfully unaware that the club's board and manager had agreed that he should be offered in a swap deal if a suitable alternative forward became available at a rival club.

Roy would never enjoy the bond with Harry Catterick that he shared with Gentleman John. However, Norma Vernon refutes the oft-stated opinion that he disliked Catterick or, for that matter, Dally Duncan at Blackburn. She claimed that her other half accepted that Harry was a disciplinarian – and appreciated what he brought to the club in terms of organisation and tactical nous – but it was always in his rebellious nature to see how far he could push the boundaries of anyone's authority.

Harry Catterick's private nature, and knowledge that John Moores was peering over his shoulder, meant that he wanted full control over all Everton-related information destined for the press. So, during pre-season training, the manager introduced his new right-hand man Tommy Eggleston, who had followed him from Sheffield Wednesday, and informed the players that in future all releases and quotes would be subject to his approval and that training would be stepped up. It remains something of a surprise that the manager's virtual media embargo did not halt Roy's contributions to the *Daily Post*. Originally entitled 'The Whole Truth by Roy Vernon – Everton and Wales', the columns continued in a watered-down incarnation under the title 'Says Roy Vernon' until the end of the 1962/63. Though he no longer reflected on wider footballing affairs in this column, he was still seemingly free to write about Everton's recent fortunes and their upcoming fixtures. Upon joining Everton, Roy was engaged to pen his thoughts and opinions in the weekly article. Averaging 1,500 words each in length, they were well-crafted, enlightening and insightful. For some unknown reason, his words weren't highlighted in the sports pages but inserted alongside updates on amateur football, Rugby League, horse racing and local golf. Assisted, but not ghosted, by Horace Yates, he addressed a wide range of strategic and topical issues in the beginning.

His favourite subjects were players' contracts and the abolition of the maximum wage, the televising of games, the age-old dilemma of club-versus-country, the perils of football management, the advent of substitutes in football as well as his impressions of his new teammates. As for his gift of prophecy, the Welsh oracle predicted that England would win the World Cup in 1966 and the formation of a super league composed of England's top clubs.

In summary, Roy vilified the concept of the maximum wage and the clubs' abilities to retain players' registrations, even at the end of contract periods. Notably, he praised George Eastham, who had taken Newcastle United to court over their obstruction of his desired move to Arsenal. No doubt Eastham's willingness to challenge his employer struck a chord with Roy's near-mutinous streak.

Equally vocal about financial matters, Roy professed that the wage ceiling of £20 per week during the winter and £17 during the summer was harmful to the game and should be done away with. He proposed: 'Clubs should pay their players what they can afford with guaranteed minimum rates graded for the different divisions.' He did add, however, that every member of a team be paid alike. His proposals mirrored those of the Professional Footballers' Association. Subsequently, under the leadership of Jimmy Hill, the PFA called its members to take industrial action on 21 January 1961. While Everton and a handful of other wealthy clubs sought gain by luring away their rivals' stars, Jim Wilkinson, the Blackburn chairman, argued that an increase to a £30 per week maximum wage would be suicide for many clubs. However, on 18 January, Football League secretary Alan Hardaker persuaded the clubs to abolish the maximum wage in order to avoid strike action from the players. Promptly, Fulham agreed to pay England ace Johnny Haynes £100 per week – seven times the average manual wage.

In general, Roy was critical about how footballers were treated by those in positions of power: 'Soccer players are the poor relations in the entertainment business. The somewhat less responsible members of the football fraternity who dash about in expensive sports cars create an entirely wrong impression. The typical footballer cannot afford luxuries. It is as much as most of us can do to stretch our income to take in some sort of economical family car. Would I encourage my son to be a professional footballer? No, not as things are in 1960. Although football will be my life so long as I can kick a ball sufficiently intelligently to appeal to a football club, I would prefer to see him take up something more substantial, like one of the professions. Of course, if he proved to be a lad who eats, drinks and sleeps football, I would not raise a finger to stop him.'

True to form, he didn't hesitate to express his opinions about his new boss and new club: 'The facilities at Goodison Park cannot fail to impress. Those who have grown up there are inclined to take it all for granted but to a newcomer the luxury is breathtaking. I soon learned that the idea of making Everton the Arsenal of the North was more than mere propaganda. When Mr Carey outlined his big plans, I knew that it wasn't sales talk. I've always considered him to be a man of his word and honestly believe that steps have been taken to make it the finest club in the land. I feel flattered to have been chosen to take part in the great revival. During my early days at Ewood, Mr Carey helped me find my feet by playing me on the wing for the simple reason that I was not strong enough to take an inside position against players of weight, class and ability. He was almost like a father to me. His door was always open.

In one column, he referred to his neighbours' plight in the Second Division: 'They have dropped only one point in their last six games and yet at their last home game there were only 26,302 spectators. I have seen Liverpool at close quarters and was pleasantly surprised at their quality. If they were only able to play that type of game in First Division company, I don't think there is much doubt that their gates would be rivalling those of Everton. It can, of course, be argued that before they taste the fruits, they must earn them, but I know just how hard it is trying to get out of the Second Division. You may read from time to time about players of repute with clubs in the lower tiers asking for a move in order that they can play with First Division sides. It is not entirely lack of loyalty or selfishness that prompts this. They realise that their play is in danger of deteriorating outside the top flight and a footballer's career being as short as it is, they cannot always afford to wait for a team to come along. It is not always a question of pounds, shillings and pence. Important though money is, contentment and a place in the right atmosphere counts for a great deal.'

Clearly proud to be a born-again Evertonian, he addressed the club's participation in the North American International Soccer League. The club skipper proclaimed: 'I don't think anyone will doubt now that Everton are worthy representatives of British soccer to take part in the New York tournament. Apart from Spurs I doubt if there is any club in the league who would be accepted generally as a better proposition, and we at Everton would doubt even that.'

It has been well-documented that Harry Catterick did not trust the press. One anecdote encapsulates the manager's desire for complete control of information emanating from Goodison. Mike Ellis had been appointed as the Merseyside football correspondent for the Daily Herald and was taken to the stadium to be introduced to the manager. Initially Catterick had been welcoming, offering drinks and telling Ellis: 'I'll do anything I can to help you.' However, just moments later Ellis walked into the player's lounge. Roy called out to his former school friend. On realising that the club captain was a long-time friend of the journalist, things soon changed. 'Harry's face was a picture. From then on, our relationship was difficult,' Ellis admitted.

On occasions, Vernon's lifestyle and maverick ways made the local papers. In October 1961, the *Daily Post* outlined his involvement in a car crash: 'Roy Vernon, Everton's 23-year-old forward, had a narrow escape when his car hit a lamp standard in Dunnings Bridge Road, two miles from his home. Factory workers going home from the night shift helped him out of his car. One told Vernon: "We thought you had been electrocuted. There was a bright blue flash as the car hit the lamp post." Vernon, who contributed Everton's goal in the 1-1 draw at Chelsea on Saturday, arrived back with the rest of the team on Saturday night. At 6.30am yesterday (Sunday), after visiting friends, he was driving to his home in Lydiate, alone. As the car rounded a traffic island near Bootle golf course, it went into a skid on the wet road. Vernon was taken to Bootle General Hospital where one stitch was inserted in a nose wound before he was allowed to go home. Yesterday he said: "It was a frightening experience. I am a lucky man."' The newspaper, however, didn't include any quotes from his wife or his manager.

Stories about the Blue Dragon's inseparability from tobacco are legion. Contemporary photos invariably have him with a Senior Service cigarette held 'twixt his fingers or lips, the only exception being once he had run onto the playing field. He would claim that he puffed on them without inhaling, but with a sixty-a-day habit the damage would be done over time. One technique he skilfully mastered was water-defying smoking. Not a single former teammate, when interviewed for this book, failed to mention this aquatic party trick. 'He was the master of smoking in the shower on account of his skill in cupping his hand and tilting his head to shield the lit cigarette from the deluge,' remembered Stoke City's George Eastham. 'If dunked by teammates into the communal post-match bath, he would resurface with the cigarette still lit, having been held inside his mouth.' Everton teammate Derek Temple, meanwhile, recalls the smoker's efforts to remove the tell-tale traces from his hands: 'His hands used to be brown with tar and nicotine and he'd have a packet of Brillo pads. He'd go in the bathroom and would rub with them to try and clean his hands.'

Then there are his nocturnal habits. Liverpool centre was only a thirty-minute drive from Lydiate and players from both senior clubs could easily enjoy the bright lights afforded by the big city. Brian Labone voiced his concerns about the discord this led to in the dressing room: 'Perhaps it had something to do with the cultural revolution of the early 60s. Whereas the local lads were more conservative and homely, the rebels – all signed by Johnny Carey – were young men from out of town with more than a few bob in their pockets in an exciting city with all its attractions. They were such snappy dressers that I thought of them as "The Walton Rat Pack". Where to start? There was Alex Parker, who I nicknamed Frankie Vaughan; George Thomson, suave enough to audition as the next James Bond; Mickey Lill, who took ages combing his precious locks to mirror those of Tony Curtis; Alex Young, with his delicate, cherub-like looks and Royston, Talacre's Frank Sinatra. In hindsight, the boss had his hands full.'

The Royal Tiger Club, located close to the Mersey Tunnel entrance, was a perennial favourite and, in the days before smartphones and social media, players were assured a degree of privacy during their evening jaunts. Whilst Johnny Carey may have had an easy-going attitude to his players' extra-curricular activities, his successor adopted a more controlling approach.

Two months after the Goodison board had advised potential buyers that they were open to offloading their Welsh maverick, the directors declined an approach from Highbury in the region of £35,000. The club's minute books recorded: 'It was agreed that we could not part with Vernon at the moment.' No explanation is given. But perhaps one reason for their reluctance was the rich vein of form that he had hit in his second full season on Merseyside.

That 1961/62 campaign – the first under Harry Catterick – saw Everton finish behind Tottenham, Burnley and champions Ipswich Town. For Roy – now sporting a neat short hairstyle in place of his trademark quiff – it was a rewarding one which provided a prolonged spell playing in tandem with Alex Young. From the start of the season, the pair would become virtual ever-presents. The blonde Scotsman's lack of brawn was more than compensated by his rare football intelligence, speed of thought, immaculate poise, sublime ball control, balletic balance and expert timing of his salmon-like leaps. Their partnership would blossom into one eulogised nearly six decades on.

Through a combination of hard work on the training ground and something approaching football telepathy, they dovetailed beautifully. 'We worked extra hard at improving our understanding and blending our talents,' recalled Alex Young some years later. 'More specifically, we concentrated on exploiting his electrifying acceleration over five to fifteen yards and his fierce shot. He had the knack of making perfect contact with the football. Of course, English football boasted some top-class footballers in the 60s but the only one to come close to striking the ball so sweetly was Bobby Charlton. Together we practiced cushioning balls towards his lethal right boot and clipping balls into space behind defenders for him to run on to.'[2]

One former player, who prefers not to be identified, was a teenager on the club's books at that time and saw the unique blend at first hand: 'When Taffy and Alex played together in practice games, it was mesmerising, like watching two men with a shared brain. They seemed to know where the other was or was going to be.'

Mick Meagan was more than a little impressed by the way the two Celts dovetailed: 'Alex and Taffy were forwards who didn't think defensively. They had this telepathy between them – they didn't say much but they knew what the other was going to do. You rarely heard them calling for a ball – they expected you to know where they were and what they were going to do next. Both were so good on the ball that they had this knack of taking the piss out of defenders. Clearly, Alex and Taffy enjoyed playing together and I enjoyed playing alongside them. One was a saint and one was a bit of a rogue.'

After a poor start – blamed in part on preparations disrupted by the American tour – Everton's 1961/62 season gained momentum. The highlights included a 6-0 thrashing of Nottingham Forest in early October with two goals from Jimmy Fell – a left-winger signed for a bargain fee from Grimsby Town – a brace from Roy plus others from Jimmy Gabriel and Alex Young. Both of the Welshman's strikes were well-worked. First, Young dribbled the ball into the eighteen-yard box before sending over a carefully-weighted pass to the unmarked Vernon, who breasted the ball down and hit it into the corner of the net. For his second, the centre-forward lobbed the ball to the far post where Bingham headed it inwards, and Vernon side-footed home.

Another highlight was the 5-1 hammering of Manchester United at Goodison in early December, with two more goals from Vernon and others from Collins, Fell and Young. On this occasion, Roy netted with another entry in his catalogue of superlative goals. Merseyside journalist Michael Charters gushed: 'The ball broke for Vernon and Nicholson to chase. Vernon withstood Nicholson's close challenge and cleverly lobbed the ball over Gaskell's head into the roof of the net.'[6] Remarkably, it was bettered by Roy's second on 32 minutes, which made the score 4-0: 'Thomson made a terrific 35-yard pass to Vernon who with a clever body swerve collected the ball and took it away from Nicholson in the one movement and ran some thirty yards before hitting it past Gaskell.'[6]

Journalist Alan Ridgill added his observations: 'Everton were cheered off at the interval, yet slow hand-clapped during the second-half. United were 5-0 down at half-time and I wouldn't have given the Manchester side much chance of finishing without ten goals rattled past them. Roy Vernon was a venomous dart who repeatedly raced down the middle like a guided missile, and was always bang on target. Everton's lack of success in the second-half was the penalty of over-confidence.' The result advanced Catterick's men to third place in the table and dropped United in the relegation zone.

Better still was to come. Roy gave one of his finest ever displays against high-flying Burnley on 10 February 1962. Leslie Edwards, a veteran of the Merseyside football scene, was in raptures and compared the Walian to Jimmy Wilde, the 'Mighty Atom' of boxing: 'Having seen most of the great inside-forwards of the past forty years – James, Mannion, Revie, Haynes, Greaves, among them – I have come to the conclusion that we have one to beat the lot. He's only starting his career, weighs little more than ten stones, has a rather knock-kneed stance which makes him look anything but a footballer, and has a Celtic temper and temperament. His name? Roy Vernon. Position? Anywhere and everywhere – at lightning speed – he can do his side a bit of good.'

He continued: 'Vernon is a natural. You couldn't coach or counsel him in any way, unless it were to hold his tongue and temper. And yet if you succeeded in doing that you might denude him of so much of his sting he would cease to be what he is now, the anchor man of an attack which would surely drift hard on to the rocks if things were otherwise. Anyone seeing the entertaining 2-2 draw on Saturday and not knowing the players would surely seize on Vernon as the dominant figure. His extraordinary control of the ball, whether gathering it and moving off in the same movement or carrying it with him; his well-developed sense of locality whether it be of a teammate or the goal frame; his sense of anticipation and the speed of his awareness of a situation, these make him a player in a hundred thousand. Vernon's virtuosity does not end there. He has drive, guts and a shot so fierce that he rates with his old compatriot, Jimmy Wilde, the boxer, who was known as "The ghost with a hammer in his hand." Like Wilde, Vernon puts them to sleep before they know what has hit them. He did it twice against Burnley, whose defence is knit so close any forward line is apt to lose itself among the threads. This was his greatest game. His spark of genius could swing any match Everton's way.'

Vernon's form was such that it seemed ludicrous that the club even considered of dispensing with his services. However, to the acute disappointment of most Evertonians, the time was up for another of their favourites. Bobby Collins was now the wrong side of thirty, sometimes outspoken and often absent through injury, and so Harry Catterick and John Moores decided it was time to move him on. Always on the lookout for a direct replacement, the manger moved to bring in the metronomic Dennis Stevens from Bolton Wanderers. Catterick did previously have a gentleman's agreement with Don Revie to sign Billy Bremner from Leeds if Collins went in the opposite direction, which he duly did, but the young Scotsman – who had been suffering from a bout of homesickness – ended up remaining at Elland Road. It meant Stevens came in instead.

Collins had been a talisman at Goodison. Arriving shortly before John Carey, he almost singlehandedly instilled professionalism and a steely desire to win – frequently at any cost – in a team that was more used to flirting with relegation. Harry Catterick was now left with the task of naming a new club captain. Centre-half Brian Labone was too young, but both Billy Bingham, the experienced winger, or Alex Parker, the experienced right-back, seemed a logical choice. Instead, Catterick gambled on a much riskier candidate. The news came as a shock to Roy himself: 'All the players wondered who the next skipper would be. As we boarded the London train for our next game, the boss said that he wanted to see me in his compartment. "You are the next captain of Everton. You know what I expect from you but on the field, you will have the responsibility. I wouldn't give you the job if I didn't know that you can do it." I was delighted – really, at last, I was losing that "Wild Welshman" tag and here I was, the captain of the new Everton.[1]

Why did Harry Catterick choose someone known for being a self-absorbed player who walked a thin disciplinary line, both on and off the pitch? First, there was the expectation that Roy's supreme confidence would rub-off on his teammates, and that confidence would also mean he would not be dimmed by the weight of the captaincy. Also, there was the hope that the added responsibility might temper his wilder extremes and help him channel his energies positively. Of course, the Everton boss would roll the same dice, with less success, with Alan Ball in 1970.

Roy claimed that the added responsibility was no burden due to the high quality of teammates and pre-match preparations: 'It didn't worry me a scrap. The manager and trainer lay down policy and tactics, and the boys have enough intelligence to carry out their duties without a lot of prompting from the skipper.[1]

An unbeaten run from late February – starting shortly before the sale of Collins – to the end of the season culminated in a fourth-place finish. The league fixtures were rounded off in fine style, with Roy netting a hat-trick in an 8-3 humiliation of relegation-bound Cardiff City in the penultimate game of the season – the pick of the three being an exquisite lob over Graham Vearncombe, the Wales international goalkeeper.

For Roy, it was a very productive season – arguably the most consistent of his Everton career – yielding 26 goals in 37 league appearances of which, having taken over spot-kick duties from Bobby Collins, three were from the spot. It should have been four, but uncharacteristically he fluffed his effort at White Hart Lane on 24 March 1962 and Bill Brown saved his attempt. It was the only miss of his senior career. His willingness and ability from the spot dated back to his North Wales youth football days. 'Penalty taking is not for the faint-hearted and I think Roy only ever missed that one spot kick at Everton,' recalled Derek Temple. The technique, honed through years of practice on the training ground, was relatively simple. From a short run up, Roy would strike through the ball, hitting it low and hard into the corner of the net, more often than not to the keeper's left. Being the cocky personality that he was, it was not unknown for him to point to where he was going to hit the ball, safe in the knowledge that the power and precision would prevent a save, even if the goalkeeper did dive the correct way.

Even though the new captain came second to Alex Young in the affections of many, he was worshipped by some younger fans, amongst them Stephen Stokes: 'Roy was just a great player who was worth the admission money on his own. My father was a dock worker with limited income, so he'd take me to the match once every month. It was always a joy to be told that we were going to the match as it was to stand on the Goodison Road terraces and marvel at Roy. In those days the players walked up about six steps from the tunnel out onto the playing area. As a matter of courtesy, the visitors took the field first and then Everton came out to the sounds of "Z-Cars". If I close my eyes, even now, I can picture Roy Vernon emerging from the tunnel, seeing his back with that black hair, long white neck and that huge number ten on his blue shirt.'

At the conclusion of the 1961/62 season, Roy's talents were highlighted by Bill Fryer of the *Daily Express*: 'Put a beret on him, and from 100 yards range he would look like a knitting needle. But don't be deceived: Royston Vernon, black-haired, Welsh-looking of 5ft 8in and a mere ten stone is not only one of Britain's greatest inside-forwards, pound-for-pound Vernon is also one of the toughest.'

He continued: 'I don't want to make his head swell but Vernon has the craftsman's ball control, a super-kiddological feint, the sharp acceleration and manoeuvrability of a fly, the psychic anticipation of a mind-reader, a sharp brain and a powerful shot. He is also still apt to chuck about what little weight that he has. "What about that then?" I asked this splendid Everton skipper, reminding him that he had been sent off twice. "First time I deserved it," he said. "Second time I didn't. But, in any case, I was too fiery then. It was immaturity. I'm 25 now and, after eight years in the game, I am calmer."' The arrival of an ambitious multi-millionaire (who forbade the local press from referring to him in those terms) committed to reviving the fortunes of a regional club was viewed with more than a little suspicion nationwide, especially in London. John Moores's dream of taking Everton and Merseyside football from the doldrums of the 50s to the peak of the British game had been built on a series of shrewd signings. While the arrival of Bobby Collins had changed the ambitions of the club, the partnership of Vernon and Young announced its return to the top. The Toffees had finished the season strongly and looked forward to the pursuit of glory and silverware in the 1962/63 season.

CHAPTER 5

Season to Remember

'Taffy had a short fuse. If someone kicked him accidentally
or intentionally, he would seek immediate retribution.
It was a combination of self-preservation and madness.'

Brian Harris

FOR EVERTONIANS BORN BEFORE 1955, THE EVENTS OF 1962/63 ARE burnt into their retinas, their memories and their royal blue souls. Indeed, it was one to remember.

Bright-eyed and bushy-tailed – having recovered from a tour to South America during which Wales faced Mexico and Brazil twice as those two nations prepared for the 1962 World Cup finals staged in Chile – Roy Vernon looked forward to the new campaign, which kicked off with a precarious trip to Burnley, a recognised contender for the title.

Mirroring Real Madrid in an all-white kit, the Everton side featured Ray Veall – a raw teenage recruit from Doncaster Rovers – at outside-left. The game was an end-to-end cracker and generated massive roars of appreciation from the near-capacity crowd at Turf Moor, especially when the Everton skipper sent an early rocket narrowly wide and scraped the post with another. Third time proved lucky when he rifled home a twenty-yard shot after his first attempt had been charged down. Though his contributions were halted briefly when the referee warned him about his overly enthusiastic challenges, Roy responded by waltzing through the Burnley defence before feeding the ball via Alex Young to Billy Bingham to make it 2-1. Almost immediately after that, the inside-left released his Scottish partner, who expertly rounded the keeper and lobbed home with precision. The 3-1 win was heartening for a team that had notched only three victories on the road during the previous season.

Four days on, the Toffees approached the fixture against Manchester United with great confidence. In an equally enthralling contest, Harry Catterick's team exhibited brilliance seen rarely at post-war Goodison and swept into a commanding lead. To their credit, Matt Busby's men mounted a fightback and, driven on by Denis Law, narrowed the deficit. The final 3-1 scoreline elevated Everton into third-place in the embryonic table, the club's highest position for almost a quarter of a century.

So far so good. Everton's line-up against Sheffield Wednesday, their third match of the season, included the controversial addition of Johnny Morrissey. The former Anfield favourite, who had signed for the Toffees from Liverpool that summer, was impressed by his new leader: 'Roy led by example. Captaincy isn't always about shouting and yelling. Some captains are different – we spoke.' The left-winger observed – at close hand – the potent blend of Vernon and Young in an impressive 4-1 win: 'Taffy tended to play a lot through the middle and didn't drift out to wings. Alex was the drifter and the provider whilst Taffy, always direct and fast, got in behind defences. He liked to play off the centre-forward and Alex was his ideal partner because of his exceptional ball control and vision. It was a great partnership.' Days later, Harry Catterick's men continued their rich vein of form with a 1-0 success at Old Trafford. Late in the proceedings, Roy took care of business from the spot after Johnny Morrissey had been fouled by Shay Brennan.

The four-game winning streak ended abruptly at Craven Cottage. Possibly troubled by the hot conditions or more likely by over-confidence, Everton lacked both rhythm and balance and lost 1-0. With Fulham more physical and not giving Vernon and Young time to indulge in their artistry, the match descended into a bad-tempered affair in which the inside-left was kicked black and blue by Fulham's Eddie Lowe.

Before the start of the next home game, the Everton fans gave former manager Johnny Carey and his newly-promoted Leyton Orient team a cordial reception. There would be no niceties, however, from their team. The *Liverpool Echo's* Leslie Edwards could not believe that Everton did not reach double figures. In his eyes, the 3-0 scoreline – which included a penalty converted by Roy – should have been far greater, and the reason it wasn't was due to profligacy in front of goal and acrobatic goalkeeping: 'Under brilliant lights on a carpet of vivid green turf, which played fast under the effect of the dew, there could scarcely have been a better demonstration of how the game should be played. It was a fabulous performance as individuals and as a team. They rained in shots, hammered in headers and had such a grip in their half-back line that Leyton must have thought that they were trying to stop a runaway steamroller.'

Looking down the table at the other 21 teams after six fixtures, Catterick's men edged an even more vigorously contested affair against Leicester City, yet another legitimate contender for the title, by a margin of 3-2, which included the familiar notation: *Vernon (pen)*. Inexplicably, their reign at the top of the table was cut short when they slipped up again in London. This time lowly Leyton Orient embarrassed them 3-0 – a penny for Johnny Carey's thoughts after the final whistle.

After coming to terms with this short, sharp, shock of reality, the Toffees rebounded and rediscovered their best form with convincing wins over Bolton and West Brom, victories which were followed by an agonising 2-2 draw with Liverpool, promoted back to the top flight the season before. The first Merseyside derby for eleven seasons started in the most controversial of circumstances. In the first minute, the ever-alert Roy nicked the ball away from Reds goalkeeper Jimmy Furnell and stroked it in the net. As the home fans celebrated wildly, the referee had a change of heart and awarded a free-kick to the embarrassed stopper. Subsequently, he explained that in harrying Furnell, he had caused him to lose his footing. In 1978, Bob Paisley, the Liverpool assistant manager during the early 1960s, confessed to having duped the referee and robbed Vernon of a goal. Speaking to Michael Charters, in the wake of Kenny Dalglish's copycat goal against West Bromwich Albion, he explained: 'The only time I have seen a similar goal was sixteen years ago at Goodison. Roy Vernon was disallowed just such a goal. It was a perfectly good goal. You don't think Everton can claim it after all these years, do you? Our keeper Jimmy Furnell was a bundle of nerves. He rolled the ball too far and Vernon was in like a flash to put it in the net. Furnell didn't know what had happened. I thought that he had been injured. The referee was walking away signalling a goal when I ran on the pitch, threw the sponge at Furnell and told him he was "injured". I shouted to the official that I was attending an injury. He came back, saw me rubbing our keeper's face and disallowed the goal.'[6]

Notwithstanding the encouraging start to the campaign, Harry Catterick continued to seek improvements to his expensively assembled team. In September 1962, he attempted to sign Bryan Douglas from Blackburn, much to Roy's pleasure. The pair had kept in touch, Douglas occasionally inviting him to share a night at the dog track and a drink or two in Blackburn, sometimes with Alex Young and Jimmy Gabriel in tow. As usual, the approach by Everton was made through an intermediary but, after weighing the pros and cons, the player and his family decided to remain in their home town. Catterick would have to wait another three months before strengthening his squad.

During this period, partly down to Catterick's distrust of all things related to the media, television and film news cameras were something of a rarity at Goodison. However, the brilliance and near-perfect harmony of Vernon and Young was captured during Everton's visit to Molineux on 6 October 1962. That afternoon, the Blues defeated Wolves, another title contender, by a score of 2-0. With the visitors leading by 1-0 with fifteen minutes of the game remaining, the cameras caught Roy receiving the ball in his own half from right-back Mick Meagan. With immaculate control and sublime body swerves, he befuddled three opponents, advanced into the centre-circle and pinged a delightful pass for Alex Young to slide into the net without breaking his stride. Many journalists concluded that it was the best Everton had played all year.

After scoring penalties in the frustrating 1-1 home draw against Aston Villa and in the impressive 3-1 home win over Ipswich, the reigning champions, Roy looked forward to travelling north of the border for the second leg of the Inter-Cities Fairs Cup tie against Dunfermline Athletic. Everton had beaten the Scottish outfit 1-0 at Goodison between the Villa and Ipswich games, in the process becoming the first team from Merseyside to compete in European competition. However, they were humiliated by a physical Dunfermline side at East End Park, and their 2-0 defeat and subsequent exit at the first stage had significant ramifications.

Manager Harry Catterick's nature was to give his players a jolt at the merest hint of complacency or underperformance. So, prior to the trip to Manchester City the following weekend, Roy was unceremoniously dumped into the reserves and replaced by Frank Wignall. When the news broke that the Everton captain had been dropped, the local press went into overdrive, speculating as to the reasons behind the decision. Leslie Edwards proffered that Roy's temperament did not sit well with the demands of the captaincy: 'In one match recently, Vernon should have known better than to go to a linesman who had just made an adverse decision and put on a show of dumb dissent – placing two forefingers to his eyes was the method used.'[6] The more plausible rationale for his demotion was that, spot kicks aside, the inside-left had scored only twice in eighteen appearances that season and had looked sluggish, almost apathetic, at Dunfermline.

Even though he was the club's top scorer in the Central League, Wignall struggled at Maine Road. Nevertheless, he persevered to bag an equaliser, going some way to vindicating Catterick's gamble. However, come the next match at home to Blackpool, Roy was back captaining his teammates as they swept away the Tangerines 5-0. The match was notable for the presence of Leonard Williams, who played Sergeant Twentyman in the popular *Z-Cars* television show. The actor would die from a heart attack days later and it is understood that the programme's theme tune, which had been aired at Goodison since the beginning of the season, was subsequently played in his posthumous honour. This went some way to establishing 'Theme from Z-Cars', performed by John Keating and his Orchestra as an enduring pre-match staple for almost six decades.

Roy didn't score against Blackpool but was in the goals at Nottingham Forest – his brace being his first from open play since 25 August 1962 – in a midweek seven-goal thriller. Hailed by travelling Evertonians as the most enthralling game so far, both sides produced football of the very highest calibre. Down 2-0 down after fifteen minutes, Everton showed great character to fight back and triumph by 4-3 and take over top spot. The Blue Dragon's second goal was magnificently executed. Collecting a fifty-yard pass from Alex Parker, he drew keeper John Armstrong and finished with aplomb.

After a controversial last-minute defeat at Ewood Park, Everton bounced back with a 3-0 home win against Sheffield United. Roy bagged a brace, one of which was hailed as the finest of his career. Witnesses claim that the inside-left received a pass on the halfway line, beat one defender with a body swerve, progressed thirty yards via a corkscrew run, repeated the body swerve to get around two other defenders before firing a thunderbolt which sent the goalkeeper the wrong way.

Come early December, Everton recorded a hard-earned 0-0 draw against Tottenham, the title favourites and their closest rivals, at White Hart Lane, and that was followed by a more disappointing point at home to West Ham. Still, they had reached the halfway point of their campaign top of the table, two points ahead of Burnley. As for Roy, he had netted seven from penalties and a meagre six goals from open play.

Thankfully, the Welshman found his shooting boots for the visit of high-flying Burnley to Goodison. Alongside Alex Young, he had an exceptionally productive day and netted in the important 3-1 win. The following week's trip to frost-bound Hillsborough would be the last time he would kick a ball for weeks as the harshest winter in living memory took its toll. Everton went from 22 December 1962 until 12 February 1963 without playing a league game. The Toffees were outplayed by the Owls for most of the match, but at 2-1 down Alex Young netted a very late equaliser when Springett could not hold Roy's shot.

In an era before under-soil heating was in widespread use (Goodison's pitch had a pioneering, and not altogether successful system), the schedule of football fixtures was decimated. Harry Catterick used the enforced downtime wisely, moving with trademark stealth to bolster his squad. First, he dashed to Ibrox to snatch Alex Scott, the pacey Scotland right-winger, from the clutches of Tottenham for a fee of £40,000. Next, the manger returned to Hillsborough to sign Tony Kay, Sheffield Wednesday's hard-tackling and talismanic half-back, a club record fee of £55,000.

Meanwhile, with Bellefield and Goodison icebound, Everton trained on the sands at Southport. Roy recalled: 'We had that horrible winter break and for weeks on end were unable to play. Of course, we kept training. As the tide retreated, out would come the balls and we would run, sprint and play six-a-sides. Despite the inclement weather, we grafted. Let no one tell you football is easy. Alright, footballers only work two or three hours a day but after these sessions many virtually crawl back into the dressing rooms.'[1]

For the devil-may-care Welshman, these were halcyon days that he would look back on fondly and laugh at how 'The Rat Pack' would lead arch-disciplinarian Harry Catterick and his lieutenants on a merry dance around the night-spots of Liverpool – that is once they had received their wages on a Thursday. 'We were winning matches,' he wrote. 'Alex Scott and Tony Kay had arrived: now we had our championship team, with steel and power in defence together with class and speed up front. However, I think the team spirit in the dressing room was largely responsible for a lot of our success. But this spirit was built up off the field. Thursday night was the lads' night out and almost every member of the team would be in the local nightclubs. The Everton manager soon became aware of this and his dreaded dawn patrol was introduced. It consisted of Tom Eggleston and

Ron Lewin, who went out in their cars to spot players out clubbing. One night we decided to outwit them. We parked outside our favourite nightspot, locked our cars and set off in taxis for another club. We had a good night out. The next morning, two red-eyed coaches watched us sign-in, shaking their heads in bewilderment. Eggleston would remark: "How the hell do you do it? We did not leave your club until 3.30am." We couldn't help laughing – most of us had been home before 1.00am by taxi, knowing that Tom and Ron would be patiently waiting to nab us.'[1]

Derek Temple smiled at Roy's brave riposte when challenged over his nocturnal lifestyle: 'We had a few playboys in the side. On one occasion, the manager cautioned his captain: "This has got to stop. Your car was spotted outside the Royal Tiger on Thursday night," but Roy replied: "Listen Boss, we play hard off the field and hard on it. When it affects how we're playing, then you can send for me and have a go." That was Roy!'

No doubt such activities would land modern day players in the social media spotlight and in the dock with managers. Yet for Roy and his colleagues, it was a safety valve in the cauldron of the local football scene: '"Why," you may ask, "do professional footballers go to nightclubs at all?" I think it is because of the pressure on them. Training is harder, wages are higher, but everyone is under pressure to win. To be successful, nowadays, you must win. Apparently, a good entertaining game of football coupled with a defeat is of no use. Regardless of the methods, you must not lose. That is the code of today's game. Little wonder individuals find relaxation in a few beers. Let's face it, you don't get punished for these offences – you get punished for being caught.'[1]

Back on the pitch, the Merseysiders had managed to complete two FA Cup ties in January – with comfortable victories at Barnsley and Swindon – with Roy contributing three goals. Finally, league football resumed after a four-week hiatus. Despite the beach and dune training regime, Everton were slow out of the blocks, comprehensively outplayed 3-1 at Filbert Street by a Leicester team very much in the title race. Roy's goal was scant consolation. In his match report, Horace Yates praised the inside-left: 'Vernon was the only forward who caused real anxiety around the Leicester goal and valuable though much of his defensive play may have been, I am one of those who consider Vernon is essentially an attacker.'[5]

Meanwhile, Tony Kay was making an impression on his new teammates, opponents and the supporters at Leicester. 'More than once the crowd took exception to his tackles and every time he touched the ball he was hooted,' Yates observed. 'It made not the slightest difference to this human dynamo. When he was greeted with another demonstration as he left the field, his only response was a huge impish grin.'[5]

The rustiness associated with the Big Freeze was still evident when the Toffees failed to breach a resolute Wolverhampton rearguard at Goodison. For Roy, it was a frustrating draw: 'The skipper had one of those days when his jinking, wheeling, side-stepping dribbles were gobbled up by the massively effective Wolves tackling. He tried to do too much individually.'[6]

The Toffees bounced back fleetingly with a home win over Nottingham Forest before being eliminated from the FA Cup via a hotly disputed penalty in a bruising fifth round tie at Upton Park. This injustice was forgotten after comfortable wins at Ipswich and against ten-man Manchester City. By and large, Everton had struggled on the heavy, grassless pitches. Roy had failed to score in five games but did rediscover his form in a 4-3 loss at Highbury.

After another unexpected setback on the road, this time at Sheffield United, Everton travelled to Villa Park on April Fools' Day and secured a much-needed victory. Michael Charters summarised the upturn in the form of the front pairing: 'The side was unrecognisable from the disjointed outfit at Sheffield. The most marked difference was in attack, where Vernon and Young played with tremendous skill and dash. Vernon recaptured his old form of fighting through tackles, making ground at top speed and distributing the ball well.'

However, the great display of the night came from the blonde bombshell, whose contribution to the fine entertainment of a thrilling game was described by Harry Catterick: 'One of the finest centre-forward exhibitions I have ever seen.'[6] High praise, indeed, from a manager who had a distant relationship with his number nine. The win left Everton in third place, three points behind Tottenham.

It was a measure of Roy's rising status within the game that he was featured on the cover of the February 1963 edition of *World Sports* magazine – an iconic colour image of him on the lush green Goodison pitch, volleying an orange ball for the benefit of the cameraman. The accompanying article by Walter Pilkington entitled 'One Man Who Nearly Makes a Team' was extraordinarily long and verging on fawning in its appreciation of the player's innate ability and capacity for captaincy. An abridged version is reproduced below:

'Johnny Carey knew what he was about when he took Roy Vernon onto the

Blackburn Rovers staff as a youth of sixteen. Like all great players he had no illusions about his value in an era marked by the acute dearth of class inside-forwards; no false modesty about how far he could go, given the opportunity.

'A complex character, he is a perfectionist whose Celtic temperament is impatient over shortcomings, including his own. For Roy Vernon, in whose nature there is by no means a sense of inferiority, is his own severest critic. Maturity has softened rancour but he still cannot conceal irritation when a colleague has not done what appeared to Vernon to be obvious. Since he took over the captaincy he has calmed down in this respect. Despite his slight build Vernon was always ready to mix it with the toughest, particularly in his Blackburn days ... he is not now as readily provoked. Vernon's readiness to improvise and take command in the true sense of the captaincy is the more welcome because it is so astute.

'Watching his objective scheming, his finesse and artifice is a fascinating study in quickness of thought and action. A clever dribbler in the minimum of space, he is a master in the declining art of beating an opponent by body-swerve.

'Many players are good dribblers, but few are able to combine skill and subtle positioning which is Vernon's hallmark of class. Most of his goals come through this sixth sense. He keeps the ball moving, looks ahead and draws upon the surprise element in his resources in rapidly rising up and exploiting a situation. One man cannot make a team, but Roy Vernon at his best is as near to doing so as is humanly possible.'

Back to the title race and the next home fixture on a blustery Easter Saturday. Disappointingly, the hosts could not find a way past a resolute Blackburn side. Although Roy, making his 250th league appearance, had the ball in the net twice, both his strikes were chalked-off. Therefore, it is little surprise that the man in black was on the end of some ire at the final whistle: 'Referee James Carr was booed, and some orange peel and rolled-up newspapers were thrown'[6]. Disallowed goals aside, the Everton captain was in scintillating form: 'Vernon brought some class to the game with a superb run in which he swayed his way through half-a-dozen Blackburn men. When he tried to chip the ball into the far corner of the net, he put too much strength in his shot.'[6]

Two days on, Everton made the short trip to Anfield and came away with a point after another gritty 0-0 draw. According to Leslie Edwards: 'A more impressive contest one could scarcely imagine.' Not surprisingly, Roy was at the centre of the game's most contentious moment when he dashed through the

Liverpool defence, only to be upended by the chasing Ron Yeats. No penalty was awarded by the referee. In fact, his tally of goals had suffered from the reality that the Toffees had not been awarded one during the past nineteen matches. Despite playing extremely well, he had netted only once in his last nine outings.

With so many fixtures rescheduled, the league programme was extended by four weeks. Even so, Everton were required to fulfil six fixtures in fourteen days towards the end of April 1963. Though victorious at Blackpool, Catterick's team appeared disjointed. Two days later, Everton again underperformed in a home draw against ten-man Birmingham. The following morning, they travelled to St Andrew's for the return fixture, their third game in four days. Although in control, the Toffees lacked a cutting edge until Roy netted towards the end and placed Everton alongside Tottenham and Burnley one point behind Leicester with a game in hand. Roy would confess that the invaluable strike had an element of fluke about it: 'My "jammiest" goal of the season was certainly that one against Birmingham at St Andrew's at Easter. Tony Kay centred, a defender mis-headed and the ball dropped at my feet. I took a terrific swipe towards the goalkeeper's right, but as he dived, the ball skidded off my feet and rolled into the opposite corner of the net.'[1]

This narrow victory set up Tottenham's imminent visit to Goodison, a potential decider in the race for the 1962/63 league title. Evertonians were desperate to get tickets for the clash. In the local newspapers, stories emerged of some forking out £10 for a 3/- ticket and one supporter exchanging his Ford Anglia for a stand ticket. With over 67,000 crammed into the ground and thousands more milling outside, Everton won comfortably, albeit by only one goal. 'Everton were faster and better than Spurs at every stage,' claimed Michael Charters. 'Vernon was very much the striker in the front line, making a series of top speed breaks down the middle.'[6] The decisive goal came after sixteen minutes. Meagan cleared the ball down the left-flank to Kay, who fed Vernon on the wing. He crossed high for Young, who leaped above the centre-half, hung in the air and headed the ball into the Gwladys Street net. The local journalist observed the goal and its aftermath: 'Vernon, almost at outside-left, clipped the ball high, right-footed, to make it hang in the wind and offer Young a meagre chance of heading a goal. Brown left his line and struggled to challenge the centre-forward with that remarkable propensity of his for jumping half his own height. The Everton spearhead soared over his one opponent, John Smith, and edged the ball, almost gently, high over the line. The applause literally shook the place. I'll swear the press box moved inches up and down from the reverberations of the din.'[6]

The first half ended with a flurry of chances for Everton to increase their lead. Morrissey and Stevens both hit the upright, a feat repeated in the second half when Vernon chipped Brown beautifully, with Morrissey's follow-up shot ricocheting wide off Tony Marchi. It was Gabriel and Kay, so solid in the half-back line, who laid the platform for the win, but Vernon and Young were once again the men to draw widespread praise.

Looking down on all rivals with just five games to play, Goodison could taste glory. Ever the man for the big occasion, Roy discovered his best form and netted six times during the run-in. At home against the Gunners, he hit the target with a rasping shot, but with keeper Gordon West badly injured in a collision, Everton had to fight hard to earn one point. At Upton Park, their free-flowing football put them in control of the proceedings. Though they fell behind against the run of play, the number ten equalised when Young skilfully flicked the ball for him to beat the keeper from eight yards. Some ten minutes afterwards, Derek Temple netted the winner. This win in East London opened a three-point lead over Tottenham and Leicester, though Harry Catterick's men had now played one game more.

With only three games remaining, a combination of anxiety and the opponents' defensive tactics caused Everton to struggle against Bolton at Goodison. Eventually, they took the lead when Young out-jumped his marker and nodded the ball for Vernon to place it beyond the keeper – a mis-hit, he would confirm afterwards – and ignited a massive roar of relief from the near-packed crowd of 52,000. The penultimate game involved a very comfortable victory – perhaps too comfortable – over ten-men at The Hawthorns. Young bagged a brace; Roy converted a penalty and West Brom donated an own goal. The 4-0 scoreline meant that two points in the final fixture would guarantee an unbeaten campaign at home and, far more importantly, the first silverware to come to Goodison since 1939. The significance of another title – Everton's sixth – is reflected in the tallies of today's elite at that time. Some 57 years ago, Arsenal had earned seven titles, Liverpool five and Manchester United five. Tottenham had won two crowns, while Chelsea and Manchester City had nabbed one each.

Prior to the final match against Fulham, all Evertonians were aware that victory would guarantee that Spurs, five points behind with two games in hand, could not overhaul the Toffees. On the eve of the match, the proud club captain used his

Daily Post column to issue a rallying call to the royal blue faithful, urging them to play their part: 'Here we are – at the last fence! Everton have defied defeat at home in the last 39 matches and must go all out against a team which beat us earlier this season. If we can strike our true blend I don't think even Johnny Haynes would be good enough to keep us from our goal. Even at this late stage, we are not taking anything for granted.'

He added: 'Like our supporters, the players would dearly love to see Everton a goal up in the early stages. If it does not come, I appeal for patience. The crowd can give us that extra push which will send Fulham tottering. Our aim is not only to win this match but to end the season in a blaze of glory with one of our best exhibitions of football, with the crowd given something to remember the match that clinched the title. That aim will be more easily accomplished with your help. You may say it's up to us, and of that there is no argument, but almost equally true we can say that a lot depends on you. When we go out to smash Fulham tomorrow, remember it will be our way of saying "thank you". Come what may, you can take it from me that there will be 100 percent effort in this grand finale. We'll be listening for you!'

Matchday was warm and sunny, a startling contrast to the glacial conditions that had dogged much of the season. Decades after the event, Alex Parker recalled the mood as kick-off approached: 'Most of the lads suffered from nerves before games to some extent but on this day the tension in the dressing room was unbelievable. Harry Catterick and Tommy Eggleston were having a quiet word with each of the players. Tony Kay was bawling and shouting about the place, trying to make people think that he wasn't nervous. Roy was trying to crack jokes. Alex just sat there.'[6] Gordon West added: 'I went through my pre-match routine of throwing up in the toilets – and I wasn't even playing.'

Any nerves carried onto the pitch from the dressing room were quelled after five minutes as Roy, undaunted by the enormity of the occasion, collected a pass from Parker and dribbled past Alan Mullery and keeper Tony Macedo before slotting home at the Park End from an acute angle. Only three minutes later, he capitalised on confusion between the same two opponents to double the lead in almost carbon-copy style. After Johnny Key had beautifully volleyed home a Haynes cross for Fulham, the two-goal margin was restored when Roy's free-kick rebounded to Alex Scott, whose low shot eluded Macedo. With Everton's stars in their stride now, they peppered the Fulham goal with shots. Michael Charters described the club captain's interplay with Alex Young as 'a sweet moving duet'.[6]

Watching in awe was a future Everton shooting star in fourteen-year-old Joe Royle: 'I was invited to the match when Everton were courting me. I was in the stands with my parents. Roy was awesome – one-on-one and the keeper didn't have a chance. He had such quick feet and such a hard shot. I was a first-year apprentice when Roy left the club therefore remember him more as a fan. He would have been a superstar today, his value would have been immense. Alex Young used to say to me that Roy was a superstar.'

The second half was a more sedate affair, but with five minutes left Young flicked on Dunlop's clearance for Roy to slide the ball home at the Gwladys Street end, completing a famous treble and putting the result and title beyond doubt. When the whistle blew, some young fans ignored tannoy announcements and the ring of policemen to join their triumphant heroes in a lap of honour. One supporter gave Roy a rattle which he enthusiastically twirled above his head. The elated captain was also photographed holding aloft the team mascot, eleven-year-old John Murray, wearing a blue shirt with number ten sown on the back by his mother.

Sadly, the mascot would be only thing that Roy got to hold aloft. With the destination of the title uncertain before the match, the Football League had refused permission for the iconic trophy to be taken to Merseyside in anticipation of a coronation. Its absence, however, did little to detract from one of the greatest afternoons in a golden decade at Goodison and the zenith of his memorable career. Match reporter Edgar Turner described the scene: 'In this carnival of colour, balloons, streamers, excitement and joy, there surely could not have been anything better even over in Rio. It was one of the most memorable experiences I have had on world soccer grounds.'

Having made it back to the dressing room and toasted the triumph with champagne, the team accompanied John Moores, Harry Catterick and the coaching staff to the directors' box in the Main Stand to receive the adulation of the crowd below. Tens of thousands packed the lower part of the Goodison Road terraces and the neighbouring area of the pitch to salute the champions. The chairman raised his hand in response to chants of his name before Roy addressed the crowd, thanking the ecstatic gathering for their support and acknowledging the contribution of his teammates and the management team. According to Michael Charters: 'It was a brief speech and expressed all that had to be said.'[6]

The journalist summarised the events in the *Liverpool Echo*: 'Has there ever been an atmosphere, an excitement, a thrill, sports-wise, to equal that at Goodison Park on Saturday? Old-timers who have seen the great football moments in this city over the past four decades say there has been nothing like it since Dixie Dean broke the goalscoring record in 1928 in the last game of the season on the same pitch. It was a privilege to be in the historic ground again, this time to see Everton win the Football League Championship.'

Without question, captaining Everton Football Club to its sixth League title was the high point of Roy's career. When the dust had settled, the history books were to record that the squad, expensively assembled by John Moores, finished with 61 points, six more than Tottenham, and that Roy had netted 24 League goals, two more than his Scottish partner. It should not go unnoticed that Dennis Stevens and Johnny Morrissey had contributed seven each, while Billy Bingham and Jimmy Gabriel had added five each. The latter voiced his thoughts on what the Vernon-Young combination brought to the team: 'Taffy and Alex spearheaded our winning challenge for the league by scoring the goals we needed to get the job done. Taffy was as sharp as a needle; he could play deep in the midfield, forward in midfield, upfront and was captain in every sense of the word. I feel that he almost single-handedly won the league for us.'[3]

Tony Kay affirmed how the title was won: 'Every man in the 1962/63 side was a dedicated and talented pro who worked hard every single day. The matches were just the icing on the cake. Behind those fantastic performances were endless hours of training: tactics, skipping, sprinting, runs up and down the sand dunes and in the sea at Ainsdale come hell or high water, set pieces, discipline, blood, sweat and tears. We all missed our kids growing up – Christmas, birthday parties, family holidays, births, deaths and marriages – because we were hungry for success and nothing would stand in our way.'[10]

Nearly a decade later, Roy accepted the crucial changes made by Harry Catterick to the more open approach preferred by Johnny Carey: 'I've not forgotten that we were one of the first teams to take the title by winning a tactical battle, as well. We tightened up tremendously in defence when we were playing away from home, and we won a lot of games by the only goal.'[6]

In the souvenir edition of the *Liverpool Echo*, the skipper acknowledged the unstinting support of his teammates: 'The team spirit given to me as captain, and to Mr Catterick, as manager, could not have been better. I think that the right team won in the end.' In the same publication, an ecstatic John Moores paid rich tribute to the captain: 'Roy Vernon has been a fine captain. Giving him the honour has ensured that we get the best out of him. He played magnificently at West Ham when we had temporary injuries – worked like stink. You saw how he played against Fulham; he couldn't have done more. In defence or attack, always on the ball all the time. Others maybe don't need the inspiration of captaincy to keep their games at the top level. Roy is a real Evertonian and never more so than when leading the side. He's a great Evertonian at heart. Need I say more?'

Perhaps the last word belongs to one of the greatest Blues of all-time – Brian Labone, who would captain his one and only club to FA Cup glory in 1966 and the league title in 1970: 'Towards the end of the Fulham game, I twigged that my dream was about to come true. Along with Taffy, Alex, Gabby, Westie and the other lads, I would be acclaimed as a member of an Everton team to win the title. Indeed, it was a season to remember.'

The week-by-week events of the victorious campaign are captured in Appendix A entitled 'Blue Dragon's Fire-Breathing Season.' It includes summaries of all 42 league games – with every Everton goal described in detail – plus eyewitness accounts from the men who were there – the players, the coaches and the fans.

CHAPTER 6

So Near, So Far

'Taffy wasn't a classic mover like Alex Young. He was more the Ferret type: in and out, in and out. When I led the line for a few games I found him so easy to play alongside. He was always in space. Back then, the atmosphere was electric, especially in floodlit games at Goodison. You would get a shock just by touching the air. Vernon and Young loved the way it put an edge to their play. They were incredible.'

Jimmy Gabriel

CHAIRMAN MOORES SAW TO IT THAT THE PLAYERS WERE REWARDED for delivering the club's first post-war silverware. In an era before foreign package holidays became the norm, the players and their partners were whisked off to sunny Torremolinos. Roy Vernon was impressed by the club's generosity: 'The Mersey Millionaires, as we were now called, were well treated. We went with our wives to Spain for a fortnight's holiday – all expenses paid. A great success story, a great triumph and let's be honest, a great club.'[1]

A 64-page booklet was published by the club to commemorate the success. Words credited to Roy, but no doubt edited by a journalist, revealed his candour in reviewing the season and looking ahead to fresh challenges: 'There have been odd moments when – running true to my "temperamental" tag – I pondered about leaving Everton, just as I left Blackburn. But in the past year or so I have come to count my blessings. Maybe the responsibilities of captaincy have helped to mellow my outlook, which – in the past – has been rather fiery at times.

'Off the field, the chairman has been my guiding light, especially in looking to the future. Now I'm really beginning to learn that this life of football is a short one, if a merry one. As for Mr. Catterick, he has always been firm but fair. A good combination. And one which Roy Vernon, the so-called rebel, respects. And I cannot forget the aid which trainer Tommy Eggleston has given. You couldn't find a better man, anywhere, than Tom. He works us hard but there is always a purpose, and you realise that if the aim is to make Everton great, it is also making you the master of your trade.

'There are folk that say money cannot buy success. But Everton have proved it can, if you buy wisely. If the need arises, Everton will plunge, yet again, into the transfer market. I don't regard myself as indispensable, either. If you are part of an outfit chasing honours you must be able to produce the stuff that wins you large crowd bonuses. You earn it, but fans contribute their whack. If you stop earning it, you must be prepared to make way for someone who will earn it more. Every player knows that; every player gives 100 percent. And that's what we will be doing next season. If we don't win the European Cup – or, at least, put up a glorious fight in the effort – it won't be the fault of the chairman, the manager, the trainer or players.'

Roy claimed that landing the title gave Everton the opening to become the first British team to win the European Cup, as well as the challenge of defending the Championship crown: 'The following season brought new challenges. The European Cup, our first sortie into Europe, but before that we played Manchester United in the FA Charity Shield. We opened in great form, fresh from our holiday. Training had been hard but now we were in the mood to win everything before us. How well we played in that match. We won 4-0, the crowd were gloriously happy. So was Little John and as we raised the Charity Shield to our supporters, I remarked to him, "The first of many this season." His smiling reply left me in no doubt that it had better be.'[1]

Staged at the home of the First Division champions, the Toffees ran their rivals ragged and did more than win the FA Charity Shield match, they walked away with it. In fact, they came close to taking the Mickey out of the men from Manchester during the final fifteen minutes. The game is best remembered for the chaos associated with the second goal, a twice-taken penalty of dubious origin and doubtful conclusion. There are differing accounts of what happened. Journalist Dan Evans recalled: 'In the 54th minute Maurice Setters was unlucky to have been adjudged to have brought down Vernon. The inside-left feinted as if to take the kick, bringing [the goalkeeper, David] Gaskell prematurely to his knees. Skipper Cantwell protested and was promptly booked. Vernon at last took the kick only for Gaskell to bring off two great saves from him and from Gabriel's rebound shot. United swarmed forward in congratulation, only for the referee to consult his semaphore signalling linesman and order the kick to be retaken. Apparently, Cantwell had moved back into the area. Vernon stepped forward for a second chance and hammered this one home.'

This day of triumph would, ironically, signal the beginning of injury concerns which would ultimately signal the end of Roy's days in royal blue and white: 'Holding the Charity Shield up I little realised that a fierce tackle by Maurice Setters had injured my knee. It was only a little sore, but I only started to feel anxious about it after a couple days, particularly when my sprint times were well down. At Goodison we sprinted against the stopwatch. Apart from Derek Temple, I was easily the fastest player on the staff. Tommy Eggleston, quick to spot my loss of form and pace, noticed it and I confessed to a little soreness in my knee. Then came a series of visits to a specialist who could locate no trouble or damage to the cartilage.'[1]

Prior to the start of the new league campaign, Harry Catterick announced that the captaincy would be decided on a match-by-match basis: 'If ever I feel I can improve on any position it is my job to do so. That goes for the captaincy, too.' Though many fans speculated that Tony Kay was being groomed for the role by Catterick, Roy lead the team throughout the 1963/64 season whenever selected.

Unwittingly, Roy missed the league season's curtain-raiser, a home victory over Fulham in which Tony Kay deputised as captain. He returned and scored in the second fixture at Old Trafford, during which United exacted revenge for the Charity Shield capitulation by running out 5-1 winners. Knee troubles kept him on the sidelines for several matches, with the race on to recover in time for the first match of the European campaign. It was Everton's misfortune to meet Internazionale in the preliminary round of the European Cup. The Italian team, managed by Helenio Herrera, was a daunting obstacle. Since joining Inter Milan in 1960 after a period managing Barcelona, the Franco-Argentine had refined the famed *Catenaccio* defensive system to incorporate a sweeper. Although his teams were associated with ruthless defensive solidity, this one boasted the creativity of Luis Suárez, complemented by the attacking flair of Brazilian right-winger Jair, left-winger Mario Corso and inside-forward Sandro Mazzola.

Herrera visited Merseyside a fortnight before the first-leg to witness Everton lose a seven-goal thriller against Burnley. Post-match, he was quoted as praising home supporters as 'the magnificent twelfth man'. Herrera made it clear that Inter Milan's mission would be one of containment: 'We aim to close every avenue to our goal and will be happy with a draw or even a one-goal defeat.' Accordingly, Horst Szymaniak – the veteran German half-back – was drafted into the team to help rebuff the Everton attack. In the build-up, the *Liverpool Echo's* Michael Charters warned of the underhand tactics likely to be witnessed: 'Body-checking, jersey-tugging and general niggling are to be expected. It is hoped that Everton will maintain their poise in what will surely be a cauldron of noise and excitement.'[6]

The countdown to the match was dominated by Roy's battle for fitness: 'The knee still troubled me and I missed a couple of games before we were to meet Inter Milan. I played that night having gambled and, in my book, I'd say it was a calculated risk that so nearly paid off.'[1]

Everton took to the pitch in their all-white strip to accommodate Inter Milan's blue and black stripes. Despite the home team's efforts and enthusiastic vocal encouragement from all four sides of the ground, the match ended goalless. However, for several seconds some 62,000 Evertonians, along with the club captain, thought that the deadlock had been broken: 'A long ball was played towards Dennis Stevens, who nodded it on. I was at full speed and flew past three startled defenders – jumping over legs, dodging elbows to reach that ball and smash it with all my force inside the near post. Goodison erupted twice that night – the first time when I scored and the second when the referee pointed to where I had scored from. Almost unbelievably he gave me offside, one of the worst decisions I have ever experienced.'[1]

There are few doubts that the goal, if allowed to stand, could have changed the post-war history of Everton Football Club. Inter Milan progressed to eliminate Monaco, Partisan Belgrade and Borussia Dortmund before defeating Real Madrid in the final. Lifelong Evertonian Tony Onslow reminisced that Roy Vernon had evaded the shackles of the German giant: 'Nonetheless, Vernon had a brilliant night. Everyone thought he had scored at the Gwladys Street end – it was nowhere near offside, not in a million years – but the referee disallowed it and we knew it was not going to be our night.' The match official was Gyula Gere from Budapest, Hungary. For the record, he was dropped by FIFA and retired after making other serious mistakes in the European Championship match between Austria and Greece in 1967.

To rub salt in the wound, Roy aggravated his knee injury but was picked to play in a win at Hillsborough just three days later, scoring in a 3-2 victory. The second leg of the European tie was contested on the following Wednesday at the San Siro Stadium. The portents were not good. Injuries arising from the intensive league programme had impacted the squad, with several walking wounded. Jimmy Gabriel was deemed unfit to make the trip and three youth players – Colin Harvey, Barrie Rees and Roy Parnell – travelled with the party, ostensibly for big match experience and to lug the skips containing the kit on and off the team coach.

Poor weather saw the party stranded at Manchester Airport for most of the day. Eventually rerouted via London Heathrow, they did not arrive in Italy until late evening. After a morning training session, Harry Catterick named his line-up and dropped the bombshell that, to fill the void left by Gabriel, eighteen-year-old Colin Harvey would make his debut at inside-right, with Dennis Stevens moving to right-half.

On home soil, Herrera felt able to field a more attacking line-up and introduced Corso, the experienced Italy international forward, in place of Szymaniak. As for the match, it was abrasive and petulant, with Everton sticking resolutely to Catterick's defensive game plan. Michael Charters declared it 'a game ruined by flying feet and fists'.[6] Still, the journalist could not help but marvel at the hosts' interplay when freed from the defensive system deployed at Goodison: 'Their variation in pace and quick-fire passing in down-the-centre-moves is something we rarely see in England. They have a tremendous amount of talent but are volatile and more than a little given to play-acting when brought down.'[6]

Openings were few. Vernon and Young saw little of the ball. However, Scott was able to waltz through the home ranks, only to screw his shot wide from twelve yards. That said, Everton gained composure as the first half progressed, causing frustration and unrest on the terraces. Eventually, though, the Toffees buckled. The sole goal of the tie came just after half-time when Jair, fed by Carlo Tagnin, lashed a sensational strike into the roof of the net.

While the Toffees were out of the competition, granted with their heads held high, the victors progressed to the final in Vienna. Their win over Real Madrid ensured that the title remained in Italy, with AC Milan having won at Wembley the previous year. Clearly, the Merseyside club had the misfortune to be drawn out of the bag against the eventual champions before the real competition had commenced. Inter Milan were an exceptional side and would make it a double in 1965 by defeating Benfica in the final staged at the San Siro.

While Catterick's men travelled home with praise ringing in their ears from the manager, the chance of truly putting Everton on the European map had gone. There was little time for navel-gazing as just three days later the club were embroiled in a 2-1 defeat at Anfield. With Young unavailable, recovering from a gash to the thigh sustained in Italy, Roy's goal was no more than a consolation.

That October, the *Daily Mirror* revealed that the Everton captain was one of two British players targeted by AS Napoli, the cash-rich club backed by shipping magnate Achille Lauro. It was claimed that the Neapolitans had sought the opinion of John Charles, who had been at AS Roma during the 1962/63 campaign, on his international teammate. Whatever the truth of the story, it quickly died. However, speculation about Roy being unsettled continued. Subsequently, Harry Catterick spoke to him about the rumours that he would be seeking a transfer. 'Vernon told me that he knows nothing at all about such reports,' the manager told Leslie Edwards. [6]

With Roy affected by ongoing knee problems and his partner struggling with massive blisters covering the soles of both feet, their performances were a tad off-colour during the festive period and both were rested for the league fixtures in mid-January. They returned for an FA Cup match at Elland Road where Roy rediscovered his scoring touch via an infamous penalty.

In his absence, Alex Scott was selected to take spot kicks and had converted one against Ipswich Town the week before the fourth-round tie. Therefore, when a penalty was awarded at Leeds, he stepped up to take the kick. Norma Vernon watched the events unfold: 'Alex missed but the referee ruled that the keeper had moved and ordered a retake. Alex went to pick the ball up, but Roy snatched it from his hands, placed it on the spot and blasted it into the net. Everyone went mad!'[9] This goal earned a replay at Goodison where both Roy and Jimmy Gabriel, playing as an emergency centre-forward, netted to put Everton through to the fifth round.

Moving onto early 1982, shortly after Trevor Ross's crucial miss from the spot in an FA Cup thriller at West Ham, *Liverpool Echo* writer VJK reflected on a time when an Everton penalty always ended up in the back of the net and highlighted the incident: 'Roy Vernon, he of knobby knees and flat feet, was decidedly not the model for Roy of the Rovers. But his spot kick in an FA Cup tie at Leeds in January

1964 was heroic. Everton were 1-0 down with not many minutes to go when they were awarded the penalty. It was Alex Scott, not Vernon, who first stepped up to take it. Elland Road was as silent as a church. Three-quarters of the crowd were praying he'd miss. The other quarter were beseeching the heavens to let him score. Scott muffed it. Or did he? The referee had noticed Sprake moving before the kick was taken and said take it again. There was no chance of Scott having a second go. He looked like I felt – on the verge of a nervous breakdown – and slowly walked away. Vernon, the captain, looked towards Jimmy Gabriel. He shook his head. Alex Young? He turned his back. Vernon stood with the ball tucked under his arm and everyone knew that the buck stopped right there. Strangely, Vernon plonked the ball down on the spot, gazed piteously at Sprake, took three paces back and wham, it went in like a bullet an inch from the post with the goalkeeper collapsing in the opposite direction. Vernon just turned and trotted back to the centre. The spectators went wild, but the reactions of his teammates seemed strangely muted. It may have been that they were less hysterical in those days. It may have been that Vernon was acting slightly superior. It might have been that they were all shell-shocked. Two things I know for certain. One, it took incredible nerve for him to hit a penalty with such pace and precision that no keeper on earth could have saved it. And two, we stuffed them 2-0 in the replay.'

Alex Scott had slightly different recollections: 'I was appointed penalty taker in Taffy's absence at Turf Moor [another fixture Vernon missed at the beginning of January]. The only other candidate was Sandy Brown and his approach was somewhat hit and miss. He claimed: "If I don't know where the ball is going, then the keeper must have no idea either!" Anyway, we were awarded a spot kick, which I powered past Adam Blacklaw and we went on to win 3-2. The following week we hosted bottom-of-the-table Ipswich and again I scored from the spot about ten minutes from the end to rescue a point. Taffy returned for our visit to Elland Road. Trailing 1-0 against the Second Division side, we were awarded another penalty. Fortunately, after my effort was saved by Gary Sprake, the ref whistled that the keeper had moved, and the kick was to be retaken. After I had bent down to pick up the ball, Roy pulled it away from me. I saw fire in his eyes as he growled: "Eff off Scotty, I'm taking it. Unlike you, I know what I'm effing doing." Wisely, I decided not to argue with the captain, especially after he had demonstrated that he knew exactly what he was effing doing. Taffy took a step backwards and dispatched the ball into the corner of the net and Everton into an equally combative replay.'[2]

February 1964 brought a trip to Anfield and an opportunity to exact revenge for the defeat at Goodison. Whilst some players struggled with the expectations of a local derby, Roy flourished in the cauldron of local rivalry: 'No one needs to be told of the intense rivalry between these two great clubs. The atmosphere is electric. To lose is unbearable – to win is to know the height of elation. I think that the people of Liverpool are fantastic supporters: knowledgeable and fiercely proud of their clubs.'[1]

Alex Young's injury-enforced absence again saw Jimmy Gabriel pressed into service as a centre-forward. In the previous match – the FA Cup replay against Leeds – both had scored. The ad-hoc spearhead proved similarly impressive against the Reds. Gabriel disclosed: 'The greatest thing I ever wanted to do – all midfielders and goalkeepers are like this – was play centre-forward for Everton against Liverpool. I always wanted to do that. The game ended 3-1. I scored one and made two for Taffy. I loved to play with him, it was perfect – we fitted like a glove. I was decent in the air and could flick balls down and he was like lightning, getting in behind defenders, so we were laughing. I remember the game especially because Big Ron Yeats was picking me up and Little Gordon Milne was picking up Taffy. There was a free-kick from the right, and I said to him at the last minute, "Let's do a switch here." I pulled off Big Ron and he stayed on the left-hand side, and Taffy pulled on to him. It meant that I was being marked by Gordon Milne. The cross came over, I beat him in the air, headed it back across. Taffy was too quick for Yeats, he got in, bang, one-nil. Then I got a ball on the edge of the eighteen-yard box and, quite honestly, didn't know what to do with it. The defenders had backed off and I thought I'd toe poke it with my left foot. It went right into the far corner of the net, so that was two-nil, which was amazing. In the second half, after Ian St John had scored, we got another free-kick on the right. I jumped up early on Yeatsie so that he carried me up. I nearly got a nosebleed I went that high but was able to head it down to Roy, who banged it in the net and that was the end of their comeback.'[4]

For Norma, watching from the stand, this was her husband at his very best: 'He was phenomenal that day. We got home and were having our tea when the phone rang. It was Bill Shankly who offered his congratulations to Roy for playing so well. That was amazing'[9]

A fit-again Young would line up with Vernon at the end of February and the pair contributed five goals over two matches together. Even so Harry Catterick had become convinced that a more physically imposing forward was required to get the team through the run-in, and it was to Ewood Park that Everton turned once again for attacking inspiration. Fred Pickering had been pulling up trees wearing the Blackburn number nine shirt, having been converted from left-back to replace Derek Dougan. His hat-trick at Goodison in November 1963 may have convinced Catterick that he was the ideal marksman. Anyway, a club-record fee of £85,000 secured his services in mid-March.

Pickering's arrival was not met with universal glee. Many supporters assumed that it would spell the end for their idol Alex Young. Their fears appeared justified when Pickering claimed the number nine shirt for the visit of Nottingham Forest and Young promptly lodged a transfer request. Despite the reservations held by the Goodison faithful, Pickering made up for his lack of grace with an appetite for goals: three crackers on his debut in a 6-1 annihilation.

After the debutant missed a gilt-edged opening after just five minutes, cries of 'We want Young' emanated from the Gwladys Street terraces. These were quickly extinguished when he scored on the half-hour mark: 'Pickering took the ball across a well-packed defence, flicked it sideways just a pace or two until he had a sight of goal. That was enough. Wham! From 24 yards he hit such a power drive that no goalkeeper on earth would have had a chance of saving.'[5]

Not to be completely upstaged by his new strike partner, Roy scored with a fierce drive after 59 minutes, whilst Dennis Stevens weighed in with a brace. On eighty minutes, Pickering secured the match ball, latching onto Alex Scott's cross. Horace Yates wrote: '"What will we do without Alex Young?" asked the doubters. Pickering showed them. Club welfare must always be paramount to individual idolatry.'[5] The veteran journalist declared prematurely that the impressive outcome marked the beginning of Everton's coronation as back-to-back champions – a feat last achieved by Wolverhampton Wanderers at the end of the previous decade: 'It is my firm conviction that they will retain their title of champions of the First Division with plenty to spare.'[5]

Meanwhile, Roy was summoned before the FA Disciplinary Committee in Sheffield in connection with a caution he received in a home victory over Birmingham City. At the conclusion of the hearing, the FA announced: 'The commission decided that they were satisfied Vernon had adopted an aggressive attitude towards an opponent, after being tackled, and that the referee was justified in administering a caution.' The resultant fourteen-day ban saw him miss an away win at Ewood Park, a disappointing draw at home to West Bromwich Albion and an away defeat of Blackpool.

Then, unpredictably, the title challenge imploded. Three days after winning at Bloomfield Road, top-of-the-League Everton travelled to The Hawthorns with Roy restored to the number ten shirt and Alex Young on the right-flank in place of Alex Scott. Improbably, Mick Fudge, an eighteen-year-old only called up by the Baggies due to injuries, scored a hat-trick to sink the out-of-sorts visitors. Even though Roy had levelled the scores after Fudge's opener – collecting the ball ten yards inside the opposition's half, beating three men and fashioning a vicious shot – the Midlanders again raced into a lead. Roy's second goal, a first-time shot from a Temple centre, was too little, too late and West Brom ran out 4-2 winners.

The *Daily's Post's* Horace Yates was perplexed by the lacklustre performance which had jeopardised the title challenge: 'One wondered why Everton took so long to infuse the fighting fury they reserved from the closing stages when their position was already impossible.'[5]

Now in second place behind Liverpool and with four fixtures remaining, there was still a chance of retaining their crown. However, any hopes were eliminated in the following match at lowly Stoke. For all but the first twenty minutes of the encounter Everton were a distant second-best to the Potters and deservedly trailed 2-0 at the interval. An unlikely comeback through goals from Gabriel and Pickering was to be in vain when winger Keith Bebbington cut in and unleashed a shot past Andy Rankin in the final moments.

Back at Goodison, Harry Catterick's men could only manage a 3-3 draw with Wolves. It was rumoured that Gigi Peronace, the first of the super agents, who had negotiated the transfers of John Charles, Jimmy Greaves, Joe Baker and Denis Law to Italy, was in the stands to run the rule over his top two targets, Young and Vernon. However, neither played in the match.

It seemed as if things could not get any worse, but Everton's troubles were compounded with the publication of revelations the following morning of betting allegations in which Tony Kay was implicated. The 12 April edition of *The People* newspaper disclosed that Kay and two Sheffield Wednesday pals had bet that their own team would lose a game, the game in question an away fixture at Ipswich on 1 December 1962. The news forced the Goodison hierarchy to suspend the half-back, pending an investigation by the authorities. Following a trial early the following year, Tony Kay, Peter Swan and Bronco Layne were found guilty and sentenced to four months in prison plus a lifetime ban from football. It was a devastating blow to the Yorkshireman, not to mention to his Merseyside club.

Without Kay, Everton lost at Chelsea before rallying on the final day with a home win against West Ham to ensure a third-place finish behind champions Liverpool, with Manchester United in second. 'The manager chopped and changed the side and we dropped seven points in the final five games,' said Sandy Brown. 'Remember it was two points for a win back in 1964 and we finished five points behind Liverpool. During this spell the club organised Dixie Dean's Testimonial match. Taffy said that the timing was crazy, especially after Alex Young had picked up a knock and had to miss the important League game against Wolves. The benefit game involved an English Players side versus a Scottish Players side selected from the two Merseyside giants. Bill Shankly managed the Scots and insisted on including Roy in his team. Unfortunately, Taffy McVernon had to miss the match through injury. Jimmy Hill, our Northern Ireland international, took his place.'

On the subject of proud Scotsmen, Sandy Brown retained fond memories of Roy as a teammate but less so as a club captain. Back in 2002 he reflected: 'Taffy was an expert negotiator – for himself. I had moved to England after the maximum wage had been abolished but was a little wet behind the ears. Delighted to sign any contract placed in front of me, my wages were double those I had enjoyed in Glasgow – a basic of £28 per week plus another £10 when in the first team. Not bad for kicking a football on a Saturday afternoon? Gordon West disagreed and claimed that I was being paid less than my teammates and much less than Alex, Gabby and Taffy, who were on £50 plus all sorts of bonuses. He told me not to worry and that our skipper would sort things out for me. Subsequently, Taffy and I met with Harry Catterick and Bill Dickinson to discuss my terms. The manager was angered by my request for another tenner. He called me an ungrateful Jock who was lucky to have been signed by the reigning champions of England. As for the secretary, he encouraged me to leave his office before the club reduced my wages by a tenner. The following day, I overheard Taffy bragging about his pay rise to £60 per week. He had used the meeting to promote his role as captain, top scorer and pain in the manager's neck.'[2]

Why did the team stumble when it possessed the experience of handling intense pressure? The fall-out from the betting scandal can't be cited as the prime factor because Everton's title bid had already imploded. Some believe that Fred

Pickering's arrival – goals notwithstanding – disrupted the team's balance by splitting the Vernon-Young attacking fulcrum. Roy, who in a posed photograph was seen reluctantly handing over the famous trophy to Ron Yeats, commented: 'With injuries, loss of form and more than a little bad luck, we were to relinquish our title to Liverpool – and that really hurt.'[1]

There was little time for introspection. The very next day the squad, minus the transfer-listed Alex Young and Fred Pickering, who had been called up by England for a tour of North America, boarded a flight at Speke Airport for the journey to Australia. With Harry Catterick staying home to supervise preparations for the new campaign, Tommy Eggleston and club director Edward Holland Hughes took charge of the touring party which would contest eight matches in four weeks. It was the club's most ambitious expedition since the pioneering visit to South America in 1908. The initiative was a resounding success, with record crowds turning out to see the Toffees put fifty goals past their various opposition. There was also time for leisure, including a visit to wineries in New South Wales and the local beaches. Roy performed his captain's duties, photographed greeting dignitaries at the various stopping points. Little did anyone know that these would be his final acts in this prestigious role.

At the beginning of June, the club moved to extend the contracts of Roy and Jimmy Gabriel, the pair having chosen to only sign twelve-month deals previously. Both players had earned around £4,000 per annum (equivalent to approximately £80,000 in 2019) during the previous season but believed their worth was nearer £5,000. Roy allayed concerns in the press: 'In my opinion everything is going well and I can assure everyone there is no cause for alarm. I am anxious that the public know that, and I feel sure that I am fulfilling the best interests of the club by making that fact known.'

Despite the positive spin, the negotiations reached stalemate with the clock ticking. The expiration date on the current deals was 1 July 1964, and the impasse culminated with Roy letting his contract lapse and briefly severing all contact with the club. Gabriel went onto week-by-week agreements pending a transfer or resolution in negotiations. In late July, both contract rebels were ushered into a meeting with John Moores and Harry Catterick to break the deadlock. At the fruitful conclusion of the talks, Moores declared: 'We had a nice, mutual, chat and explained the new contract which is fairly complicated. Under our terms, the players could earn up to £5,000 every year. It was all very friendly with a little bit of give and take on both sides.' Whilst Gabriel signed on the dotted line, Roy sought the opinion of his solicitor before returning to Goodison and committing for another season. A relieved Harry Catterick stated: 'To lose both or either of these players would have been a terrible blow. I regard Vernon and Gabriel as irreplaceable in their respective positions.'

It was a stance that Catterick would soon change. Little over a week before the season started Roy relinquished the club captaincy. The reasons behind his decision were not reported. Without question, Tony Kay would have been Catterick's choice as the new captain but, in view of the Yorkshireman's indefinite suspension, the well-respected Alex Parker was appointed. Unfortunately, the Scotsman, having returned from a long-term injury, would struggle to regain form and fitness before ceding his first-team place to young Tommy Wright. Subsequently, the honour was passed to Brian Labone.

'Many claimed that I was a Catterick-type of player – lots of industry and Sheffield steel,' Tony Kay revealed. 'They thought that we were best mates, but the manager was aloof with everyone. That said, "The Catt" did trust me and had made me Wednesday's captain. He was aware that I was a first-class trainer and the fittest player on the books, who needed no encouragement to run up and down the terrace steps to shorten and quicken my strides. Also, he liked the way that I marshalled the troops and refused to accept second best.'

More than simply confident, Kay was convinced that Everton had the players to win the title again and again: 'We had a decent side. While Labby was a genuine gent – and there's no place for them on a football pitch – we had three resolute policemen in Dennis Stevens, Gabby and me, and, of course, two golden boys up front. I liked both Alex and Taffy. The Scotsman reminded me a little of Albert Quixall, another blonde bombshell who didn't bleed enough apart from his blisters. Of course, the Golden Vision was far more skilful and tremendous in the air. How he hung there remains one of life's great mysteries. Also, I'm amazed that he could walk never mind sprint because he had the most awful feet which caused him agony. They made your eyes water just to look at them. As for Taffy, I didn't understand his ongoing passion for cigarettes. Without a fag in his mouth, he could have been another Denis Law who was more robust and a bit naughtier with his tackles than the Welshman. One was a bulldog, the other was an underfed smoking greyhound.'[2]

Despite these upheavals, the 1964/65 season started promisingly. Roy was selected alongside both Fred Pickering and Alex Young in a routine 2-0 victory over Stoke City at Goodison. 'Vernon was at his best when his teammates were moving fluently in the first half,' Michael Charters observed. 'He and Pickering have struck up an effective link which could produce plenty of goals.'[6] With ten minutes left on the clock, Roy was on hand to lash home the rebound from a Derek Temple shot. But perhaps the match was most notable for the debut of England full-back Ray Wilson, who had arrived in the summer from Huddersfield in a part-exchange deal involving Mick Meagan.

With Pickering, Young and Sandy Brown contributing goals, Everton won three and drew two of the first half dozen games and were in third place prior to the visit of Sheffield United in mid-September. However, optimism that the Welsh striker, freed from the constraints of captaincy, would reproduce his best form proved ill-founded. Having failed to add to his tally since the opening day, Roy pulled-up with a knee ligament injury after only ten minutes against the Blades. Gamely carrying on, he re-merged for the second half with the knee heavily strapped and switched places with left-winger Derek Temple. Horace Yates reported: 'Although everything he did was at half-pace or less, he was responsible for some very thoughtful and intelligent passes.'[5] Harry Catterick announced that Roy would miss a fortnight of action but, as it transpired, it would be mid-October before he would play again.

While injuries prevented Roy and Alex Young from taking part in the Anfield derby, their replacements Colin Harvey and Derek Temple gave breathtaking performances. Both scored in the 4-0 mauling of Liverpool. Harvey, who had not appeared since his surprise debut in Milan, claimed that wearing the Welshman's shirt – even for a handful of fixtures – was a daunting task for a teenager: 'Roy was a great footballer with a great football brain. Though we both wore number ten, he was a completely different player to me. Roy was a goalscorer whereas I wasn't, so it was a burden for me, with people expecting lots of goals from me. Evertonians associate that shirt with goals, going back to players like John Willie Parker. That's why I wanted to wear number six. Roy always played off the number nine. He was such a good reader of what was going on around him that he got chances, and when he got them, he took them. He could read play and drop off – he wasn't just an out-and-out marksman – he was a more all-round player. He could play a pass as well as score a goal. It was almost a telepathic relationship between Alex and him, and a hard act to follow.'[1]

Having graduated to the first-team squad, Harvey would get a close-up look at Roy: 'When I moved into the first-team dressing room I sat next to Taffy. He had a sharp tongue – if you ever said anything out of place you got it back but, that said, he was one of the better ones for making you feel welcome. I didn't like smoking so the only time I "smoked" was on a Friday morning when Taffy would come into the dressing room after being in the Royal Tiger Club the night before. He'd say to me: "A good night, last night," and there'd be a mixture of cigarette smoke and whisky on his breath!'

The first-team dressing room could be unnerving for youngsters coming up through the ranks at Bellefield. Some senior players enjoyed testing their mettle. Joe Royle, a first-year apprentice in Roy's final year at the club, explained: 'You had to knock on the door to enter the senior changing room. One or two gave you a hard time and threw their smelly socks at you, telling you to get them a pair without holes in, but never Royston. He was a superior footballer and the first striker I recognised as lurking on the defender's shoulder, ready to go in behind, a method perfected by Ian Rush. Harry Catterick saw merit in playing Young as the withdrawn striker with Vernon stretching the opposition's defence. Together, they were awesome. Off the pitch, Royston always had a smile on his face and was an absolute rascal, but you couldn't help liking him. Some of his pranks are legendary. In many ways he was a coach's nightmare, but it's all about what they do on Saturday afternoons, and he was exceptional – one heck of a player.'

In April 1990, *The People* published an article attributed to Joe Royle. It read: 'Roy Vernon, the Welsh striker was a legend and once almost gave the reserve team trainer a heart attack by threatening to go out and play with an umbrella. It was a typical winter afternoon, with the rain lashing down, and Vernon was making a rare appearance in the second team. "We'll get pneumonia in that," said Vernon, "I'm taking my brolly with me." They all laughed but as the team lined up to go out Roy had the umbrella in his hand. "You're not serious, are you?" said the trainer. "Dead right I am. If I can't take this I'm not playing." The trainer, by then, was almost on his knees begging Roy to stop fooling around. But he ran up the tunnel and got to the edge of the pitch before throwing the brolly into the dugout.'

Not surprisingly, Roy made significant impressions on other youngsters advancing through the youth development programme. 'Taffy was a character and a bloody good footballer,' George Sharples reflected recently. 'He was hard on the field, didn't show any nerves and was skipper of the ship when we won the league.

In that role, he didn't hesitate to give you a royal bollocking when you needed one but then that was it. Taffy was as straight as a die. There would not have been an Alex Young but for him, they complimented each other in a breathtaking partnership. Watching them together was like poetry in motion – it was bloody marvellous. Off the field he was a different person. Taffy had immense charm – it was part of his make-up.'

Alex Wallace added: 'I was a youth player but have vivid memories of Mr Vernon – that's how we referred to the first-team pros – and his addiction to cigarettes. He was a chain smoker. In those days, we used Vicks sticks as inhalers to remove nasal congestion and kick-start our senses. These sticks were white and shaped like a cigarette which you would break in half to release the vapours. However, Taffy used to walk out of the tunnel holding it to his lips looking like he was smoking his way onto the pitch before snapping, inhaling and stamping it out with his boot.'

Andy Rankin admired his dedication: 'Roy was a consummate pro who liked to practice his immaculate penalty technique. Occasionally and much to his annoyance, I would save one in training – by luck more than judgement. As a forfeit, Roy would take over between the sticks. More often than not, I would be intimidated by his mere presence and miss the target, or Roy would make an overly-dramatic save. After paying my dues in the stiffs, I made my debut thanks to Fred Pickering scoring a hat-trick for Blackburn against Gordon West. A couple of outings later, I saved a penalty from Ralph Brand at Ibrox. Roy told everyone in the dressing room that he had taught me everything that I knew about stopping spot kicks. If I needed to pick someone to take a penalty to save my life, Taffy would be at the head of the list.'

After missing seven games, during which time Everton had slumped to eighth in the league, Roy returned and scored in a comfortable win over Valerengens of Oslo in the Inter-Cities Fairs Cup at Goodison. This outing came at no little cost as his knee complaint flared up again. It was to become a pattern for the season – multiple comebacks curtailed by recurring knee problems. Thereafter, he missed two more games before reappearing for the December 1964 clash with Leeds which has gone down in the annals as one of the most notorious confrontations the English game has seen. Modern day fans talk about bear-pits and cauldrons of fanaticism, but when it comes to an intimidating atmosphere little compares to that day. The match was later dubbed 'The Battle of Goodison'. Everton were aware of the reputation of Leeds, a team of rugged individuals that included Bobby Collins – deemed surplus to requirements by Harry Catterick in 1961 – and had expected a fierce battle. They had met the then Second Division outfit in the FA Cup several months earlier and both ties had been littered with uncompromising fouls. Indeed, the replay at Goodison had enraged the hostile crowd of 66,000. It should be noted that back then football was more physical with little theatrical flopping to the ground, even less feigning of injury and absolutely no writhing and rolling around the pitch. And, it goes without saying, that no player hit himself with someone else's arm to hoodwink match officials.

Since those FA Cup clashes, Harry Catterick's side had introduced Fred Pickering, forfeited Tony Kay and collected only six points from the final seven games to concede the league crown to Liverpool. Everton had started the new campaign well and been buoyed by a 4-0 win at Anfield and the signing of Ray Wilson, but soon after that victory their home form collapsed. Inexplicably, Everton had achieved four disappointing draws and one disheartening defeat at Goodison in the league prior to the arrival of Leeds and had dropped to eighth in the table, four places behind the team across the park.

Back to the November 1964 battle. After a couple of reckless fouls by Bobby Collins on Derek Temple and Billy Bremner on Fred Pickering, plus a cynical one by Johnny Morrissey on Jack Charlton, the match exploded. In the fourth minute, Johnny Giles left his stud marks on the chest of Sandy Brown, who retaliated by pole-axing his opponent with a monster left-hook of staggering power and precision. He was duly sent off. The incident mirrored Desperate Dan in *The Dandy* comic, who would knock the bad guy off his feet with 'POW', in a word balloon. Decades later, when interviewed by David France at his Blackpool home, Sandy explained: 'Johnny said my parents weren't married!'

Shortly after Brown had been dismissed, Goodison turned ugly with 44,000 frenzied Evertonians baying for blood. Hate radiated from the terraces and any Leeds player who strayed within throwing distance ran the risk of being struck by missiles such as coins, bottles and other projectiles fired from all corners of the ground. What followed on the pitch remains one of football's most savage confrontations. As the men in blue stood toe-to-toe with those in white, the violence turned brutal and 'The Grand Old Lady' grew angry.

Cursed by the absence of Tony Kay, who would have banged more than a few Yorkshire heads together, Roy, the thinnest man on the pitch, and Bobby Collins, then of Leeds and the smallest man on the pitch, choreographed the warfare. Along with Norman 'Bite Your Legs' Hunter, Jack Charlton, Johnny Giles, Billy Bremner, Jimmy Gabriel, Johnny Morrissey and Dennis Stevens, they were lucky not to join Brown in the showers.

In the combat zone, the men in blue stood toe-to-toe with those in white and 44,000 Blues demanded Yorkshire blood. Goodison had an unsavoury reputation for its frenzied crowd and tribal hooliganism. During a clash with Tottenham in November 1963, idiots in Gwladys Street had been thrown darts at keeper Bill Brown. As a result, arcs were added to the walls behind both goals to distance potential perpetrators from visiting goalkeepers. Consequently, the *News of the World* proclaimed that we were the 'roughest, rowdiest rabble who watches British soccer'. Predictably, some Blues took it was a badge of honour.

As the Leeds game deteriorated into anarchy, the perception that visitors were getting away with foul after foul incensed the crowd and the November sky rained cushions from the Bullens Road Stand and pre-decimal coins (the old penny was about 1.25 inches in diameter), bottles and other missiles from all four terraces. Any Leeds player brave enough to stray within fifteen yards of the touchlines ran the risk of being struck. And of course, for poor goalkeeper Gary Sprake, there was no hiding place.

Things came to a head in the 35th minute when full-back Willie Bell launched a two-footed tackle at Derek Temple near the touchline. It was around neck high and one of the worst seen outside a wrestling ring. As the Everton winger was being carried off by the St John Ambulance attendants, 'The Grand Old Lady' exploded into violent rage. Recently Les Cocker, the Leeds trainer at the time who had demanded that Bell feign injury and stay down, noted the response from the Goodison staff to his request for assistance: 'Get your own effing stretcher!'

Who can forget the photo of the two captains – 'The Little General' at 5ft 3in and 'The Last of the Corinthians' at 6ft 1in – leading their teams off the pitch? Years down the line, Brian Labone told co-author David France that it was the only time he had been frightened by the home crowd. He saw hate in the contorted faces of the fans yelling obscenities at him, some of which were his neighbours in Maghull. Brian recalled: 'I learnt a lot from Bobby during my younger days. During training I challenged him for a ball and he flattened me. I was shocked by his aggression, so the next time I tackled him harder and he smiled: "You're learning son." Wee Bobby added ruthlessness to any team and relished hostile environments.

For him, the Battle of Goodison was the Promised Land.'

Some participants have claimed that the referee had intended to abandon the game but changed his mind on police advice. Alex Young recalled: 'The ref came into our dressing room and spoke to us like we were school children. He cautioned that if we didn't stop kicking each other and start playing football, he would report us to the Football Association. He had no idea that if we were to return to the pitch it would be warfare with no prisoners taken by either side.'

The local constabulary issued its own ultimatum via the tannoy system that the game would be abandoned if any more cushions were thrown. Cushions? Older Blues will recall that the wooden seats in the Upper Bullens Road stand were so uncomfortable that most patrons rented cushions. An inch or so thick and measuring the size of the British standard bum in the 60s, it was the rectangular prototype for a plastic frisbee and could be thrown considerable distances using the most primitive backhand and hammer techniques.

Most fans were surprised when the teams returned to the pitch. However, the ten-minute ceasefire had done little to soothe the hostility of the fans or the fury of the combatants. Many of the latter adopted a kill or be killed mentality and the match continued to seethe with an undercurrent of aggression bordering on thuggery to its bitter end. There was no invasion of the pitch when the final whistle blew. Most likely everyone was either exhausted or too disgusted. Post-game, angry mobs pelted the Leeds bus with missiles and had to be dispersed by mounted police from the adjacent streets. As for the referee and his linesmen, they were advised to remain in the changing rooms for several hours until the angry supporters had been removed from the vicinity.

Some 25 years on, in the aftermath of a not quite as rambunctious Hall of Fame evening, David France quizzed Bobby Collins about his part in the infamous game: 'Aye, it was a brutal affair with lots of nasty tackles – some blatant, some sly. I don't know what Goodison expected. I was just as small, just as competitive and played no different than during my three seasons there. Both sides were naughty. I'm not sure who won the war and we won the match.'

'The wee man was extra combative that afternoon,' Alex Young reflected. 'He was such a master of the game as well as the dark arts that he was voted Footballer of the Year at the end of that season. Also, he had a win-at-any-cost attitude and demanded the highest standards from his teammates. It was something he shared with Alan Ball.'

Everton were penalised for nineteen fouls, whereas Leeds committed – in the eyes of the match officials – only twelve. However, it was the arrogance of Don Revie's team of perfect villains, skilled at upsetting their opponents – who in turn would forget to play football in order to fight fire with fire – without winding up the referee which fuelled the flames. Even though Leeds squeezed out a 1-0 victory, there were no winners that afternoon. Sandy Brown was suspended for two weeks. The hosts were fined £250. The visitors were vilified as 'Dirty Leeds' – a bunch of thuggish yobs who would stop at nothing to win a football match. The appalling scenes provoked some predictably hysterical press coverage and both clubs were condemned for damaging the image of football and being a disgrace to our national game.

It is telling of Roy's diminishing impact, however, that his name is largely absent from newspaper reports and was not mentioned in dispatches from the war zone. The game would also prove to be the last league outing for Vernon alongside his great pal Alex Young, as injuries limited the Scotsman to only one more appearance in the remaining 22 fixtures in that campaign. The game was not a fitting end for such an iconic partnership.

After completing games against Kilmarnock and Chelsea without scoring, Roy missed the next four fixtures. He returned for the games against Wolves and Stoke in December, again without scoring, and was therefore dropped for the next fixture at Tottenham. As expected, he wasn't pleased by Harry Catterick's decision. However, it transpired that a few weeks previously, he had been fined for turning up late to training and had also been carpeted for giving a press interview without the prior consent of Catterick – a cardinal sin in the manager's book. On this third wobble on the disciplinary tightrope, Roy had not turned up for training prior to the departure for North London. Telephone calls to his home failed to get a response so a club official was dispatched to Lydiate to seek out the elusive player at home, who had overslept. Belatedly arriving at the training ground, the inevitable summons to the manager's office was given and sentence handed down by 'The Catt.' The club put out a curt public statement advising: 'Vernon has been omitted from the team as a disciplinary measure for a breach of club and training regulations.'[6] Leslie Edwards underplayed the Welshman's reaction to the sanction: 'I understand that Vernon did not take news of his suspension kindly.' Roy would be not pull on the Everton number ten jersey for another ten games.

With too much time on their hands, it's no surprise that some footballers spent their excess cash at the races. Roy was no exception. But not satisfied with betting on horses, he and Alex Young sought to invest in their love of the sport of kings by buying one of their own. The Welshman stated: 'Alex and I are considering buying a racehorse. We would like to get a two-year-old, if we can find a good one at a reasonable price, and call it "Goodison Park".' Alex was more optimistic: 'It has always been my desire to own a thoroughbred. I reckon we should be able to pick up a good two-year-old for about £500.'[6] These ambitions, however, were not realised.

Six years later, Alex teamed up with Alan Ball to purchase a thoroughbred named Daxal. The Scotsman elaborated: 'Like true enthusiasts with more money than sense, we spent 1,500 guineas on a yearling trained by Ron Hutchinson in Newbury. Unfortunately, he lacked the blistering speed of his dam Chamosaire or his sire Kelly. Out of loyalty and friendship, Taffy would enquire regularly about Daxal's next outing but, being a savvy soul, I suspect that he never bet on Daxal to win. I've kept no photos of the horse and have sought to erase his quiet hooves from my memory but smile when I think of Daxal and Bally, only one of them was ever a winner.'[2]

Swirling in the background throughout this period was the fallout from the publication of allegations in *The People*, the newspaper that had broken the 'Football Betting Scandal' story six months earlier. Albert Dunlop, the tempestuous and somewhat troubled former Everton goalkeeper, had made a series of claims about his former club, including the consumption of purple heart stimulants and, more seriously, alleged match-fixing when Everton had defeated West Bromwich Albion in the penultimate match of the title-winning season. The allegations were refuted by the club, who launched an internal investigation led by Edward Holland Hughes. His dossier was passed to the authorities, who took no further action.

It was reported in the local press that Roy, Jimmy Gabriel and others were considering legal action, but the stories faded from the public consciousness and matters were not pursued. Most recently, Tony Kay vented his distaste for the pill-popping claims via ToffeeWeb: 'The only tablets I heard mentioned were sleeping pills the night before an away game, when we were staying in a hotel, and glucose pills in the dressing room before kick-off. I've never taken an illegal drug in my life and can't imagine any of my teammates doing so. It certainly didn't happen in front of me. I didn't hear a whisper about during my short-yet-glorious time at Everton Football Club.'[10]

However, despite shaking off such allegations, by the beginning of 1965 most commentators speculated that the chasm between manager and Vernon was too wide to be bridged. With Blackpool, Wolverhampton Wanderers and Nottingham Forest – the latter managed by Johnny Carey – touted as being keen on signing him, Roy submitted a transfer request. Harry Catterick announced: 'Vernon came to see me after lunch today. He said his reasons for asking for a transfer were that he appreciated that his football had deteriorated and feels that his game will improve with a change of club. His request will be considered by the board at the earliest opportunity.'[6]

The Everton directors approved the request but there was to be no instant exit – possibly the asking price in the region of £50,000 had dampened the ardour of some suitors. In early February an intriguing possibility was revealed by the Herald Sun, an Australian newspaper, and was picked up by the local press. It was claimed that Australian outfit APIA FC were negotiating for the acquisition of Brian Harris. The left-half was keen to move if his wage demands of £56 per week could be met by the Sydney-based club. The *Liverpool Echo* took the scoop a step further, stating that Roy was keen to join his teammate in Australia if he could secure appearance money of £80 per match. Apparently, both had been favourably impressed with the country during Everton's antipodean tour during the previous summer. However, the dream move evaporated after Harris returned to favour and regained his left-half position.

On Roy's eventual return to the first-team line-up in February for the second leg of an Inter-Cities Fairs Cup clash with Manchester United, it was evident that he struggled to influence the proceedings. His old zip was missing. Afterwards, he managed to play six league games, including wins at West Ham, Sheffield Wednesday and Blackburn. Amid speculation of a transfer to Glentoran, his final league game was at Goodison against Aston Villa on 13 March. He scored twice and helped Fred Pickering to propel Everton from eleventh place to fourth in the table. Previously, in the absence of Alex Young's prompting, he had failed to score a league goal since the opening fixture at the Victoria Ground. It was not through the lack of trying. He came close in the home draw against Blackpool at the end of February but was foiled, not for the first time in his career, by the inspired form of Tony Waiters. Michael Charters wrote: 'The most heartening feature for Everton was that it seemed like Vernon was back to something like his old form.'[6] However, it was a Blackpool player who caught the attention of Leslie Edwards that day:

'There was nothing cramped about the play of red-headed Alan Ball. This little chap – he's not much more than boy-sized – had pitch, ball and opposition tamed with sure control and artful weavings to open a channel for a pass and ability to slide the ball through the gap. He's a Denis Law of a sort who may make an even bigger impact on the game, assuming he makes the necessary development.'[6]

Roy's drought ended in an uncharacteristic manner. An early goal against Villa – via his head – from a Pickering cross got the scoring underway. This was his landmark 100th league goal in just 176 appearances for his two clubs. Despite having netted with his head already, Roy was overlooked in favour of Fred Pickering when the hosts were awarded a penalty, much to the consternation of the crowd and the watching media. Horace Yates opined: 'There is more to taking penalties than merely hitting the ball, and no-one is more worldly-wise than Vernon.' Having seen his spot kick saved, Pickering made amends by heading down a Morrissey cross for Roy to dispatch a left-footed finish into the net. As they celebrated, little did the Gwladys Street faithful appreciate that this strike would bring the curtain down on a memorable Everton career.

Sadly, Roy's bloom had wilted and, given his lack of goals, had fallen down the pecking order. He netted only four times in his nineteen appearances in league and cup competitions during his final campaign. By comparison, Fred Pickering, who was in scintillating form throughout the season, had amassed 37 goals in his 51 outings. Plainly, it was time for the 28-year-old marksman from North Wales to seek new pastures.

CHAPTER 7

The Ceramic City Slicker

'Taffy fed off centre-forwards. He was very quick over ten yards.
When you pushed balls forward for him, you knew he would get there first.
Once he got in front of people, he would score more often than not.
He was very clean in striking the football.'

George Eastham

ROY VERNON'S RELATIONS WITH HARRY CATTERICK ALWAYS BLEW hot and cold – more often the latter as time progressed – and he would joke that it was easier to get an audience with the Pope than with his boss. By April 1965, Harry Catterick was ready to cash in and move on the wayward forward. 'Taffy was too outspoken and must have upset Harry too many times,' was Alex Young's verdict. Dennis Yaeger, a young Australian player invited for an extended trial, saw the deteriorating relationship at first hand before the Villa game: 'I came over in 1964 and Roy was out of the team. The incident I remember most about him was the morning we were waiting in the foyer to get on the bus to training and Roy arrived looking very dishevelled and unshaven. One of the trainers said: "The boss wants to see you," and he replied: "I don't want to see him." In due course he departed to the Potteries.'

That year, Roy was a regular in the Wales national side and selected to play on seven occasions, during which he scored six goals. Directly after the Aston Villa game, he turned up for duty with the Welsh squad in preparation for a World Cup qualifying match against Greece at Ninian Park. With the players known to be holed-up in Porthcawl, Stoke City's Tony Waddington made a five-hour drive to their hotel. After some 45 minutes, he had Roy's signature on a five-year contract with a weekly wage in the region of £80. The genesis of the deal came about before the previous weekend's fixture. The manager, on the look-out for a long-term replacement for Jimmy McIlroy, had approached the Merseyside-based journalist Mike Ellis with a view to getting a low-key audience with Roy. Ellis takes up the story: 'Tony called me on a Friday evening asking me where he could contact Roy Vernon. I told him that he'd probably be at the Royal Tiger. He said: "Surely he won't be there the night before a game?" So, we went there and waited. It got to 9:30pm and Tony said, "He won't be coming now," then ten minutes later he appeared with a cigarette in his mouth. We waited until he went to the urinal and followed him in. "Would you be interested in signing for Stoke City?" asked Tony. Roy turned his head and replied: "If you sign me, it will be the best bit of business you ever do."'

Once Roy's blessing had been obtained, the Stoke City manager could approach Harry Catterick, who had been his teammate and manager at Crewe Alexandra fourteen years previously. With the clock ticking, a £40,000 transfer fee was agreed, and Waddington was free to make the long drive to Porthcawl to seal the deal before the transfer deadline at midnight. The Stoke boss got his man to sign the paperwork with fifteen minutes to spare. Perhaps buoyed by his exit from Everton, Roy scored for Wales in a 4-1 victory over Greece during which he and Ivor Allchurch were described in one report as 'inspired'.

Roy had been transfer-listed at his own request for about two months before Horace Yates announced his departure in mid-March 1965. The Welshman explained: 'The terms offered to me by Stoke are quite attractive. If I had waited another year or so it might have been too late to move. If you remember I was reluctant to move from Blackburn but have no regrets. Naturally, I can't leave a great club like Everton without some pangs. I've been here for five years and you cannot stay that length of time in any place without making many good friends. I've enjoyed my stay on Merseyside immensely. I appreciate what the club has done for me and can't speak too highly of the way the crowd has appreciated my efforts. The fans were simply great.' The journalist debated that, while Vernon could be impetuous, his league record with Everton was more than a little impressive: 1959/60 – 9 goals in 12 games; 1960/61 – 21 goals in 39 games; 1961/62 – 26 goals in 37 games; 1962/63 – 24 goals in 41 games; 1963/64 – 18 goals in

31 games; and 1964/65 – 3 goals in 16 games.

For the Mersey Millionaires, their former captain's exit appeared to be sound business with the club recouping its investment for a man whose physical peak had probably passed. However, Roy's departure was felt keenly by many supporters, including teenager Stephen Stokes: 'When Roy left it was like a death in the family. Fans were devastated. They cursed Catterick to the heavens. Of course, they did not know the background to Vernon's behaviour. It all came out in the wash eventually.' Others took to the pages of the *Liverpool Echo* to bemoan his departure before the arrival of a replacement. Mr J Vemas of Moreton penned this critique: 'I was amazed and disgusted on opening my newspaper to see that the club had made another mistake in selling Vernon, the best inside-forward on the books, when there is nobody to take his place. Since his return, we have been playing with more punch in the forward line and Pickering getting the sort of passes he likes.'[6]

Fred Pickering – an under-sung Everton hero – would continue to plunder goals at an astonishing rate until a debilitating knee injury derailed his career and saw him miss the 1966 FA Cup Final. He totalled 56 goals in 97 League games for Everton and five goals in three international appearances for England. Alex Young recovered from injury to play alongside Pickering and then Alan Ball. Despite his blisters, progressive deafness and his own difficult relationship with Harry Catterick, he would remain at Goodison for another four seasons. In 1968, in the autumn of his Everton career, he was hailed as 'The Golden Vision' when Neville Smith's screenplay of the same name was brought to BBC television by Ken Loach.

Although the club has had great strikers, there has not been a pairing in the intervening half-century that has demonstrated such telepathy. Looking back in 1972 Roy stated: 'Whenever I visit Merseyside, people say: "You shouldn't have left," but I think that I left at the right time. I had five wonderful, happy years at Everton. I'll always be an Evertonian but my decision to ask for a transfer was prompted by many circumstances.'[7] His wife disagreed to some extent with her husband's statement. She believed that were times he would reflect wistfully on his Goodison days, the most fruitful of his career, and wonder if he should have stayed for another year or two. Without doubt, seeing his pals lift the FA Cup in 1966 might have prompted those thoughts to enter his head. It was a rare regret in his life that he did not reach a Wembley final with any of his clubs.

Life at the Victoria Ground, with its lower expectations and greater freedom, was a breath of fresh air. When interviewed by JB of *The Sentinel* during his first full season at his new club, Roy seemed contented yet could not resist having a dig at Harry Catterick's boot-camp regime: 'I suppose everyone in football knew we were going to part company. At Everton success is not anticipated, it is demanded. Players are expected to toe the line rigidly, almost like school children. I don't like too much discipline. Stoke treat you more like an adult. If you are bombing away to the best of your ability on Saturday afternoon's they are happy. I like it here very much; the team is playing a lot of good football.'

Hailed in the local media as one of the best three or four inside-forwards in the land, the acquisition was considered one of the bargains of post-war football. He added: 'I like it here very much. The team are playing good football and I knew many of the players before I arrived which has helped a lot. I remember playing for Everton at Stoke in the first game of last season. Eric Skeels marked me so closely that the only kick of the ball I managed was in the last few minutes when I scored. Now Eric is one of my best friends, but I won't forget his marking that afternoon for some time. He is that sort of player. Give him a job and he carries it out to the letter. I find may young, strong boys coming into the game today haven't this sort of dedication.' Skeels would make 597 appearances in all competitions for Stoke.

In his memoir notes, Roy would reflect on the pleasant contrast with life at Goodison: 'The Stoke City team that I joined was nothing if not sociable – an easy-going set-up where parties and late nights were the rule rather than the exception. For me, this was the complete opposite to the discipline of Everton and I gladly welcomed the opportunity of playing the game as it came rather than I was told. Training, such as it was, was little more than a warm-up followed by a six-a-side.'[1]

Tony Waddington was arguably one of most underrated British managers of the 60s and 70s. The one-time Manchester United youth player had spent his injury-curtailed senior playing career at Crewe. After hanging up his boots through injury, he took a coaching job at Stoke and ascended to the manager's position in 1960. Inheriting a club down on its uppers in the Second Division, Waddington transformed its fortunes and the Potters earned promotion in 1963, at the end of the same season that the Toffees won the First Division crown. One coup that put the club firmly in the spotlight was the re-signing of local hero and national treasure Stanley Matthews – then a stately 46-year-old – from Blackpool. Matthews was still technically a Stoke player when Roy arrived at the Victoria Ground, but injury prevented any further outings barring a benefit match against a World All-Stars XI.

Further astute signings followed, notably former Burnley star Jimmy McIlroy, Peter Dobing, who had arrived from Blackburn via Manchester City, and the former Manchester United man Maurice Setters, who had inadvertently caused the onset of Roy's knee problems during the 1963 Charity Shield match. Another inspired swoop was Dennis Viollet, a former Busby Babe from Manchester United. Less heralded but no less effective was the £2,000 acquisition of John Ritchie from non-League Kettering. This strapping centre-forward would go on to become the Potters' record goalscorer.

The Stoke City manager sought to blend battle-hardened pros, deemed expendable by their previous employers, with young talent. The latter category boasted the likes of Terry Conroy, Mick Bernard and Mike Pejic. Bernard summarised the Stoke boss's skills in recruitment and man-management: 'Waddo wasn't a brilliant football coach, but he was a brilliant man-manager. He was shrewd enough to get one or two around him to do the coaching. The manager would look after us and all the players would run through fire for him. He would back you up to the hilt. If you did it for him on a Saturday afternoon, Waddo was always at your shoulder.'

Roy arrived at the Victoria Ground as one half of a deadline day double-swoop, with Aston Villa left-winger Harry Burrows also signing. He would reflect on Stoke's recruitment policy: 'We had players with playboy reputations who had also proved themselves more than average performers on the field of play. In fact, many so-called mavericks are the stars of today's game. What, one may ask, was the manager doing to allow this state of affairs? In retrospect I think he was buying time in which to build a stronger club with more substantial foundations than a collection of ageing stars. I think he bought good men at reasonable prices to keep the club in the First Division and to consolidate its place in it whilst other changes were made in the general format of the club.'[1]

Unfortunately, Roy's arrival in the Potteries coincided with Dennis Viollet suffering a hairline ankle fracture, robbing the public of seeing the international-class inside-forwards operating in harness. Nonetheless, Roy debuted for Stoke at Molineux on a pitch described by KW of *The Sentinel* as a 'green-fringed swamp where the ball alternately skids and stops dead in the mud'. Prior to the match, his manager outlined the free role that his expensive signing had been assigned: 'Tony Waddington said that it was irrelevant if Vernon is down on the programme as inside-left or inside-right. In Stoke's loose 4-2-4 plan, he is assigned the part of frontier ranger alongside centre-forward John Ritchie. Jimmy McIlroy is midfield schemer.' [8]

Fired by desperation, the relegation-threatened Wolves were unstoppable, but KW provided reason for cautious optimism following the 3-1 defeat for Stoke: 'On this flimsy evidence, the supporters can extend a welcome, tinged with reservation, to Roy Vernon – the Wales international inside-man – and Harry Burrows, the former Aston Villa left-winger. Neither played badly; neither inspired hat-throwing enthusiasm. There were moments when Vernon glittered like a diamond in the setting of mud and perspiration, but the sparkle was not as effective as it can be in an inside-forward.'[8]

The subsequent home match against Aston Villa provided some 20,000 spectators a first glimpse of the record signing. On a pitch described as 'ravaged', Roy did not disappoint in a 2-1 victory. In the match report published in *The Sentinel*, KW gushed over his 'flashes of brilliant opportunism' and 'elusive darts upfield' as he went close to scoring with a header and then hit the woodwork with a powerful drive. Eventually, Roy opened his account with a near-post flicked finish from a Jimmy McIlroy cross.

Roy's international rejuvenation continued when he starred in a 5-0 defeat of Northern Ireland at Windsor Park at the end of the March. With Ivor Allchurch moved across to inside-right, Roy gave a 'smooth display of soccer artistry', according to the *Aberdeen Press and Journal*. Revelling in his favoured inside-left berth, Roy notched two calmly taken goals. His first saw him wriggle past opponents to send a low shot past Irvine in goal. The newspaper described his second: 'Two minutes after the interval Vernon fastened onto a loose clearance and nonchalantly strolled through the Irish defence to leave Irvine helpless.' The domestic campaign continued with a visit to Anfield, where his Everton connections had not been forgotten by the Liverpudlians. Michael Charters reported: 'The former Everton skipper received special mention from the Kop. They chanted, to great laughter, "We'll hang Roy Vernon from the Kop".'[6] Unperturbed, he put his side 2-1 up with a well-taken strike from a Ritchie knock-down. Liverpool rallied, however, to win 3-2. The season was concluded with two victories in which Roy scored, bringing his tally to five goals in ten appearances.

The penultimate match – the last home fixture – saw Roy hailed by *The Sentinel* as the mastermind of a 3-1 victory over Sunderland: 'The Welsh International hardly wasted a ball in laying on regular chances for his colleagues.'[8] His goal was executed in classic Vernon fashion: 'Richie slipped a ball through to his partner, Vernon, who ran right round the defence, including the goalkeeper, before screwing the ball back into the net from a near impossible angle.'[8] His smartly taken goal in the re-scheduled away fixture at a sparely populated Filbert Street – just 8,00 supporters turned up – guaranteed a top-half finish for Stoke. In an end-of-season atmosphere, he was described as the game's 'only distinguished player'.[8] The Potters finished the 1964/65 in eleventh place.

Injury prevented Roy from appearing in the Stanley Matthews tribute match, his old pal Bryan Douglas taking his place at inside-left against a World XI. Matthews had called time on career in February 1965 at the age of fifty years and 5 days. However, there would be no respite for Matthew's former teammates. Stoke City, ever keen to raise its profile and bring in much-needed revenue, was a well-travelled club. In the early 60s, after the conclusion of their domestic fixtures, the club had headed to the likes of Continental Europe, South America, the USA, Sub-Saharan Africa, Morocco and Israel. In 1965, the post-season tour focussed on Scandinavia and the USSR, the latter destination proving not to the Welshman's taste, as he recounted shortly after retiring:

'If there is one thing about top-class football that I shall really miss, apart from the big-time atmosphere, it will be the tours on which players unwind and have hilarious times. Stoke's tours were some of the best I have been on, but the worst was our tour of Russia. Having arrived in Moscow, we asked where we could find some entertainment and were informed by our interpreter that there was an American bar in the city centre. Having had something to eat – I must call it something because even the interpreter was at a loss to explain what it was – we set off to the bar. It was the basement of another hotel. A wooden counter and a dirty floor just about sum it up.'[1]

He continued: 'Anyway, we had a few beers and set off back to our hotel. We seemed to walk for miles, cheerfully chattering away until it registered that we were lost. Imagine our feelings as our earlier glow faded and thoughts of hidden microphones and the secret police entered our heads. Happily, the only accident occurred as we reached some roadworks near our hotel. One of the lads stumbled into a trench and was promptly helped up by two workers. We stared at his rescuers for the road-men were, in fact, road-women complete with overalls and boots. We laughed but one of the lads swore it was Tamara Press – a legendary Soviet shot putter – out for her early morning training.'

'We moved on to Leningrad and, finally, Odessa, where we enjoyed a farewell dinner. In the best English traditions of sportsmanship, and as ambassadors of our country, we stood solemnly to toast our hosts. After we had emptied our champagne glasses, the skipper threw his glass against the wall. Quick to cover up this temporary lapse, it was explained as an old English custom whereupon the Russians promptly toasted us and proceeded to hurl their glasses again the wall. Altogether over ten glasses were broken that night and it was just down to an "old English custom".'

The start of 1965/66 season saw no significant changes in personnel, although the fit-again Dennis Viollet featured in a deeper half-back role, leaving Roy and Jimmy McIlroy to support John Ritchie in the front-line. After only three matches into the new season, the man from Ffynnongroyw was provided a wonderful opportunity to demonstrate to Harry Catterick and the Evertonians just what they were missing when the Merseysiders visited the Victoria Ground. Even though Fred Pickering struck for Everton, Roy was unable to respond in kind. He was, however, praised by *The Sentinel* for his 'persistent probing' and twice had goal-bound shots kicked off the line. It fell to Ritchie to bring the scores level from a spot kick. The match is best remembered for John Hurst – coming on as Everton's first-ever substitute in a league match – thinking he had grabbed the winner after a last-gasp header crashed into the net, only for the referee to claim that he had already blown for full time. Several weeks later, with John Ritchie sidelined by illness and Peter Dobing deputising at centre-forward, Roy enjoyed his finest game in red-and-white stripes when he bagged a brace against Newcastle United. JB resorted to prose to describe the Welshman's brilliance: 'Frankly, Newcastle might as well have been chasing a bee with a frying pan. No matter how hard, or how often, they swatted at Vernon, the inside-forward slipped through to the nectar in their goalmouth.' An unnamed teammate told the journalist how roughhouse tactics, if anything, inspired Roy: 'He is absolutely fearless and hates to lose. If he is tackled unfairly, as he was constantly today against Newcastle, the opposition better look out.'[8]

Evidence of the special attention dished out to Roy during the match was extensive bruising to both shins and a gash which required five stitches. Post-match Vernon was the talk of the press room, according to JB: 'The subject was Roy Vernon, City's slim, sharp-featured, Welsh international who had just treated us to one of the fieriest performances of his eventful career. The place was the

Victoria Ground, one hour after a Vernon-inspired side had shattered Newcastle United 4-0. We were talking specifically about the Vernon temperament which can interpose moments of sheer football artistry with the sort of incident which had earned him a booking by the referee.'

Roy's good form continued at international level as he scored in the 2-1 win over the USSR at Ninian Park on 27 October. Latterly, Wales rounded off their unsuccessful qualifying campaign with a comfortable 4-2 victory over Denmark at the Racecourse Ground, with Roy claiming two goals.

In November 1965, the BBC's *Match of the Day* cameras were present at White Hart Lane to capture the clash between Tottenham and Stoke. On a treacherous pitch, the attacking triumvirate of Vernon, Viollet and Dobing produced some brilliant interplay, full of give-and-goes. In one passage of play, Roy flicked the ball first time to Alan Bloor, who advanced before sliding it to Dobing, who was upended in the box. The spot-kick duties naturally fell to the Stoke number ten. The technique was textbook Vernon. With a minimum of fuss, he placed the ball on the penalty spot, walked away three paces, turned and arrowed the ball low to Pat Jennings's left, just inside the post. Later on, after receiving the ball in his own half, he left Dave Mackay floundering before advancing into the Tottenham half with Alan Mullery trailing in his wake. Deep into the second half, with the score at 2-2 and Spurs pressing for a winner, Roy's gamesmanship came into play. The hosts were awarded a free-kick 35 yards out. As the referee turned away, Roy trotted forward and hoofed the ball away to deny Mackay the opportunity to take it quickly. With Spurs players remonstrating and the home supporters chanting "Off! Off! Off!", the match-official – realising that something had gone on behind his back – read the riot act to the Welshman, who spread his arms in apparent innocence and astonishment.

When not on first-team duties, he would fill time in his traditional ways. Uttoxeter and Chester replaced Haydock and Aintree for his horseracing fix. As a regular patron, he was on good terms with several stable hands and jockeys and would help them out. Norma laughed: 'Once we had Willie Carson, Colin Williams and Greville Starkey all staying in one bed in our back bedroom in Endon. They were only little, so we managed!' The hospitality for the jockeys did not end there, as Roy's teammate John Worsdale recalled fondly: 'In the afternoons, when the first team had departed, the reserves used to clean up after them and discovered that Taffy would invite jockeys in to have a sauna. It was not far from Uttoxeter and they were trying to get down to the weight. Afterwards, Taffy would say: "I've had a tip off a jockey today and if you put your wages on it, you'll have a winner." And nine times out of ten it was a winner! I didn't put my wages on it as £7 was a lot, but I wasn't Taffy!'

Roy remained on the disciplinary edge at Stoke, as he had been at Blackburn and Everton. In April 1966, he was fined £25 and suspended for two weeks by the FA Disciplinary Committee for 'persistently infringing the laws of the game' against West Brom. A caution issued four months earlier was considered when the tariff was set.

These happy days in the Potters team would, sadly, not last. With John Ritchie out for several months – x-rays had revealed a spot on his lung linked to tuberculosis – Roy was robbed of his attacking foil. Then, as the season progressed, his niggling cartilage problems worsened. After receiving a kick to the right knee in a defeat to Northampton Town in mid-April 1966, he was referred to a specialist who deemed surgery to be required. Roy would miss the rest of the season and Wales's summer tour of South America. The patient was underwhelmed with the standard of after-op care received at Stoke, in contrast to what he would have experienced at Everton: 'I knew at the end of the season it was inevitable, so I had the op and then set about getting fit for the following season. Conditions were far from ideal for this. They had no medical room and no physiotherapist – all injured players had to report to the general hospital and, in many cases, had to sit and wait their turn for treatment with the general public. I wonder how many hours our players have wasted sitting in that hospital waiting room instead of having first-class attention at the ground and then getting on with remedial exercises. On top of this it was now summer, and I was left to lap the ground, run up and down the terrace steps and do my weight exercises alone. Hardly the interest one would expect when bearing in mind that I had cost them nearly £40,000.'[1]

It would be 1968 before Stoke appointed Fred Street, a medically qualified physiotherapist. Street, who had been an RAF physical training instructor before joining the NHS and gaining chartered status, would return to London and work for Arsenal and the England national team. He retains fond memories of his time with Roy at the Victoria Ground: 'He was a character who liked a smoke and a drink, plus the horse racing. In that respect, he was typical of his generation of men, not just footballers. Players had more time to indulge their interests than the average working man and were well off relative to their contemporaries.'

Stoke City finished the 1965/66 campaign in tenth place, one spot above Everton. It was a modest improvement on the previous campaign. Roy had made a meaningful contribution, bagging ten goals in his 31 league outings. That summer whilst recuperating, he returned to home turf as guest of honour at the Point of Ayr Colliery Open Day. The event was part of a recruitment drive for the mechanised pit which, according to the National Coal Board, had a 'long life'. In fact, it closed in August 1996 after the British coal industry was decimated in the wake of the Miners' Strike. Accompanied by Norma and his two sons, he declared the gala open and accepted the gift of a miner's lamp from Gala Queen, Mary Davies. It was a proud moment for his father who, having undergone an operation, left his sick bed to attend the ceremony. At that time, Thomas Vernon had retired from the boat pilot duties and was working in the engine house. Roy was amongst 2,000 locals who took the lift to the bottom of the shaft. When asked if he was glad that he chose football over the pit, the guest of honour grinned as he replied: 'What do you think?'

On the pitch, he suffered yet another setback: 'At the start of the 1966/67 season I was able to start in the usual warm-up fixtures in Ireland and felt reasonably happy when we travelled to Portsmouth for another friendly. It was in this match that I injured my knee again and, as a result, failed to command a first-team place regularly again.'[1] Roy was declared fit for the third game of the season. Playing against Fulham in a roving wide-right role, he scored Stoke's consolation goal in a 2-1 defeat, but also took a blow to the knee, sidelining him for two further months. As a consequence, new arrival George Eastham – who Roy had admired so much for standing up to Newcastle United in a contract dispute – cemented his place in the number ten shirt. Just as he returned to the first team, the sale of John Ritchie to Sheffield Wednesday sent shock waves through the Victoria Ground. Medical opinion suggested that symptoms linked to his tuberculosis-related illness from the previous season could manifest themselves again at any time. With Sheffield Wednesday manager Alan Brown desperately keen to sign the centre-forward, Waddington decided to cash-in on the player. Over time he would admit that the decision to sell Ritchie was his 'biggest mistake'.[8] The big man's physicality and ability to bring his inside-forwards into play – not to mention his goalscoring prowess – would be greatly missed.

The burden of wearing the number nine shirt and fulfilling the attacking pivot role fell to Roy and, subsequently, Peter Dobing. Both were ill-equipped for the demands of the role: 'I had been a striker when I first went to Stoke and so I suppose the transition to front-runner appeared natural. However, I wasn't physically strong enough for what must be the most unrewarding role in football,'1 Roy told *The Sentinel*: 'I like that bit of space to work in and that's why I prefer to play a shade deep.'8 Within a month of Ritchie's departure, Roy, still unhappy in his new role, had submitted a transfer request. It was rejected. However, a second request early in the New Year was met with a more positive response and he was listed as being available for transfer, albeit with a significant caveat. Tony Waddington was insistent that the player repay his four-figure signing-on fee before completing a move to another club. Stalemate ensued, and no transfer came to fruition. For the remainder of the 1966/67 season, the transfer-listed forward was in and out of the first team.

As the season neared conclusion, the Stoke boss brought in Terry Conroy, a young forward from Dublin. For someone who had not ventured outside of Ireland, Conroy was, by his own admission, somewhat naive and taken-aback by the life at Stoke. He was also grateful to Roy: 'I was twenty but very green, having come over from Ireland. Funnily enough Taffy took me under his wing. I loved horse racing and every day Taffy would have the *Sporting Life* and the *Sporting Chronicle* with him in the dressing room, whilst smoking continuously. He'd ask: "What horse do you fancy today?" and then pass on some information to me. No one else was interested in horse racing, so we had a nice little relationship. He was the older pro and looked upon me as someone who knew something about horses that he could talk to. I always said that Taffy was kind to sick animals, but he didn't know that they were sick when he backed them!'

Conroy continued: 'It was a smashing club. We had Harry Gregg, Maurice Setters – a very opinionated character – Calvin Palmer, Gordon Banks, Taffy and George Eastham. They were players of colossal ability. George was a fantastic player and we had Taffy's silken skills plus toughness at the back in Setters and Calvin Palmer – a lovely blend. Waddo wasn't a disciplinarian, he knew that these lads had form in relation to liking a drink and gallivanting but trusted them. For the first time, Taffy was treated as a grown-up and one day he said, "I hate this club because there are no rules to break." The quip was oft repeated by the sometimes-wayward star to his younger teammates.'

On the pitch, following the recruitment of the cultured World Cup-winner George Eastham, Stoke City finished the 1966/67 season in twelfth position in the

First Division. Peter Dobing netted nineteen times and Harry Burrows added another seventeen goals from the wing. In contrast, Roy contributed a disappointing four goals in his twenty league appearances. Off the pitch, the next stop was the United States. Or more specifically, Cleveland, Ohio, located on the southern shore of Lake Erie.

CHAPTER 8

Roy of the Stokers

'I remember watching the Welsh Dragons versus the Danes at Wrexham.
Vernon was in his element and scored a brace. He was a terrific footballer for club
and country. The contributions of men from my neck of the woods like
Billy Meredith, Kevin Ratcliffe and Neville Southall are unfairly overlooked by the
national media. To that list I would add Roy Vernon. If we had been
born in England and played for a southern club, he would be a household name.'

T. G. Jones

THE CLOSE SEASON OF 1966/67 BROUGHT A NEW VENTURE AS THE
Stoke City team morphed into the Cleveland Stokers for six weeks. In the afterglow
of the 1966 World Cup, two rival soccer leagues were formed in North America,
namely the United Soccer Association (USA), which was recognised by FIFA, and
the National Professional Soccer League (NPSL), which had a 'match of the week'
contract with the CBS television network. The United Soccer Association had
twelve franchises and Vernon Stouffer – the American multi-millionaire who
started the Stouffer Hotel chain, pioneered microwave dinners via Stouffer Frozen
Foods and also owned the Cleveland Indians baseball team – was persuaded to
invest in the Cleveland franchise. Like all the other start-ups, he faced a race
against time to recruit a squad in time for the competition's kick-off in late
May 1967.

Ultimately clubs from Europe (including Sunderland, Wolves, Dundee United,
Hibernian, Cagliari and Shamrock Rovers) and South America (Bangu from Rio de
Janeiro and Cerro from Montevideo) were commandeered to fulfil the fixture
obligations, with the franchises aiming to be self-sufficient for the following

season. Stouffer used his powers of persuasion to poach Stoke City from under the noses of the Vancouver franchise. Thus, the Cleveland Stokers, decked out in the Potters' customary red-and-white striped shirts, were born.

The initial fourteen-man squad – Peter Dobing and recent signing Gordon Banks, a considerable coup, would arrive later – touched down in Ohio on 21 May 1967, just five days ahead of the opening fixture. Settled in at the 500-bed Pick-Carter Hotel, the squad had access to the sports field and running track at the local university along with the gym and swimming pool at the Cleveland Athletic Club for training.

Off the pitch, the players were known to enjoy long afternoons tanning on the hotel roof plus long nights out on the town. Cleveland journalist Dan Coughlin said: 'They lived there and had wonderful times.' John Moore, the young defender, looked back on the fun during the tour and recalled: 'Jackie Marsh, Bill Bentley and I went to Taffy's room. He had been a drinking a bit too much so we picked him off his mattress and put it out on the floor in the hotel foyer and ran off. He didn't wake up. I don't know what happened except he got his own back – he wrecked our room. He had tipped it upside down. That day, I learned not to mess with Taffy.'

On another occasion, both Roy and Maurice Setters – always in cahoots – found themselves facing the long arm of the law when driving out from Fort Lauderdale. Pulled over for speeding, they were ordered out of the car at gunpoint and frisked, but managed to talk their way out of any further action. Terry Conroy was shocked by the antics of seniors pros on his first tour: 'The real eye-opener for me was Taffy Vernon and his lifestyle. He was a good drinker and smoked incessantly – sixty cigs a day would be the norm. You could turn him sideways and mark him absent he was that thin, like a rake. In North America, Waddo did not impose any rules. Maurice and Taffy went everywhere together – they were inseparable. On a day off they would drink all day and wouldn't be any the worse for wear – they had a great capacity for alcohol. The next day, Taffy would be training in sunglasses to hide the bloodshot eyes.' Harry Burrows had similarly fond memories of the tour: 'We played our home games at the Cleveland Browns' stadium, which was enormous. Also, we played a team of Brazilians on Astroturf in the first enclosed stadium, the Houston Astrodome, which had just been completed.'

The soccer club was based at Lakefront Stadium in Cleveland, Ohio. The

78,000-capacity venue was one of the early multi-purpose stadiums and became the home of the Cleveland Indians of Major League Baseball and the Cleveland Browns of the National Football League. The team managed by Tony Waddington were undefeated in their first seven matches until fading and missing out on the play-offs by a single point. Roy Vernon scored two goals for the Stokers. His first was in a 2-1 victory over Aberdeen, masquerading as the Washington Whips, the second in a 4-1 triumph over ADO Den Haag, moonlighting as the San Francisco Golden Gates. However, the small squad and intensive schedule of fixtures – two matches per week – was to put a strain on the touring party. Also, Roy was eager for news of an addition to his family. Norma, expecting the imminent arrival of a third child, was kept company by Maurice Setter's wife Nancy back in England. The baby was so overdue that Nancy herself was on holiday by the time Roy Junior entered the world on 19 July at North Staffordshire Hospital. Nevertheless, the proud new father and the rest of the Cleveland Stokers fulfilled their twelve-game schedule.

The Cleveland Stokers were pipped by the Washington Whips to the Eastern League title, thereby missing out on the national championship decider, which was won by Wolverhampton Wanderers in the guise of the Los Angeles Wolves. Somewhat surprisingly, Roy Vernon, George Eastham and Peter Dobing were named in the United Soccer Association's All-Star Select XI.

The United Soccer Association would be short-lived, merging with the National Professional Soccer League to become the NASL in 1968. Before the curtain came down on the American competition of 1967, the Stoke City manager had returned home to prepare for the domestic 1967/68 season. There he failed in a bid to sign Francis Lee from Bolton with an offer of £45,000 or, it was mooted, a part-exchange deal with Roy as the makeweight. After Lee was transferred to Manchester City for a fee of £60,000, it was disclosed that Bolton had been interested in taking Vernon on loan.

The new 1967/68 league campaign started in testing fashion with a trip to Highbury: 'We had played with a weakened team and, though beaten 2-0, were not disgraced. We went out with a strictly defensive line-up and I was the front runner, a thoroughly unrewarding afternoon in a role that I should have embraced. We had to make the best of things and, with virtually no support, I had a poor match.'[1]

Roy's below-par showing in North London led to a clash with Tony Waddington.

With Sheffield United coming to the Victoria Ground for a midweek fixture next, the manager gave a debut to Bert Hulse. Roy imparted: 'I turned up for the next match and Tony told me about half an hour before the kick-off, "You're substitute tonight." "Why?" I said, "Who is playing?" When he told me, I was livid: "I'll tell you what, I am not subbing for him. In fact, you can sub for him and if you must go on nobody will notice. In fact, if you start off playing, we'll have a better chance." Then I stormed out of the dressing room. Tony gave me a few minutes to cool off and then asked me to be sub again. I refused and I know that I should have accepted the role, for the player who went on never played again for Stoke, and I probably would have gone on before half-time.'[1] In fact the player in question, Bert Hulse – the former Northwich Victoria forward – made one further first-team appearance for the Potters.

Jackie Marsh was hurriedly drafted in to warm the bench, wearing the number twelve jersey whilst Roy headed home. The match ended all square, but it was Vernon's behaviour that caught the headlines. The club confirmed that Roy had been suspended without pay for a fortnight for what was described as a 'breach of club discipline'. Five years later, Roy would rue his reaction: 'It was my biggest mistake at Stoke and it was a long time before I was selected for the first team again.'[1]

In the aftermath of the substitute stand-off, Waddington could afford to ignore his star because he was well-blessed in the forward department with Gerry Bridgwood, Peter Dobing, John Mahoney and George Eastham all at his disposal. Finally recalled in mid-September, Roy got off the mark in a defeat of Southampton but would have to wait until May 1968 for his next league goal.

The substitute incident may have convinced his boss that it was time to move Roy on and in October 1967 he was again transfer-listed and the subject of interest from Stockport County, who were prepared to offer £30,000 for him and teammate Alan Philpott. In the end, Roy turned down the two-tier drop. As for Philpott? After playing 52 games in his eight years at Stoke, he moved to Oldham in the Third Division.

That month, October 1967, the curtain came down on Roy's decade-long international career after Wales fell to England by 3-0 in a European Championship qualifier. As one career was ending, another was beginning. Accompanying Roy on the drive down from the Potteries to Porthcawl was John Mahoney. His Stoke teammate had made his debut for his country in February, but the match had been

The mighty minnow. Roy (far left, front row) at age fourteen is dwarfed by his teammates in the Rhyl Grammar School team. Also included is Billy Russell, the future Sheffield United player (second from right, front row).
[VERNON FAMILY ARCHIVES]

Roy at age seventeen, an amateur and member of the Ewood Park groundstaff, stretches on the terraces in front of the Nuttall Street Stand.
[VERNON FAMILY ARCHIVES]

The Blackburn Rovers squad for the 1958/59 season. Back row (left to right): Mick McGrath, Ronnie Cairns, Ally MacLeod, Harry Leyland, Matt Woods, Dave Whelan, Tommy Johnston. Front row: Bryan Douglas, Roy Stephenson, Roy Vernon, Ronnie Clayton, Peter Dobing, Bill Eckersley [COLORSPORT]

Roy in action for Blackburn Rovers against Rotherham United in April 1958. After bamboozling goalkeeper Roy Ironside and his defenders, Roy coolly slips the ball into the unguarded net with his left foot in a 5-0 triumph. [VERNON FAMILY ARCHIVES]

More action: Roy scores for Blackburn at White Hart Lane in January 1959. He out-wits Maurice Norman before firing a rocket past goalkeeper John Hollowbread with Mel Hopkins looking on. Tottenham won 3-1. [VERNON FAMILY ARCHIVES]

Manager Johnny Carey congratulates Bryan Douglas on the award of his first international cap and selection for England against Wales at Ninian Park in October 1957. Roy was awarded his sixth Wales cap for his participation in the fixture which the visitors won 4-0. Also pictured (left to right): Jack Weddell (coach), Ronnie Clayton, Harry Leyland, Roy Vernon and Matt Woods. [VERNON FAMILY ARCHIVES]

Shortly after his big-money transfer from Blackburn, Roy poses in the royal blue and white of Everton at Highbury in February 1960. [PA]

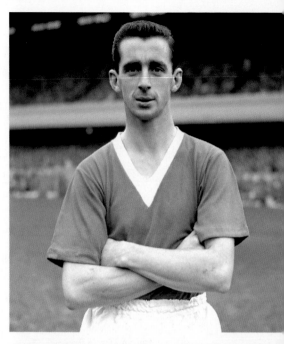

Attired in old gold shirt and black shorts, Roy stretches his long and skinny legs when attacking the Leicester City goal at Filbert Street on New Years' Eve 1960.
[DAVID FRANCE ARCHIVES]

Title clincher: In the 83rd minute, captain Vernon scores his third goal at the Gwladys Street end and completes his hat-trick against Fulham in May 1963. [GETTY]

After clinching the 1962/63 League title, Roy leads the post-match celebrations. Pictured left to right: Manager Harry Catterick, Alex Parker, Dennis Stevens, suited Gordon West (partly hidden), Roy Vernon, Albert Dunlop, Alex Young and coach Ron Lewin. [ALAMY]

The Football League elected not to present the famous silverware at the conclusion of the title clincher against Fulham in May 1963. In the absence of the trophy, Vernon, enjoying a post-match cigarette, and Jimmy Gabriel salute the ecstatic fans from the Goodison Park directors' box. [VERNON FAMILY ARCHIVES]

World-class chain smoker Roy enjoys a Senior Service cigarette after capturing the league title in 1963, while Tony Kay enjoys something more robust. [NEWSPAPER CLIPPING FROM DAVID FRANCE ARCHIVES]

The league trophy at last. This photograph features the forward-line from the title-clinching game against Fulham, namely Dennis Stevens, Derek Temple, Alex Scott, Roy Vernon and Alex Young. It was the first time that the trophy had graced Goodison Park for 24 years. [PA]

The Everton title-winning squad of 1962/63. Back row (left to right): Alex Young, Jimmy Gabriel, Alex Scott, Alex Parker, Gordon West, George Heslop, Brian Labone, Mick Meagan, Tony Kay. Front row: Brian Harris, Ray Veall, Derek Temple, Roy Vernon, Dennis Stevens, Billy Bingham, Johnny Morrissey. Missing: Albert Dunlop. [THE EVERTON COLLECTION]

Lauded for his prowess from the penalty spot, Roy is pictured driving his kick into the bottom corner and sending David Gaskell, the Manchester United goalkeeper, the wrong way at Goodison Park in August 1963. Everton won the Charity Shield match by 4-0. In the background, Brian Labone is caught with his back to the action. [NEWSPAPER CUTTING FROM DAVID FRANCE ARCHIVES]

Arguably the biggest set-back in Everton's history. Roy is congratulated by Dennis Stevens after breaking the deadlock against Inter Milan in the preliminary round of the European Cup at Goodison Park in September 1963. The goal was disallowed, and the Italian champions advanced to win the trophy. [THE EVERTON COLLECTION]

Also lauded for his ability to outwit goalkeepers, Roy attempts to knock the ball past Bill Brown in the home clash with Tottenham Hotspur at Goodison in April 1963. Everton won 1-0, a key win in the title contest. [VERNON FAMILY ARCHIVES]

Greyhound-like quick over short distances, Vernon outpaces Tottenham's Terry Medwin at White Hart Lane in March 1964. Roy scored two goals in the 4-2 victory. [PA]

The first Merseyside league derby for eight seasons. Roy welcomes Ron Yeats, the Liverpool captain, to Goodison Park in September 1962. In an action-packed contest, Roy scored a penalty and had a goal disallowed before the visitors equalised in the final minute. [THE EVERTON COLLECTION]

With the 1963/64 title in their grasp, Everton conspired to forfeit the title race to Liverpool and so were required to handover the famous silverware to Ron Yeats. Roy appears to be hesitant to do so.
[NEWSPAPER CLIPPING UNKNOWN]

The Stoke City squad in the spring of 1965. Back row (left to right): trainer Fred Mountfield, John Ritchie, George Kinnell, Bill Asprey, Lawrie Leslie, Maurice Setters, Calvin Palmer, Tony Allen, Alan Bloor, manager Tony Waddington. Front row: Peter Dobing, Roy Vernon, Jimmy McIlroy, Dennis Viollet, Stanley Matthews, Harry Burrows, Eric Skeels. [DAVID FRANCE ARCHIVES]

Roy meets the Holy Trinity. This iconic photograph captures Kendall, Harvey and Ball overwhelming Roy at Goodison Park in May 1968.

Roy poses in the red and white shirt of Stoke City in January 1967. [VERNON FAMILY ARCHIVES]

In the colours of the Cleveland Stokers (Stoke City), Roy Vernon is thwarted by goalkeeper Ton Thie of the San Francisco Golden Gate Gales (ADO Den Haag) at a sparsely populated Candlestick Park in 1967 as Aad Mansveld and Theo Van Der Burch look on. [UNKNOWN]

Wales preparing for a match against England at Ninian Park in October 1963. Manager Jimmy Murphy shares his words of wisdom with star forwards Ivor Allchurch, Roy Vernon and John Charles. [MIRRORPIX]

Roy on international duty in Budapest in November 1962 when Hungary defeated Wales 3-1 in the European Nations' Cup tie. He is captured outpacing Ferenc Sipos and Kálmán Mészöly. [DAVID FRANCE ARCHIVES]

Not known for his love of food or managers, Roy, attired in his club suit, dines with Harry Catterick and his good friend Alex Young around 1964. [VERNON FAMILY ARCHIVES]

Roy – the man about town. Immaculately turned out, Roy accompanied by Alex Young and singer Alma Cogan, were invited to judge the Miss New Brighton beauty contest in front of several thousand spectators at that town's open-air swimming baths in 1964. The winner is unknown. [VERNON FAMILY ARCHIVES]

Roy the father. At their home in Lydiate in 1963, Roy gives sons Neil (age 2) and Mark (age 4) boxing lessons as wife Norma looks on. [VERNON FAMILY ARCHIVES]

Roy the grandfather. Roy with granddaughter Christina (age 8) and their favourite pony named Jingles (or Lindisfarne Jingle Bells during equestrian competitions) in 1991. [VERNON FAMILY ARCHIVES]

Roy the husband. Behind every professional footballer is a good woman. Roy Vernon married Norma Tierney in St Mary's Catholic Church, Blackburn on 17 February 1958. They had been married for 37 years when he passed away in December 1993.
[VERNON FAMILY ARCHIVES]

Delayed recognition. Norma accepts the Everton Giant Award on behalf of her late husband at the club's end of season awards night in 2017.
[EVERTON FC]

abandoned due to the condition of the pitch. During the journey to Wales, Roy could not resist winding up his mate: 'I remember Roy saying to me, "When you are down there, in the five-a-sides just call me Prince." I was a bit innocent and did as he said. So, in training a few other the other lads were saying, "What are you calling him Prince for?" He had got me, of course – The Prince of Wales! He was a hell of a boy.'

Roy's eight goals in 32 appearances for his country was a creditable return, especially when you consider that he was occasionally deployed on the right-wing. He was awarded nine caps whist at Blackburn, another thirteen caps at Everton and his final ten caps during his time in the Potteries. It would have been more but for his knee operation in 1966. In his pomp on Merseyside he was often overlooked in favour of Ivor Allchurch.

Back on the domestic front, Stoke supporter Robert Clarke was alarmed by Roy's rapid fall from grace as injury, miles on the clock, ill-suited tactics plus a degree of apathy blunted his effectiveness, and he admitted that the forward was very much 'on the wane' by the time he saw him in action.

Clarke also outlined the perception amongst the Victoria Ground faithful that Roy was not giving his all for the Potters' cause: 'He was singled out with terrace barracking, although knowing his acerbic sense of humour Roy may have appreciated the wit. But I've not known another Stoke player who attracted what he did, a song directed at him showing the fans' dislike. He was having a particularly lackadaisical performance and towards the end of the match a song started wafting down from the 'mobs' (the name given to the fans who started them). To the tune of "Michael, Row the Boat Ashore" they sang: "Send Roy Vernon to Vietnam – Hallelujah. Send Roy Vernon to Vietnam – Hallelujah." Poor old Roy.'

The Welshman lamented how football was changing, not for the better in his experience: 'Many changes were taking place and I was getting older. The training had stepped up; we were made to work out on the famous hill at Trentham Park. Also, tactics were changing.'[1]

Long runs were the last thing that Roy had in mind, as teammate Bert Hulse remembers: 'Taffy wasn't the best trainer. In pre-season we jogged around Trentham Gardens, which were hilly. This was the thing he least looked forward to. We'd have to do three laps and after the first he'd be gone, then you'd see smoke coming up from behind a bush. It was incredible! The trainer, Frank Mountford – who didn't run with us – didn't know what was happening. It was just what Taffy did. He had been there, seen it and done it, so nothing rattled him. He used to say to me: 'I'm the fastest man over three yards – that's when you have to be at your quickest.' I missed his prime, of course, so, arguably, three yards was all he could manage.'

With Stoke preparing for a relegation battle that spring, Roy got his chance at redemption: 'I had asked for the role of coming from behind the front men into goalscoring spaces that their running had created but it was only later, when relegation was threatened, that I was to play in this way and score goals which helped to keep us up. How well I remember standing in the tunnel with Tony watching the rain come down on the morning of a vital relegation match. About five games previously he had told me that he could not play Eastham, Dobing and Vernon in the same forward line. He believed we had the skill but not the physical strength needed in such desperate circumstances. I was the odd man out but this time I didn't complain, I just hoped that physical strength would help us to a few vital points and keep us in the First Division. Well, his gamble had failed and now we were playing relegation candidates Coventry. "We're in a bad way, Roy," Tony said. "If we lose this one, we're down. You had better get to bed this afternoon and come with good shooting boots tonight." I didn't score that night, but we pulled it back from 1-3 to 3-3'.

The previous day, Roy had been sent off for remonstrating with the referee in a reserve match but was instrumental in two of the goals upon his recall to the first team. His cute flick had set up John Mahoney for the first and he thought he had levelled the match at 3-3 when he dived full length to connect spectacularly with a left-wing cross from Harry Burrows. Celebrations were curtailed when the 'goal' was ruled out for a perceived handball. As the clock ticked down Maurice Setters was repelling every ball launched at him by his former team but, in the dying seconds, his old mate had the last laugh.

Peter Hewitt was watching for *The Sentinel*: 'It was injury time when Roy Vernon, socks rolled down, collected a pass from Eric Skeels on the left and cut in towards the advancing goalkeeper. Thousands of hearts stopped beating as he coolly pushed the ball out of Glazier's reach towards the net before Dobing tapped the ball in.'[8]

Retained for the next match, away at Goodison, Roy saw his injury-hit team blown away by Everton's fast, attacking football. His own diminished status is best captured in a press photograph taken on 4 May 1968. Snapped on a sunny spring afternoon, it captures Roy seemingly rooted to the spot whilst The Holy Trinity of Howard Kendall, Colin Harvey and Alan Ball swarmed around him, taking the ball with them. Noticeably, the Toffees had invested shrewdly and advanced to another level.

Roy's most telling contribution during the relegation battles was at Craven Cottage against fellow strugglers Fulham. His decisive goal, described by *The Sentinel* as 'a stroke of Welsh genius', came a minute before half-time when he ghosted onto a long ball down the middle from Burrows, swerved past a hesitant defender and cracked in a superb fifteen-yard right-footer.

Physio Fred Street was impressed by the composure displayed when notching the crucial goal, which went a long way to securing First Division survival: 'Roy had a cool talent. Vividly, I remember his goal in the last few minutes at Fulham. We were drawing 0-0 and had to win to stay up. Roy was through on his own with the goalkeeper advancing on him and just clipped it past him, whereas a younger player might have blasted it and hit the keeper. I spoke to him after the game and said how easy he made it look. He replied, "Fred, I once did that in front of 100,000 in an international game. Today's gate was about 10,000."'

A heart-pounding draw at Filbert Street secured top flight status for another year. Roy's nous and experience had played a part in staving off relegation and was recognised by the club hierarchy: 'We were safe. It was a terrific team effort, but I was still delighted that the chairman raised his glass to me and said: "Thanks Taffy." I wish this episode could have a happy ending but, alas, it can't.'[1] Having sold Calvin Palmer and Maurice Setters, Stoke were fortunate to finish the 1967/68 campaign in eighteenth place. It had not been a good season for Roy Vernon either. He had contributed a meagre two goals in his nineteen league appearances.

The following 1968/69 season saw him reduced to a bit-part player. David Herd had arrived from Manchester United to belatedly fill the void at centre-forward left by John Ritchie. He started only five league matches and two League Cup outings. The second of those sticks in the mind of Stoke supporter Terry Simpson: 'It was a replay against Blackburn in the League Cup. It was a filthy night and the Vic was in its best condition – knee deep in mud. We lost 1-0 but when Roy Vernon came off at the end and there wasn't a spot of mud on his kit. Everybody stood in amazement as the other players had mud from earhole to earhole. Roy was like that; he didn't go diving around – he waited for the mountain to come to Mohammed.' Norma Vernon was aware of her husband's increasing disenchantment with the game: 'For Roy, teams were taking the flair players out of the game and it was all run, run, run. That was not his idea of football. The ball's supposed to do the work, you should not be running around like idiots.'

Roy's bond with Tony Waddington would have perhaps been holed below the waterline when word reached the manager of his player's behaviour when selected for the Stoke reserve XI, which also contained Denis Smith and Terry Conroy. The Irishman recalls: 'We were playing in the reserves at West Brom and Taffy had backed a horse called Torpid, trained by John Oxley. He had told me in the morning and I had gone to the bookies to put on a fiver on it, a big bet for me as I was on £30 a week. The Hawthorns had a TV in the changing room, which was unusual at the time, and Taffy knew about it. He got "injured" in the pre-match kick-about and then at 3:05pm precisely, having watched the race, came to the side of the pitch. After the referee waved him on, Roy gave me the thumbs up and said: "It won TC, at five to one!" That incident sums him up. He was all about innocent devilment. He was always one step ahead, thinking how he could gain an advantage.'

In late November 1968, Roy came on for the final half hour in the league game at Hillsborough and was kicked from pillar to post, so much so that he would spend two months on the sidelines nursing a hairline leg fracture. When he did return, he was confined to substitute duties until recalled to the starting line-up for the final few matches. In his final home match – on a miserable, wet Staffordshire night – Roy exacted some revenge on the Owls as he rolled back the years to dominate the game, hitting the woodwork twice and netting his final goal for the Potters in a 1-1 draw. He would retain his place for the finale at Newcastle, but was substituted in a 5-0 thrashing.

Plainly, Stoke had learned little from their previous flirtation with relegation and had won just nine matches all season and scored just forty goals as they narrowly avoided the trap door by three points. As for Roy, he scored one goal in his eight league appearances, three of which were as a reluctant substitute. Without delay, Stoke embarked from Newcastle Airport for an end-of-season tour which took them to Africa and then Spain. For domestic reasons Roy was not in the travelling party which drew 1-1 with Kinshasa (Congo) and defeated the mighty Barcelona 3-2.

Though no longer the player who terrorised defences with Everton, Roy was highly regarded by his teammates at the Victoria Ground. Several of his contemporaries were delighted to share their recollections of him. With no little enthusiasm, right-winger John Worsdale asserted: 'Roy was an unbelievable talent and a joy to play alongside. He could ping the ball into the net with either foot and excelled at one-twos. He loved to receive passes over the top and could master the ball without breaking stride, go past defenders and smash it into the net.'

Denis Smith, the hard-tackling defender who for a period was banned by his manager from playing against his teammates in training but progressed to make over 400 first-team appearances, added: 'He was a tough nut. But the one thing that sticks in my mind is a train journey to a reserve match at Newcastle. I was sitting opposite him – I was seventeen or eighteen, a young lad who didn't drink or smoke – and Roy got through what seemed like 100 Senior Service cigarettes. This was a Welsh international and Stoke City first-team star. Everyone talks about his drinking and smoking but he could play.' Oddly, a few of Roy's up-and-coming teammates would move on to Everton. Perhaps it had something to do with how he described his glory days to them? These young lads included Geoff Nulty, who joined the Toffees in 1978 after spells at Burnley and Newcastle. 'I was a teenager way down the pecking order at Stoke and was slightly intimidated by Roy,' the midfielder recalled. 'He walked onto the pitch as though he owned it. Once there, Roy made his own rules and did what he wanted to do. I remember the first time he was informed that he was going to be substitute. He just told the manager to piss off and did not turn up to play.'

Mike Pejic, the England international left-back, who was sold to Everton for a £135,000 fee in 1977, added: 'Tony Waddington knew how to treat individuals and Roy Vernon was a massive character who required special handling. When I joined Stoke as an apprentice the first team went on five-week visit to the USA (as the Cleveland Stokers). I'll never forget the stories the lads told me when they got back. For example, Roy Vernon and Maurice Setters were out driving. Obviously they had done something wrong or said something out of line because the local police stopped their car, pinned them up against a wall with their legs spread out wide and all the rest of it, and searched them. As a footballer, I'm confident that all his teammates at Stoke, Everton and Blackburn concur that Roy was a lethal finisher, so slick around the area. Players like Roy Vernon and Jimmy Greaves were deadly in and around the penalty area.'

Another youngster to join Everton was Mike Bernard. The rugged midfielder was signed by Harry Catterick for £140,000 in April 1972 to fill the white boots of

Alan Ball: 'Waddo was a brilliant man-manager and all the players – young and old would run through fire for him. He would back you up to the hilt if you did it for him on a Saturday afternoon. This may explain his tolerance of Roy and his vices. I had heard the stories about him having a cigarette in the shower but didn't believe them until I saw it with my own eyes. He would nod his head on one side so the water ran past his ear and wouldn't get his fag wet. Afterwards, he drove home in a Jaguar with a big brown patch – courtesy of his cigarette smoke – on the roof-lining. Roy was also a drinker. He'd come in for training on a Tuesday and, believe it or not, would be at the front during sprints. But when he started to sweat, we made him go to the back because of the stench of beer that came off him. But on a Saturday afternoon Roy did the business. Did I mention that he liked a bet? One afternoon we went to Chester Races. Taffy was betting £100-£150 a go with a bookie he knew. He lost in every race so, for the final race, he told the bookie to put his bet on the nose. We all thought he was skint and weren't aware that he was betting his car. With a grin on his face, he held his keys up, lost the race, and ended up having to get a taxi back to Stoke.'

While Roy Vernon's success at the Victoria Ground evaporated over time, Tony Waddington's team fared little better – finishing and in mid-table for three campaigns before slipping into the relegation mire for his final two. Stoke's fortunes would improve after Roy's departure, however, culminating in the League Cup win of 1972. Roy concluded: 'Nowadays, Stoke City never sign players like me. Perhaps, they never will again.'

CHAPTER 9
The Twilight Years

'Football is well represented in the Welsh Sports Hall of Fame.
There is John Charles, Ivor Allchurch, John Toshack, Mark Hughes, Ian Rush,
Ryan Giggs, Gary Speed and our own Neville Southall. But one name
surprises me – Clive Thomas. If this referee, with an ego bigger than the
Rhondda Valley, can sneak in, then there must be room for Royston Vernon.'
Ronny Goodlass

CONTRARY TO EXPECTATIONS, THE WELSHMAN WAS STILL A STOKE City employee when the 1969/70 campaign got underway. Prospects of a return to first-team duties were further diminished after Tony Waddington addressed the chronic lack of goals in his squad – Stoke scored just 40 goals in 42 games in the 1968/69 campaign – by bringing back John Ritchie from Sheffield Wednesday and signing Jimmy Greenhoff from Birmingham City. Thereafter, Roy was rooted in the reserves: 'With less and less first-team outings, I had made up my mind to move back to Lancashire. I had discussed the future with my wife and decided if I had to pack in football then I would and concentrate on something else. When you have played in the First Division nearly all your career it is hard to accept that younger players are coming in to take your place. I knew this was the case and tried to accept it in a common-sense way. We sold our house quite easily and moved to Blackburn.'[1]

Norma and Roy were keen to return to Lancashire in order to lighten the burden on her parents, who were in poor health and struggling to run the Tierney antiques, house clearance and market stalls business. For Roy, it meant long commutes to the Potteries for training and a situation soon escalated: 'I was called in and told that the directors had suspended me for going to live outside the district.'[1] The move north was against the wishes of the Stoke City manager who, in September 1969, was quoted as stating: 'We made it clear to Roy that he could not move from the Potteries to Blackburn and travel daily to Stoke. But he went. We understand that he is in business there. He is certainly under suspension from us.'

In limbo, without pay, Roy believed that his Stoke City days were at an end. Nevertheless, the impasse dragged on: 'I thought that they would give me a free transfer – surely they didn't want to pay me such high wages for playing in the reserves? I appealed to the Football Association and the day came when I had to appear at an FA meeting along with the manager and the club chairman, Albert Henshall. I thought, "At least I will know where I stand after this". But no, at that last moment the club agreed that if I lived in Staffordshire during the week, they would lift the suspension. I had no choice. I had lost three-and-a-half months' wages and had still not got a free transfer to a club nearer to Blackburn.'[1]

The lifting of the suspension did not signal a return to favour. During the stand-off, Roy had been offered a move to Stockport County with Stoke's blessing, either on loan or on a permanent transfer, but he once again spurned the Third Division club. In January 1970 Roy, along with former teammate Maurice Setters, was interviewed for the vacant player-manager's job at Wigan Athletic, then in the Northern Premier League. Subsequently, ex-Liverpool midfielder Gordon Milne was appointed to the post. Although Wigan may have been appealing geographically, one suspect's that Roy's heart was not set on entering football management.

A decade earlier, shortly after he had joined Everton from Blackburn, he gave a strong indication that he would remain in the sport he loved once he finished playing. In his *Daily Post* column, he speculated: 'What will I do when my playing days are over? Seek the security of a tried and proven business as so many of my colleagues do? Take up some job outside football? You may think that with the greater part of my career ahead of me as a player, it is a little early to spare thoughts on a subject which lies so far in the future. And yet, I have no doubts at all, if the opportunity comes my way I hope to become a football manager. If you think this does not make sense, forgive me. Players have football in their blood, and once the germ is there it is not easy to remove. Life without football seems to me to be a terrible prospect. By the time I get around to that stage, maybe there will be a 'League for the Protection of Football Managers!"

Days after the Wigan rebuttal, Roy was offered a lifeline by a past acquaintance. Alan Ball Sr. – the father of the Word Cup-winning hero – had coached briefly at Stoke City in the mid-60s. Having guided Halifax Town to promotion from the Fourth Division in the 1968/69 season, he was consolidating the Shaymen's status in the third tier and had signed Bolton's schemer, Freddie Hill. Unfortunately, Hill had broken several toes in a post-Christmas friendly match. As Ball was able to obtain dispensation to breach the limit of three on-loan players, he signed Roy for a month from 30 January 1970.

'With his reputation and history, it was incredible that he came to us,' remembers Alex Smith, Halifax's goalkeeper at the time. 'I think the manager got him because Halifax was handy for him. Can you imagine the difference between Everton and Halifax? Back then the Shay was a dump, but the team was doing okay at our level and had got promoted. Roy was a bit quiet, but it was indisputable that he had been a top player. When training was over, he was straight off. He had a Jag, so that was a bit different.'

Roy joined a Halifax side that had suffered only one defeat in the previous eleven league games. He replaced Ian Lawther at centre-forward for his debut at Stockport County on 2 February. Despite the waterlogged Edgeley Park pitch, which was only passed fit 35 minutes before kick-off, Roy made a telling contribution by advancing down the right-wing and playing in Bill Atkins to score the game's solitary goal.

Two defeats on the road followed, the second of which – on an ice-bound pitch at Gay Meadow – brought Roy up against a familiar face and Stoke training pitch adversary in John Moore, who had moved on to Shrewsbury. 'Roy spent the whole game moaning to the referee and the linesmen, telling them how I was trying to kick him,' Moore recalled. 'He didn't realise that I had calmed down by then!' Maybe distracted by the spectre of Moore, Roy wasted several chances in the 4-1 defeat and missed the subsequent match. Afterwards, the *Halifax Courier* revealed that the club had provisionally agreed a fee of £3,000 for Roy's permanent transfer to the Calder Valley, with the ball left in his court. He re-appeared in the side wearing the number eight shirt for the home 2-0 defeat against Barnsley on 28 February. This turned out to be his last appearance in the Football League. With the loan period concluded Roy returned to his parent club. Transfer talks continued, but no agreement was reached.

Alex Smith believes that his teammate had concluded that Alan Ball's methods were ill-suited to a player of his vintage and waning work ethic: 'Ball was very aware tactically – he had people watching the teams and his own way of playing – but he was a slave driver. He had this philosophy of: "If my lad can do it, anybody can do it." We used to train a little bit on The Shay and did a lot of the running. We didn't need a training ground, just hills, and there were plenty of those in Halifax. If you knew anything of Roy and how he played you know that he wasn't that type of player – it was a culture shock for him. You had to do it with Alan, but Roy didn't buy into that. We played with four upfront with the two biggest and fittest wingers in the country. When the opposition were breaking on the right, our left-winger had to track back, and the right-winger had to come all the way back and send the full-back round on cover, so we always had an extra one in defence. Alan had his own system. It got results, but you only buy into it for a couple of seasons.'

On 28 March 1970, with Everton one match away from securing the league title, Roy was interviewed by Stan Liversedge of the *Liverpool Echo* and compared his title-winning side of 1963 with the champions-elect of 1970: 'I've seen Everton on television and they're a tremendously skilful side. Our half-back line of Gabriel, Labone and Kay had more devil but the Kendall, Labone and Harvey line compensates with its skill. Sometimes I think about some of the youngsters I knew – players like Colin Harvey and Jimmy Husband – and wonder what would have happened if I'd stayed and fought for my place. Would it have been different? But you make decisions and I can't really say I've any regrets.'[6]

A week after this article was published, Roy was released a few weeks early from his contract by Stoke City. This enabled him to enjoy a brief and lucrative cameo in South African football. Former Stockport and Blackburn Rovers forward Frank Lord had arranged for several British players to guest for clubs in South Africa and George Eastham, Roy's recent teammate at Stoke, had been over during the previous close season and put a word in for him to join Cape Town for three months. 'It was an experience I thoroughly enjoyed,' the North Walian mused.[1]

On his return to England, he was lured back into the domestic game at non-League level with Great Harwood Football Club. This small-town club, sandwiched between Blackburn and Burnley, had enjoyed a permanent presence in the Lancashire Combination, albeit in the lower reaches. All that changed in 1967 when Derrick Keighley, a local haulage entrepreneur and owner of Dutton Transport, embarked on a spending spree to improve the club's fortunes.

In came the likes of former Rovers players Bob Jones and John Bray, the latter as player-manager. Having been crowned Combination champions in 1969, Great Harwood joined the newly-formed Northern Premier League and Keighley continued his investment in players to make the club competitive in the new environment. Bryan Douglas – available after seventeen years at Rovers – joined. The following year, Ronnie Clayton was recruited after resigning as player-manager at Morecambe. In September 1970, Keighley persuaded the Blue Dragon to spurn the advances of Lancaster City and throw in his lot with his upwardly-mobile club.

Pete Jackson, who joined Great Harwood after being released by Rovers in 1967, was impressed by the impact the owner's outlay had on the club and himself: 'It was an unbelievable time, really. Derrick was putting the money in and bringing ex-internationals and experienced league players like Adam Blacklaw – who won the title as a goalkeeper with Burnley – Ronnie Clayton, Bryan Douglas and Roy Vernon, to name but a few. He must have been paying a lot of money out – rumour has it that the ex-pros were getting about £25 a game whilst we were on £7 to a tenner.'

Inside-forward Geoff Shaw – another player recruited from Rovers' youth ranks – recalls the sensation that something special was happening at the Showground, Great Harwood's home, under Keighley's largesse: 'It was a fantastic period for the club. In addition to signing some top players, the owners built a new clubhouse, so we'd get back from away matches at faraway places like Morecambe and Goole to enjoy performances by big names such as Bernard Manning and The Swinging Blue Jeans. You felt something of a star as you walked off the coach and into the cabaret room. Also, because Derrick Keighley was friends with Manchester City's director Peter Swales, Dennis Tueart and Peter Barnes were invited to open the floodlights.'

Roy made his home debut in an FA Cup qualifier over Leyland and then saw off Lancaster in the next round. In November, Great Harwood contested a first round-proper tie against Rotherham United. The match, which had been postponed due to the condition of the pitch on the Saturday, kicked off on a dismal Tuesday afternoon. Many local employers allowed their staff to finish early and some 5,000 fans crowded at pitchside. Rotherham boasted John Fantham, ex-Sheffield Wednesday, Neil Warnock, yet to embark of his career of managing seventeen clubs and counting, and a young Dave Watson, who went on to play for Sunderland

and England. There was a flurry of goals in the first half, with Roy levelling the scores at 2-2. However, as the match progressed, the fitter Yorkshire team coped better in the energy-sapping mud and won 6-2.

Fred Cumpstey, who had grown up seeing his three heroes in harness at Ewood over a decade earlier, found it difficult to see them in the red of Great Harwood: 'It was a bit sad, like seeing them in a testimonial. It wasn't the same.' The likes of Pete Jackson, however, relished playing alongside the stars they had idolised from the terraces. Roy, unsurprisingly, stood out: 'He was different to them all. Not only was he a quality player, but he was something special. He was only ten stone wet-through but, with no backlift, would rifle the ball into the net. The Showground was not the best of surfaces – in fact it could be a mudbath – but he used to wear Adidas rubber soled football boots. I can picture him in them now. He seemed to skate over the pitch, going around opponents as he just had this balance to him. He never seemed to get dirty.'

Teammate Geoff Shaw volunteered one of the Welshman's epithets on the subject of avoiding going to ground: 'Taffy wasn't mad keen on getting his knees dirty. If teammates ended up on the ground he used to say something like: "If you were meant to do that you'd have been born with studs in your backside."'

Because Roy would not make himself available for all away fixtures, Shaw deputised at number ten: 'We had a great partnership – he played all the home games and I played all the away games! If I arrived at the ground and Roy's car was in the club car park, I knew that he'd be playing, but if it was parked out on Hill Street (near the dog track) I knew that he'd come to say that he had a muscle strain.' Shaw recalled Roy telling his Great Harwood teammates about the trials and tribulations of the Tierney business and attending auction houses: 'He once joined his father-in-law at an auction. Apparently, Roy was bidding for something and some pain in the neck at the other end of the room, that he could not properly see, was bidding too. The other bidder kept upping the ante. When he got back to van, he said to his father-in-law: "Sorry, I ended up paying much more than I wanted to but some bloke at the other end kept upping the bids." His father-in-law replied: "That was me, you idiot!"'

Pete Jackson revealed that on the away trips Roy did make, he was a popular source of anecdotes throughout the journey: 'He was a character and such a down-to-earth lad. He would hold court and tell all sorts of tales about his Everton days with the likes of Johnny Morrissey. I wish that I had written them all down. He'd also tell us how he'd had an interest in dogs that were twins – allegedly they'd race the poor one for a few weeks and then swap it for the good one without anyone realising and have a bet on it.'

Although getting long in the tooth for a forward that had a devastating burst of pace as a key attribute, hints of the old quality remained. Gerry Glover, whose Everton career overlapped Roy's briefly, was playing for Runcorn, and remembers coming up against him at Great Harwood: 'Roy was the finest striker of a ball I've ever seen. His technique was pure quality and he scored a couple of goals against us.' It was at Great Harwood where Roy delivered his witty riposte to being labelled a has-been: 'I'll never forget one remark made by a youngster as we left the pitch. "You're a has-been," he said. "Yes son," I replied, "but it's great to have been. I doubt whether you'll ever go."'

Another famous epithet attributed to him at Great Harwood was when his manager shouted in frustration: 'Roy, the midfield can't find you if you are standing still!' As sharp-tongued as ever, Roy responded: 'If they can't find me when I'm standing still, how the hell do you expect them to find me if I'm running around?'

At the end of Roy's first season at the Showground – which aside from the FA Cup run, yielded a disappointing 29 league points – Douglas and Clayton were released. Roy was retained for the 1971/72 season, but his contract was terminated by mutual consent when halfway through its term. A harbinger had been his self-substitution at half-time in one match. Geoff Shaw tells the tale: 'I remember one game on a very heavy pitch; it was pouring down with rain and everybody was getting covered in mud. At half-time the manger was giving us a dressing down, telling us that we needed to play the ball long. Then he looked around and said, "Where's Roy?" We could hear the shower running – he has subbed himself!' Having retired, Roy would confess that it was difficult to rouse himself: 'It was a nice little club but there's no atmosphere playing in front of a crowd only 200 or 300 strong. Derrick Keighley continued to bankroll Great Harwood Football Club. However, it folded in 1978 after the benefactor transferred his interests to Blackburn Rovers. The club was subsequently revived as Great Harwood Town, but this reincarnation ceased playing in 2006.'

For Roy, the disillusionment of playing fifth-tier football after years at the very top was not the only reason that compelled him to finally hang up his boots. With his father-in-law having passed away that year, Roy was obliged to concentrate on the Tierney family business, therefore, the Vernons moved into her parents' home on Infirmary Road. With no background in antiques or house clearances, Roy's primary role was to act as 'muscle' for moving furniture and the driver when conducting clearances, mainly on the Fylde Coast. He also helped on their two markets stalls on Wednesdays, Fridays and Saturdays.

'We had contracts with auctioneers in St Anne's and did probate – anything that did not come under the hammer we moved for them,' Norma recalled fondly. 'If a solicitor had a house to empty, we went over and gave a price – we were rarely turned down, so we must have been fair – then we would empty the house and leave it in immaculate shape. People didn't see much of Roy, but he worked hard. Sometimes it would be three trips in a day. We only did it to help my mum when Dad was ill, then gradually they became reliant on us and we got used to doing it. We brought the boys up with money out of the Tierney's business.'

'Roy's company used to do clearances from big posh houses,' Dave Parker, a friend and neighbour in Blackburn, recalled. 'After I told him that I wanted a new carpet for my own house, Roy replied: "Don't buy one – I'll get you a good one." And true to his word, the following week he turned up with one out of a big posh house. The pile must have been two inches thick, because we ended up having to plane the doors down.'

Harry Leyland, who had played alongside him at Blackburn and owned several stalls at Blackburn market, noted: 'I was surprised when he moved from Rovers to Everton, my previous club. At the time, I didn't think it was a step up for him. Back then, the Rovers had so many international stars like Douglas and Clayton that I don't remember too much about Roy except that he was immaculate on the ball and off the pitch. Upon his retirement, our paths crossed often at the local market. Strangely, we talked about the antiques business and dog racing, but never about football.'

This tough work schedule precluded any involvement in professional football. It was with regret that he turned down the opportunity of returning to South Africa in 1972 to play for Hellenic, George Eastham's team. By then his lingering desire to pursue a career in coaching or football management had long since evaporated. His wife elaborated: 'He thought of going into coaching, but I don't think he'd have stuck with it to be honest – people like to tell you what to do. Roy was his own man – he liked flair players.'

Although a footballing folk hero in his adopted home town, Norma noted that her husband kept a relatively low profile: 'He didn't go into town an awful lot –

he was a creature of habit. He'd go into the local for last orders or sometimes to the Halfway House on a Wednesday night as he liked Country and Western music and, of course, he went to the dogs. He did not socialise a lot, only with friends into dogs.'

This view is reinforced by Dave Parker, who recalls how Roy was always good company but never treated as a star in his adopted town: 'There were five or six of us knocking about at local pubs such as The Ivy, The Infirmary Hotel and the Horse Load. Roy was one of life's characters who liked life in general, going out and enjoying himself. It was very rare that we talked about his football career, we were too busy playing darts, shooting pool and drinking. Once he had hung up his boots, it was behind him. We did go to presentations when the Blackburn and District League needed a celebrity. Even then, he kept himself to himself.'

Norma recalls how Roy, for a short time, unexpectedly became a greyhound owner: 'Arthur Danson, the chairman of East Lancs Coach Builders, held a party one Sunday afternoon. His greyhound had delivered five pups and we were all given one. We called her "Birthday Girl" as it was my birthday when we got her. Roy kept her at home for about two days, but the puppy was driving him mad, so it went to the trainer's kennels. He wasn't someone who would take the dog for a walk.' Sadly, Birthday Girl's racing career was modest and failed to reap riches for her new owners.

His wife revealed that her other half did things in fits and starts: 'Roy would have an interest for so long and then he'd go, "I'm not going there, I have had enough of that." He used to go to the dogs at Preston, but he was one of these who was all or nothing. He would go for a few months and then say, "Why I am doing this? It's boring," and he would give up and then he would get talking to old buddies and he would start again.'

There was one thing that he never got tired of doing. Roy embraced the adage: 'No cowboy was faster on the draw than a grandfather pulling a baby picture out of his wallet.' He doted on his grandchildren. His son Mark revealed: 'My daughters rode ponies and horses. Dad would come to the local equestrian shows, especially with Christina – our second eldest – who rode a pony called Jingles. He looked after her when my mother and my wife were busy at the shop and market stalls. She had him wrapped around her little finger – they did everything together from dressing up to baking. The kitchen often looked like a bomb site when Mum got home from work. Dad would say: "We've been baking," and Christina would offer round the cakes and biscuits they had made.'

Only a very occasional visitor to Ewood Park – finding that the style of play exhibited by teams lacked improvisation – he told a journalist in 1974: 'I was soon disillusioned. The football I played is different to the game we see today – it's too stereotyped now.'[5]

'Dad often said that he'd had a great life through football but was a realist and knew that when his playing days were over he had to focus his energies on his business,' Roy's eldest Mark added. 'A few years after he had finished playing, he claimed there was too much coaching in the modern game and there wouldn't be the likes of George Best anymore because they were taking individualism out of the game.'

He would relent in the late 70s and visit Ewood again on an occasional basis. However, his more frequent sporting appearances were on the green baize at snooker tournaments. In July 1983, one such charity event saw him make an unwelcome return to the media glare when he was banned from driving for eighteen months and fined £200 at Chorley Magistrates' Court. Roy had been playing in a charity tournament in Charnock Richard when stopped by police as he drove home too slowly. He pleaded guilty to drink-driving. In mitigation, his legal representative explained: 'My client was drinking between matches but became very successful and reached the final, which meant that he stayed longer than intended. He had arranged with some friends to be picked up but, when that did not materialise, decided to drive home.'

Visits to Liverpool were even rarer, though he did make the trip for Harry Catterick's testimonial match in May 1978. His sometimes-fractious relationship with 'The Catt' was forgotten as Roy accepted an invitation to the directors' lounge. Another visit was to the 'Tribute to Everton's Forwards' celebration staged in Southport hotel as part of Kevin Ratcliffe's testimonial year programme on 20 April 1989. Given that Ratcliffe was the only other Welshman to lift the league championship trophy for Everton, it was appropriate that Roy was there. He was joined by a stellar array of attacking talent in Graeme Sharp, Dave Hickson, Andy Gray, Derek Temple, Alan Whittle, Gary Lineker, Bob Latchford and Adrian Heath. Sadly, the evening was darkened by the Hillsborough Disaster, which had occurred five days previously. Exhibiting no little compassion, the attendees raised over £6,000 on the night for the LFC Relief Fund.

Over time, the rigours of playing top-level football for so many seasons –

coupled with having hundreds of pain-killing jabs in order to be declared fit – returned to haunt him as he struggled with arthritis in his back. His wife claimed that, during their years together, her other-half had kicked the smoking habit several times, only to succumb to temptation again: 'He'd smoke for months – then he'd stop and give up for twelve months. Then he'd be offered a Hamlet cigar and be off again. Roy was one of these binge people – it was all or nothing with him.'

Most likely smoking precipitated the onset of lung cancer, which prematurely ended his life at the age of 56 years. Once diagnosed, he was admitted to hospital and underwent surgery to remove the cancerous lung. This was adjudged to be a success, seemingly halting the spread of the disease, but the subsequent medical bulletin given to Norma relayed bad news: 'A few months after the operation, I took a call from the surgeon. He said: "I am very sorry, but the cancer is in Roy's other lung and we are talking about a matter of months now." I didn't tell the boys as they would have made a fuss because Roy was feeling quite good at the time and was going out playing snooker. I thought, "It might be two years, so why should I say something now?" But once you go down that route of it being unsaid you can't go back on it. However, one day Roy came home and said: "I can't even finish a game of snooker these days." He knew and I knew.'

Picking up on the theme, Roy once told Norma: 'If anything happens to me you must get married again, because it is a long lonely life if you are on your own. But do yourself a favour – don't marry someone like me. Marry someone with plenty of money to look after you.' Although said in a humorous manner, she knew that, deep down, Roy meant it and was thinking of her: 'We went to Tenerife on holiday just before he died. One of our sons drove us to Manchester Airport. Roy had lost his confidence in lots of things – when you're ill, it does that to you. He said, "I don't think I could have driven us here." He had a panic attack in the airport, saying, "I don't think I can do this," so I sat him down and he had a cup of tea. He pulled himself together and enjoyed the holiday. He did say, "If I had my time again, I would take more time off to go on holidays." But that's hindsight for you.'

She continued to agonise: 'Back home he wasn't eating – it was still unspoken that it was terminal. I rang Macmillan Cancer Care and they came around and said, "You need help." I rang the hospice and got him in that day. The doctor there had been at Accrington Stanley. He said: "Don't think that just because you are here, you're not coming out. We're going to get your tablets sorted out." He returned home after two weeks and died there about three weeks later. It was a morning and I was the only one in the house with him. It was a hell of a shock but at least he was at home.'

Roy Vernon died on Sunday, 5 December 1993. A minute's silence was observed at Ewood Parker that afternoon prior to Blackburn Rovers' clash with Chelsea. One Evertonian, Tony Kelly, sent a touching message to the *Liverpool Echo* upon reading the news: 'I would like to express my sadness at the passing of my all-time idol, Roy Vernon. In my opinion, alongside Bally, he was Everton's finest. I had the privilege of seeing every league and cup appearance Royston made for Everton. His ball skills, pace, vision, eye for goal, and shooting were second-to-none.'

Alex Young, when informed of his old teammate's death, also paid tribute in the *Liverpool Echo*: 'Roy was one of the greatest Everton players and certainly one of the best I ever played with. He was unrivalled as a penalty taker, always driving the ball hard and low into the corner of the net. Opponents found his greyhound-like speed difficult to cope with. Roy was, of course, a deadly marksman from inside and outside the penalty area. Also, he was a dear friend of mine, although I have not seen him for some years. It is sad that he has died at what, these days, is a young age.'

The Golden Vision, along with Jimmy Gabriel, Colin Harvey, Alex Parker, George Sharples and many other Evertonians attended the funeral, held at Woodland United Reformed Church in the Cherry Tree district of Blackburn. As the cortege paused outside Ewood Park, former Blackburn teammates – including Bryan Douglas, Ronnie Clayton, Harry Leyland, Keith Newton and Fred Pickering – were assembled with their heads bowed.

Gabriel would reflect on what his old Everton teammate meant to him: 'There were some great Everton forwards, but I have to say that Vernon and Young were the best that I played with in an Everton team. For me, they are forever on my mind when I mentally revisit my days as a player. Both brought something special at a time when the fans needed to believe that their team could be winners of trophies and still play entertaining football.'[3]

The service was followed by a committal in Pleasington Cemetery. There, someone slipped an envelope into Norma's hand as she got in the cortege car. She opened it during the journey to find a touching card from an anonymous Evertonian. It read: 'They speak of Alec Young. They speak of Brian Labone. But in my eyes, Roy Vernon was in a class on his own.'

In the years since his death, Roy's brilliance at Ewood Park, Goodison Park and the Victoria Ground has sometimes been neglected. His early passing was one factor. At Blackburn, supporters would continue to spot Ronnie Clayton and Bryan Douglas at home games, a reminder of their greatness, whilst a new generation of heroes in blue-and-white halved tops would land the league title in 1995 under Kenny Dalglish. At Everton, Roy lacked an advocate to keep his flame burning brightly. 'Cannonball Kid' Dave Hickson was venerated by Bill Kenwright, the current chairman, and Alex Young had been immortalised as 'The Golden Vision' by the eponymous 1968 BBC television play and more recently in the documentary entitled 'Alex the Great'. On the international stage, despite winning 32 caps and representing his country at the World Cup finals, he was trumped by Welsh giants such as John Charles, Ivor Allchurch and Cliff Jones.

Then in 1999, Roy Vernon was returned to the consciousness of the Everton family when he was included in the 75 inaugural inductees into Gwladys Street's Hall of Fame – a independent initiative, voted by Everton fans worldwide, to acclaim their greatest heroes since the club's formation in 1878. His wife received a standing ovation lasting over one minute from the 750 vociferous supporters gathered at the Adelphi Hotel. Then some eighteen years on, Norma accepted another award to mark her husband's selection as an Everton Giant – a select group of former players and managers – at the club's end-of-season awards ceremony. Subsequently, a plaque was unveiled by her and son Mark on the brick wall of the Goodison Road Stand – fittingly, close to those of Alex Young and Bobby Collins.

Be it Roy of the Rovers or Taffy of the Toffees, he brought joy and exhilaration to the millions passing through stadium turnstiles in the North of England. He burned brightly, often incandescently – a cigarette twixt his lips, a swagger in his stride, a song tripping off the tongue, always ready with witty aside. Although he died too young, one suspects that the proud son of Ffynnongroyw wouldn't have had it any other way.

The Blue Dragon had been a great player, a maverick, a smoker, a gambler, a joker and much more who defied his managers off the pitch and delighted them on it. At one time or another, he had planned to tell the story of his life and made extensive notes for that purpose. Hopefully, this biography reflects what Roy Vernon had set out to write – warts and all. It is long overdue.

APPENDIX A

Blue Dragon's Fire-Breathing Season

'We won the title as I wanted to win it: with brilliant teamwork,
sound methodical football and brimming confidence.'
Harry Catterick

THIS APPENDIX DETAILS EYEWITNESS ACCOUNTS OF THE WEEK-BY-week progress of Everton's 1962/63 season as they challenged for the First Division title. It was honed from writings in the matchday programmes secured in The Everton Collection as well as the archives of the *Liverpool Echo* and *Daily Post* and is peppered with recollections from the men who were on the pitch, the training ground and the terraces during the campaign. Their observations, including those of the co-author David France, provide a novel insight into the highs and lows of a 42-game programme.

Some people's memories were much better than others. Other people's opinions were more candid than others. However, all were helpful. Most interviews were conducted face-to-face. Those with Brian Labone, Alex Young, Gordon Watson, Brian Harris, Alex Parker, Alex Scott and Gordon West were prompted by exposure to the contents of the matchday programmes and souvenir publications from 1962/63. They took place several years after the death of Roy Vernon in 1993 and have been edited to focus on his contributions.

Now to the Mersey Millionaires and the pursuit of silverware in season 1962/63. Having invested a small fortune – or rather a small part of his giant fortune – on attracting the players who had finished fifth in 1961 and then fourth in 1962, John Moores trained his sights on traditional silverware, so much so that the club declined to participate in the League Cup, instead deciding to focus on just the league campaign and the FA Cup, Gordon Watson, a veteran coach at Bellefield, outlined the flaws within the expensively assembled side: 'Harry Catterick had developed a first team which pretty much picked itself. Of course, it was essentially Jackie Carey's side, with Gordon West in place of Albert Dunlop and Dennis Stevens in place of Bobby Collins. Their names still slide off my tongue – West, Parker, Thomson, Gabriel, Labone, Harris, Bingham, Stevens, Young, Vernon, Veall plus Meagan and Temple. Two issues needed to be resolved – the lack of pace of the wide-men and full-backs and the questions about the leadership of Taffy from near Talacre. Of the other candidates for the captaincy, Brian Labone and Jimmy Gabriel were considered too young and Alex Parker and my favourite, Billy Bingham, were too old. Indeed, the Irish veteran's first-team place seemed to be in jeopardy, as the Sunday newspapers were rife with speculation that the manager had tried to sign Peter Brabrook from Chelsea that summer.'

Though overlooked for the role of skipper, Brian Labone affirmed his optimism that the 1962/63 season would be rewarding: 'We had made a poor start to the previous campaign, with only four points from the first seven games, yet had finished only five points behind Ipswich. In my eyes, we had played like champions most of the time and I felt that if Taffy and Alex – I called them 'The Dynamic Duo' and 'The Effing Goodison Darlings' – could reproduce their magic then we could bag a trophy or two.'

Unbeknown to the club chairman and management, Alex and Roy agreed to a wager. In simple terms, the loser would hand over one week's wages to the one who bagged the most league goals if Everton won the title and their teammates or their boss didn't get wind of the bet. Even though Alex suggested that penalties should not be counted as 'real' goals, Roy eventually prevailed and therefore was super-confident that he would £50 better off in early May.

The following nine months would prove to be arguably the most eventful in his football career. As luck would have it, Everton's fixtures began with a difficult excursion to one of the founding members of the league – Burnley. The Turf Moor club was managed by Harry Potts, a former Everton player. In August 1962, they coupled the silk of Jimmy McIlroy and Ray Pointer with the steel of Brian Miller and Tommy Cummings and were formidable rivals. In fact, they had finished runners-up to Ipswich in the league – with Everton two points behind them in fourth place – and to Tottenham in the 1962 FA Cup final the season before.

PART 1:
INCANDESCENT START

HAVING FAILED TO SIGN PETER BRABROOK DURING THE SUMMER, Harry Catterick made only one refinement to the side which had completed the previous campaign with an 8-3 thrashing of Cardiff and a convincing 3-2 victory at Highbury. He introduced Ray Veall, an exciting yet raw teenager recruited from Doncaster, in preference to Derek Temple on the left-wing. It was a bold move.

Fixture 1: Saturday, 18 August 1962
BURNLEY 1 EVERTON 3
Bingham, Vernon and Young
Attendance: 37,100

The match was an end-to-end cracker in front of a near capacity crowd, some 14,000 higher than the Turf Moor average. As expected, Roy Vernon – who had amassed 28 goals in 40 league and cup games during the 1961/62 season – was regarded as the club's most lethal threat. Early on, he lived up to his reputation by sending one rocket-like shot narrowly wide and scraping the goal post with another. While the home side opened the scoring through centre-forward Ray Pointer in the eighteenth minute, Vernon equalised when he lashed home the rebound from his own free-kick with such power that it threatened to rip the netting from the woodwork.

The Everton skipper's contributions were halted briefly when the referee warned him about his overly enthusiastic challenges. Unperturbed, he responded by dancing through the heart of the home defence to feed the ball via Alex Young to Billy Bingham, who beat Adam Blacklaw with a fierce drive to make it 2-1 on the hour. By now, the travelling Evertonians were in full voice. Their demands of 'We want three!' were met in the 74th minute when Vernon released his partner Young. The classy centre-forward used his immaculate control to round the goalkeeper before lobbing the ball into the net with expert precision.

It was a heartening display for a team which had notched only three victories on the road during the previous campaign. The media and the travelling Evertonians concurred that the top performers at Turf Moor were Vernon and Young. The former was in scintillating form and the latter ended the theory that his best football was reserved for Goodison. The following Monday, Horace Yates – the veteran journalist of the *Liverpool Echo* – declared: 'Blunted and bewildered, the home side was run into the ground. I can hardly remember a cockier Everton side. Surely, this performance is a foretaste of things to come.'

The local newspaper also mentioned fine contributions from Billy Bingham, Mick Meagan and Brian Labone. Many years on, the Everton centre-half confessed his early-season confidence: 'I thought of Ipswich as one-season wonders and really fancied our chances along with the usual suspects like Spurs, Wolves, Leicester and possibly Burnley. The Turf Moor club had some pacey forwards and that afternoon John Connelly was a real handful and drove more than one nail into the coffin of George Thomson's career.'

David France, who thanks to his paper round was a season-ticket holder for the Ground section of the terraces, reminisced: 'Most of my match-going pals worshipped Alex Young, even before he was acclaimed "The Golden Vision". Next in our popularity stakes were Royston Vernon (we called him by his full name), Jimmy Gabriel and Alex Parker. I had looked forward all summer to watching them in action but missed the opening match. I joined my father – who alternated between Goodison and Anfield – to witness the Reds' return to the First Division. Consequently, I enjoyed the debut of a youthful and spotty-faced Alan Ball for Blackpool and a defeat for Liverpool.'

Four days on, Alex Parker replaced Mick Meagan and a full-strength line-up opened the home campaign against Matt Busby and the pride of Manchester. Having lost only two of their last thirty or so games at home, Roy Vernon and his teammates approached the contest with confidence enhanced by the news that Bobby Charlton, United's golden boy, would be absent. In the first matchday programme of the season, John Moores reinforced his desire to emulate Tottenham's accomplishment of capturing the league and FA Cup double in 1961: 'Last season we finished one place higher than the previous one. Nothing but top place will satisfy.' The Everton chairman added: 'Today, we look forward to a good, entertaining game of football – worthy of the great names of the clubs.' He must have been a soothsayer because his Mersey Millionaires enjoyed their second memorable victory within five days in an enthralling contest.

EVERTON 3 MANCHESTER UNITED 1

Young 2, Parker

Attendance: 69,501

Rarely had Harry Catterick's team exhibited such brilliance. For the opening hour, Roy Vernon and Alex Young were unplayable. Firing on all cylinders, the Toffees swept into a commanding 3-0 lead and had the massive crowd – the biggest since the 75,000 recorded for the clash with Burnley in 1960 – roaring its support. Then, out of the blue, Busby's team mounted a recovery. Driven on by Denis Law, who had been recruited for a British record fee of £115,000 one month earlier, United took control. With wingers Ian Moir and Johnny Giles tormenting defenders Alex Parker and George Thomson, United overwhelmed their hosts and pulled one back through Moir. Through tiredness or a possible change in tactics, the home side was required to defend resolutely throughout the final half hour, so much so that Vernon, his teammates and the home supporters were relieved to hear the blast of the final whistle.

The local papers ignored the Blue Dragon's contributions to focus on those of the two blonde Scotsmen who had dominated the proceedings – Denis Law and Alex Young. The former was an all-action man with lightning speed, whereas the latter personified a football virtuoso with exquisite artistry. 'Remind me to ask Parliament never to give the Scots home rule,' Leslie Edwards suggested to his *Liverpool Echo* readers. 'They would surely keep to themselves such wonderful footballers as Alex Young and Denis Law.'

In retirement, Gordon West reminisced about playing in such a big match: 'I was a novice – a nice way of saying wet behind the ears – and more nervous than usual in front the biggest and noisiest crowd I had ever experienced. No doubt I threw up in the changing rooms – I usually did at Goodison. It was a game of two halves. Labby was required to man-mark David Herd, who was a big money signing from Arsenal, while Gabby tried to muzzle Denis Law, who had just returned from his unhappy spell at Torino. In the second half, it was one-way traffic – headed towards me. At times, I feared that we would squander the benefit of Alex's super goals, which were worthy of winning any football match.'

Despite the 70,000 bodies squeezed into Goodison, David France – then a diminutive schoolboy – managed to see all our goals: 'The opener after fifteen minutes was breathtaking. Dennis Stevens's cross found the head of Alex Young, who nodded the ball upwards and over veteran Bill Foulkes before volleying into the net. This exquisite piece of skill had the crowd open-mouthed in disbelief. Then only thirty seconds on, perhaps a little longer, Billy Bingham's cross found the same blonde curls and the ball was glided skilfully over keeper David Gaskell. Shortly before the interval these strikes were augmented by Alex Parker, who had returned from a cartilage injury. He dispatched a thunderbolt courtesy of his underutilised left foot.'

The Scotland international, who was the inaugural member of the Mersey Millionaires, divulged: 'I fancied myself as more of a half-back than a full-back and loved to have a pop from outside the box. My strike against United wasn't only my finest goal but also my finest kick of a leather football. Sadly, it occurred after Alex had performed his party pieces and has been long forgotten. More important, the result lifted us into third-spot – the club's highest standing for almost a quarter of a century.'

The next home game, just three days later, provided an opportunity for Harry Catterick to gain revenge against his former charges who had inflicted his new club's heaviest defeat by 4-0 in September 1961. Traditionally labelled a yo-yo team, Sheffield Wednesday had developed into one of the best sides in the land under the stewardship of Catterick and his replacement Vic Buckingham. The Everton boss made a couple of changes. George Sharples deputised for the lame Jimmy Gabriel – who had made fifty plus consecutive appearances – and Johnny Morrissey made his debut after his controversial move across Stanley Park in place of Ray Veall.

Fixture 3: Saturday, 25 August 1962
EVERTON 4 SHEFFIELD WEDNESDAY 1
Vernon 2 (1 pen), Stevens, Young
Attendance: 51,504

In a rugged encounter, Wednesday took the lead when Bronco Layne headed home Eddie Holliday's immaculate cross after twenty minutes. Parity was restored almost immediately when Wednesday's Tony Kay fouled Dennis Stevens inside the area. Geographically, it was a very close decision. Without any fanfare, Roy Vernon hammered his spot kick past keeper Ron Springett. It remained a tight contest until the balance of play shifted in the home side's favour when Tom McAnearney was injured. The right-half had fouled the Everton skipper but, like many before him, had limped away from the confrontation, and in an age before substitutes the visitors had to continue one player down. The Toffees embraced this extra-man advantage to take the lead on 35 minutes thanks to Dennis Stevens and a healthy deflection of his shot.

Blessed by such serendipity, the Vernon-Young combo tormented the opposing rearguard before the club captain made it 3-1 in the seventieth minute after he latched onto a pass by Billy Bingham. Though his fierce shot rebounded off Springett, the Welshman reacted to nod the ball across the goal-line. Yes, a headed goal by the Blue Dragon. Within no time at all, this rare effort was bettered by his playmate. In his match report, local sportswriter Michael Charters described Young's goal as 'a most perfect thing'. It evolved from a cross-field pass by Brian Harris which found the unmarked number nine on the right-wing, and from there Young clipped it beyond the goalkeeper as if scoring from such an angle was a mere formality. Everton continued to exert control and Springett was required to make a series of heroic blocks at the feet of both Vernon and Young. To their immense credit, the home fans applauded the England international at the final whistle.

These majestic contributions of the Dynamic Duo had maintained the club's 100 percent record and elevated it into third place in the First Division. Leslie Edwards – a colleague of Charters – summarised his observations: 'Young's immaculate collection of the ball, smoothness of his onward glide and impudence of his shot were touches of genius. In addition, the fiery contest will be remembered for the agility of Springett and the tireless excellence of Kay – when he wasn't getting into the bad books of the crowd and the referee. The number six demonstrated that he is one of the finest as well as one of the toughest men in the game.'

Brian Harris also remembered the performance of his opposite number vividly: 'It's rare that the man of the match is on the receiving end of a good hiding, but Tony Kay was outstanding – simply outstanding – that afternoon. He was as influential as Dave Mackay at Spurs and the late Duncan Edwards at United. Of course, little did I know that within months he would have pinched my job.'

Decades later, Alex Young reflected on the bright dawn: 'Seven days is a long time in football. Both Taffy and I were delighted to have made a such a rewarding start. Our pre-season optimism was strengthened by the canny signing of John

Morrissey. I've never understood why our neighbours sold him – especially to us – for only £10,000. He was some player.'

Fixture 4: Wednesday, 29 August 1962
MANCHESTER UNITED 0 EVERTON 1
Vernon (pen)
Attendance: 63,675

One week after the home triumph over Manchester United, the teams met again. Given the impressive start to the new campaign by the Toffees, the trip to Old Trafford was cited as something of a litmus test. As anticipated, it turned out to be a fast-moving encounter with no punches pulled. Following United's dominance during the final thirty minutes at Goodison, the home side concentrated on stifling the threat of the Dynamic Duo. But with their midfield now stretched, they became vulnerable to penetration by both Dennis Stevens and Brian Harris. While both teams created chances and both David Gaskell and Gordon West made top-class saves, Everton came closest to scoring with Harris and Vernon rattling the crossbar and Billy Bingham having a goal-bound shot hacked off the line by none other than Denis Law.

The crowd of almost 64,000 maintained a raucous atmosphere until about ten minutes from full time when the outcome was decided by an uncontested penalty decision given after Shay Brennan had impeded Johnny Morrissey. Again, with little commotion, Roy Vernon secured both points. Following the victory, Horace Yates was full of praise for the half-back line: 'Labone is sufficiently mature to become a full international, whereas Gabriel curbed Law and laid claim to the Scotland right-half position equally emphatically.' Left-half Brian Harris, who was a forceful presence that day, pronounced: 'Of course I remember the game. It was the one and only time I was on the winning side at Old Trafford. Usually we got thumped 4-0 or even 5-0. More than anything, I can picture Taffy's precise execution of his spot kick in such hostile surroundings. Bobby Collins and Tommy Jones had previously missed penalties at Old Trafford but unlike them he had ice-cold water in his veins and a twinkle in his eyes.'

The club heralded the impressive team performance and the milestone of four wins in four games in the matchday programme issued on 6 September: 'The directors feel it was a pity that 50,000 more of our supporters could not have been at Old Trafford. From a football point of view, it was one of the best exhibitions ever staged.'

Alex Parker enjoyed playing at Old Trafford: 'More than anything, I loved its towering floodlights. While the stadium didn't look anything like it does today, it generated and cradled an ear-splitting din when we were defending at the uncovered Stretford End. The frequency of the noise – the vibrations per second – made the hairs on my neck stand up straight. United fans loved to swear at opponents and, crammed behind a flimsy-looking picket fence – were so close that you could see the individuals effing and blinding at you. Anyway, that night, we out-played an unimpressive Man Utd side. After marking Johnny Giles – a tricky and somewhat timid wide-boy in those days – out of the game, I helped "Angel Gabriel" in his battles with "Denis the Menace". It was a bloody contest best suited for Liverpool Stadium.'

The double over United hoisted the club to the pinnacle of the league for the first time in 23 years. 'With the evidence of four matches as a guide, it now seems the appropriate moment to stick out one's neck and suggest that this will be Everton's year,' proclaimed Horace Yates. 'Like all good sides they will require their share of good fortune mainly in freedom from accidents, but all the signs are abundantly evident that the team has welded into a superb combination.'

As for the royal blue wager, it was heating up, with both forwards averaging a very impressive statistic of one goal per game.

The next destination was the nation's capital where Everton had experienced a miserable tally of two wins, six draws and eleven defeats since the infamous 10-4 humiliation at White Hart Lane in 1958. Because their hosts had finished the previous season one point above the drop zone, Everton had expected a rewarding trip to Craven Cottage. Confidence was buoyed further by the news that Johnny Haynes and Bobby Robson were missing from the Fulham line-up. Would this be Everton's lucky day?

Fixture 5: Saturday, 1 September 1962
FULHAM 1 EVERTON 0
Attendance: 30,58

Things didn't go according to plan in London. Possibly troubled by the heatwave temperatures or more likely by overconfidence, the players were unrecognisable from the ones who had triumphed at Turf Moor and Old Trafford. Fulham were more physical in the tackle, much quicker to the ball and never gave Everton's expensive stars time to indulge in their artistry. Lacking both rhythm and balance, Catterick's side played poorly and the match descended quickly into a bad-tempered affair involving four or five belligerent skirmishes. From a royal blue perspective, Jimmy Gabriel battled everyone in a white shirt, especially Graham Leggat, Dave Metchick and Maurice Cook, while Eddie Lowe reciprocated against any blue shirt that crossed his path – more often than not Roy Vernon. Although Brian Harris, Gordon West and Alex Young received extended treatment for knocks at one time or another, no one was badly hurt. Perhaps more amazingly, no one was booked or dismissed. Ironically, George Thomson – the most composed defender on the pitch – came closest to being dismissed when he flattened Leggat from behind.

Gabriel – still only 21 – played like a man possessed and the home supporters booed him every time he touched the ball, made or even contemplated a challenge and strayed towards the touchlines. Undeterred, the right-half continued to grapple and scuffle in aid of the cause. Before the interval, however, he was warned by the referee that his next offence would be his last. With the Scotsman now on his best behaviour, Dennis Stevens and Roy Vernon picked up the baton.

As for the football, the winning goal was scored by Fulham after 22 minutes. A long throw by right-back Jim Langley was misjudged by Gordon West and Stan Brown took advantage as the young keeper lay on the ground. This sloppy goal, however, wasn't against the run of play because Everton had struggled to create any clear-cut chances. During the final thirty minutes, the visitors managed to stretch the home defence but the closest they came to getting level was when Vernon evaded his robust markers only for Tony Macedo to tip his delicate lob over the bar. Distracted by his skirmishes with Lowe, the Welshman had an inconspicuous outing as both striker and captain.

The local media were unimpressed by Everton's display and credited only Thomson and Harris with decent performances. Leslie Edwards observed: 'Everton were not half the team they had been in earlier matches. Perhaps Fulham brought them down to their level. To be fair, if they had taken advantage of the mistakes made by West the match would have been settled long before the end.' He added: 'The weaker the opposition, the more necessary it is to get them beaten quickly.'

West who was a nineteen-year-old at the time, admitted: 'Even though I was the most expensive goalkeeper in the world, everyone knows that I had periods of indifferent form during my twelve-year career at Everton, but that afternoon was my first truly awful stinker. It was a stinker with a capital 'S' and I wanted the River Thames to overflow and sweep me away. No one blamed me to my face, but I was aware I had let down my teammates. Labby still claims that I couldn't have caught a cold that day.'

Alex Young – yet to be worshipped as The Golden Vision – added: 'Painfully, the so-called Mersey Millionaires were brought down to earth by tactics of the London beggars. I don't want to be disrespectful, but Taffy and I were kicked black and blue for ninety minutes. It was brutal. Labby was too much of a gentleman and left the retributions to Gabby. As the rough stuff intensified, I could see my partner getting angrier and angrier and expected him to explode like a Disney cartoon character. I had a calming word with him, but he took no notice. He never did when he was consumed with rage and hate.'

Fixture 6: Wednesday, 5 September 1962

EVERTON 3 LEYTON ORIENT 0

Bingham, Gabriel, Vernon (pen)

Attendance: 51,542

Licking their wounds, Everton returned home to prepare for the return of a familiar face. Three months after being discarded by John Moores in the back of a London taxi, Johnny Carey had been appointed to the position of manager at Leyton Orient in July 1961. There, he had enjoyed immediate success and gained promotion from the Second Division as runners-up to Liverpool. It was to be the East Londoner's only adventure in the top tier.

In the first ever league meeting between the clubs, the Toffees overwhelmed the Orient with a mix of fast and fluid play. It was a one-sided contest in which Bingham, Stevens, Young, Vernon and Morrissey were rampant and rained crosses, shots and headers at the opposition's goal, much to the delight of the royal blue faithful. The bombardment was so intense that Bill Robertson – the veteran keeper who had been first choice at title-winning Chelsea in 1955 – made one miraculous save after another throughout the proceedings and received a near-deafening ovation at full-time.

Also, for that matter, did Alex Young. With the Dynamic Duo purring at its very best, the number nine out-smarted the Orient defenders continually with his superior ball control, delicate feints and elegant body swerves. That September evening, he did everything with God-given flair. That is everything but hit the target. The Scotsman struck the upright on two occasions and even found the net with another rocket shot, but the referee decided to give a free-kick instead of a goal due to an infringement in the build-up.

In his second biography published in 2008, Alex Young reflected on the fixture: 'I don't remember much about the match other than the frustration of scoring a top quality goal only for referee Jack Taylor to ignore the advantage rule, disallow my strike and award us a spot kick – because Brian Harris had been brought down in the area – which, of course, Taffy converted. I don't think the famed Wolverhampton butcher liked me. Four years down the road, he denied me a good goal and a blatant penalty in the FA Cup final.' As for the goals? Billy Bingham was involved in the first two. He scored in the opening minutes and then supplied an inch-perfect free-kick for Jimmy Gabriel to head home.

As expected, Johnny Carey received a friendly reception and his team attempted to play aesthetically attractive football. Even though they were outclassed, it must have been some consolation that he had recruited many of the Everton stars and that the victory had returned them to the top. 'I liked Johnny Carey – he had been a world-class footballer,' said Alex Young. 'Possibly because the Irishman had sued his ex-employer for wrongful dismissal, he was banned from the home dressing room. Nevertheless, Taffy and I chatted with him after the match. He wished us well.'

In the *Liverpool Echo*, Leslie Edwards raved about the performance: 'At Craven Cottage, Everton had been slow, temperamental and torpid. Against Leyton Orient, they were fast, clean and clever. The miracle was the visitors did not lose by double figures. There would have been ten goals if they had not struck the bar or post three times, had two deserving penalty claims disallowed and found Bill Robertson playing like a man with three pairs of hands.' With great enthusiasm, he concluded: 'The exhibition was as fine as we have seen since the days of Dixie Dean and company.' Even though the Everton manager had reaped ten of the available twelve points, he sought to strengthen his flanks and made approaches for two outside-rights recently capped by England, namely Mike Hellawell of Birmingham City and John Connelly of Burnley. Both were hailed as speed merchants. On the left-wing, he focused on two renowned dribblers from Scotland, namely Davie Wilson of Rangers and Eric Stevenson of Hibs. For one reason or another, none of his initiatives were productive.

The home fixture against Leicester City provided an opportunity for further verification of the club's ambitions. Before the match, Catterick cautioned his men that they were about to meet one of the more muscular sides in the country. Managed by Matt Gillies and containing more than a few hard cases, the visitors also boasted the likes of Gordon Banks, Frank McLintock and skilful playmaker Dave Gibson and were touted as potential contenders.

Fixture 7: Saturday, 8 September 1962
EVERTON 3 LEICESTER CITY 2
Stevens, Vernon (pen) and Young
Attendance: 48,738

Everton gained the upper hand directly from the kick-off. Gordon Banks kept out Roy Vernon on a couple of occasions before the skipper slotted home his fourth penalty of the new season in only the seventh game. It was awarded when Alex Young was brought down by Ian King in the 25th minute. Leicester, however, drew level when a mistake by a flat-footed Mick Meagan was punished by Jimmy Walsh. Towards the conclusion of the action-packed half, the Dynamic Duo set up Dennis Stevens to net from a narrow angle.

Shortly after the restart, the number nine made it 3-1. It was no ordinary goal. Without question, it was an extraordinary goal. Michael Charters waxed lyrical: 'Young's goal was a sheer delight. The build-up involved a long cross-field pass by Harris which was picked up by Vernon, who swayed his way into the box before passing to Young. The centre-forward side-stepped a couple of tackles and coolly placed the ball beyond the reach of Banks.'

This remarkable piece of artistry sent the old stadium crazy but also served to stimulate the visitors, who responded with no little skill of their own. Fashioned on the great Hungary and Austria sides of the 1950s, they used short probing passes coupled with positional flexibility in which Frank McLintock and Graham Cross regularly changed positions to unlock the home rearguard.

Another defensive mistake let their rivals into the game in the 71st minute when the Blue Dragon, back on the edge of his own penalty area, tried to guide the ball into the hands of West but only succeeded in cushioning a perfect pass to the feet of Howard Riley, who had no trouble scoring. The unforced error was the low point in a rather impotent second half for the skipper. The Foxes launched a battery of offensives and the outcome remained finely balanced. With a bit more luck, the visitors could have had another three goals. Of course, they didn't, and the hard-earned victory brought Everton's tally to six wins and twelve points from seven games.

Many years later, Alex Young confessed: 'Ian King and I grew up in Loanhead. We were members of the same youth club and played football together day-in and day-out for years. Let's say that I knew his weaknesses and wasn't too surprised when he brought me down.' As predicted it had been a robust game. 'It was out of character for me to get involved in fisticuffs on or off the pitch,' Brian Labone remembered, 'but I'll never forget Albert Cheeseborough because I almost came to blows with the big lug. Leicester were an intimidating yet talented side who nearly snatched the double, ending in fourth spot and as FA Cup finalists at Wembley.'

For the coach Gordon Watson, who knew a bit about football having played alongside Dixie Dean, Tommy Lawton, TG Jones and, at the time, had been on the Goodison payroll or thirty years, it was a key victory: 'While some matches are forgotten within 24 hours, I remember this hard-fought encounter and its aftermath. Tommy Eggleston confided to me that he thought our boys were likely champions. Believe me, it was out of character. He wasn't someone to make such claims.'

Perched at the peak of the English football ladder, Harry Catterick's men were being hailed as genuine challengers – even in London. One week on from the demolition at Goodison, Everton headed south for another encounter with Johnny Carey and friends. Rather than risk aggravating Jimmy Gabriel's injury, the manager selected eighteen-year-old George Sharples at right-half.

Fixture 8: Wednesday, 12 September 1962
LEYTON ORIENT 3 EVERTON 0
Attendance: 21,847

Both teams contributed to a magnificent display of fast, skilful and entertaining football. Though 0-0 at half-time, Everton had created countless scoring chances

– with Bill Robertson saving from Vernon, Young and Stevens – and had looked favourites to capture both points. In contrast, Gordon West didn't have anything to do before the interval.

Shortly after the break, the Everton captain should have opened the scoring but delayed placing his shot into an unguarded net only for Robertson to appear from nowhere. The Orient keeper almost defied gravity by throwing his significant bulk full-length and knocking the ball to safety. With young George Sharples struggling and Brian Harris playing below par, Orient grew in confidence. With no fear of failure, they took the lead after 52 minutes following an uncharacteristic misunderstanding between Brian Harris and Brian Labone, providing winger Norman Deeley with a gift. As Everton intensified their efforts to draw level, full-length saves by Robertson denied Roy Vernon, Johnny Morrissey and others. His displays of athleticism were punctuated by a simple side-footed goal by Gordon Bolland and a delightful glancing headed goal by Dave Dunsmore to ensure a 3-0 home success.

In the *Echo*, Michael Charters sought positives in a disappointing display: 'Everton will long remember Bill Robertson. Last week, he kept the Toffees to a 3-0 winning margin by his efforts alone. Last night, he was the man responsible above all others for the hosts reversing the previous result. He made five great saves, aided by luck on a couple of occasions, and long before the end the rampant forwards must have felt that whatever they did, they could not get the ball around him.'

The result was a wake-up call. Looking back, Brian Labone pondered: 'The final scoreline was a real shock. Orient would win only five or six games that season and were well and truly relegated. Our humiliation was like that experienced at Second Division-bound Carlisle in 1975 – except that we bounced back in 1963. The setback, however, brought out the worst in some people. Taffy criticised me and my fellow defenders. His words were brutal and out of order. In response, I suggested he scrutinise his own inability to beat an overweight and over-the-hill goalie. Worse still, the club's massive spending in the transfer market and formidable start to the season were showcased that evening on *Sportsview*, BBC Television's flagship sports programme. I heard that Peter Dimmock couldn't believe the result relayed from Brisbane Road. They assumed that Everton had won by 3-0.'

Alex Parker was more philosophical about the encounter: 'Thank goodness I didn't play. The state of the changing rooms at Brisbane Road sent a clear message of the battle ahead. Let's just say they were primitive. Some of my teammates claimed we were a bit unlucky, whereas I thought we were a shambles. Afterwards, Taffy threw a tantrum when I joked that we'll play worse and win. He was livid about how we let in three soft goals. Most of his fury was a result of the fact that he had been physically abused for ninety minutes. I wondered if things would have been different if Wee Bobby had been in the side. The little fellow knew how to look after himself and his teammates.'

Having lost at Fulham and Orient and slipped behind Wolves into second place, Everton travelled to the home of another founding member of the league, Bolton Wanderers, for their ninth fixture in four weeks. After their previous experiences at Burnden Park, they expected a bruising get-together, with the notorious left-back Syd Farrimond and his industrial strength tackles.

Fixture 9: Saturday, 15 September 1962
BOLTON WANDERERS 0 EVERTON 2
Bingham, Gabriel
Attendance: 27,404

As it transpired, Roy Vernon, Alex Young and their fellow forwards ran riot throughout the first 45 minutes. Undeniably, the Welsh ace was Bolton's tormentor-in-chief, and he set the tone by shoulder-charging the ball along with goalkeeper Eddie Hopkinson into the net. Initially, the referee awarded the goal but changed his mind, much to the chagrin of the noisy following. Apparently, the stopper's feet were off the floor when impact was made. By half-time, Vernon had carved out enough chances to put the outcome beyond reasonable doubt only to be denied by the amazing agility of Hopkinson. The Bolton keeper touched one Royston rocket onto the crossbar before denying him with an even more sensational dive. Both saves were applauded by home and away fans alike. Horace Yates was impressed: 'Hopkinson gave as a display of goalkeeping as good as anyone could wish to see.'

The Everton skipper had enjoyed a sparkling game but, subsequent to him being brought down by Graham Cunliffe and his appeal for a penalty had been ignored, needlessly augmented his reputation as something of an abrasive character by clashing with Fred Hill. The referee separated and admonished both men. Incredibly, no one was booked.

Five minutes into the second half, Billy Bingham dribbled in from the touchline and exchanged passes with Dennis Stevens to enable the Ulsterman to open the scoring. The Burnden crowd reacted wholeheartedly to more displays of agility and guts by Hopkinson to deny Young, Stevens and Morrissey. Eventually, Everton faded. With the threat of The Dynamic Duo no longer as troublesome, the home side was able to exert increasing pressure, which caused Brian Labone and Mick Meagan into uncharacteristic mistakes. Thankfully, Fred Hill, Wyn Davies and Peter Deakin missed the resulting chances to level. Then, seven minutes from time, Johnny Morrissey's shot was saved by Hopkinson and Jimmy Gabriel headed the loose ball into the net. During the goalmouth scrimmage, the left-winger took a kick in the face. No doubt his pain was tempered by the final scoreline of 2-0.

Horace Yates was encouraged by what he had witnessed: 'Everton, interrupting their sequence of two defeats in London, not only got their third away victory at Burnden Park but matched last season's entire yield of winning points away from home with only five games played. This represents a remarkable advance and, if maintained, must make the team a genuine championship proposition.' He concluded: 'They have more difficult trials to surmount than Bolton and if this realisation leads to an acceptance of opportunities, Hopkinson or not, they have no need to be apprehensive.'

Gordon West was impressed by his opposite number, who went on to play over 500 first-team games for Bolton: 'Before I joined Blackpool and was seduced by the deeds of Big Tony Waiters, my heroes were Ron Springett at Sheffield Wednesday, Alan Hodgkinson at Sheffield United and Eddie Hopkinson. All three goalies were short and acrobatic. In fact, Eddie must have been no more than 5ft 8in in his orthopaedic boots. His occasional anxieties with the high crosses were compensated by incredible courage, cat-like reflexes, smart positional sense and consistency. That day he was simply amazing, and produced one of the finest displays I've ever witnessed. He made our skipper question his abilities to put the ball into the net.'

The city of Liverpool came to a standstill in mid-September 1962 as it prepared for the first league derby in eleven seasons. Though managed by Bill Shankly, the red neighbours were something of an unknown quantity, having been promoted to the top flight at the start of the 1962/63 season. With their neighbours still finding their feet, Evertonians were confident of a home victory. The Blue Dragon confided: 'I don't mind letting you into a secret, I expect to see Liverpool perish against our half-back line – Gabriel, Labone and Harris. There isn't a better one in any club team.' Ron Yeats, the Anfield captain, spent the run-up to the match ringing Alex Young, his ex-Army colleague, to inform him that he would not be getting a kick. He disclosed: 'Living with Alex every day for two years during my National Service, I'd seen all his moves. I knew what to expect.'

Fixture 10: Saturday, 22 September 1962
EVERTON 2 LIVERPOOL 2
Morrissey, Vernon (pen)
Attendance: 72,488

The matchday programme highlighted Everton's standing as the first club of Merseyside by summarising the more modest honours earned by their neighbours: 'Liverpool have won the First Division five times and the Second Division four times. Although they have yet to win the FA Cup, they have twice been finalists.' The contest started dramatically. In the very first minute Vernon robbed keeper Jim Furnell to score, only to hear the referee's whistle for a foul. It took months for the club captain to come to terms with the baffling decision and express his frustration – 'I was staggered. There was never anything approaching a foul' – whereas Ron Yeats expressed his relief: 'I could see the colour return to Furnell's cheeks when the goal was disallowed.'

Tony Onslow, a lifelong Evertonian, remembers one incident in particular: 'Early in the game, the ball was played out by the Everton defence to Roy Vernon, who rushed towards the Park End goal with Ron Yeats hot on his heels. Just before the giant pivot made his tackle, our inside-left let fly from 25 yards. His shot hit one post then the other post and rebounded into Jim Furnell's chest.'

The Toffees continued to boss the proceedings. Dennis Stevens had another strike disallowed by the referee, this time for offside, before Vernon drove home a penalty kick in the 29th minute, awarded when Gerry Byrne handled. The old stadium erupted as he chalked up his fifth successful spot kick of the season. However, the crowd was much quieter ten minutes before the interval when Kevin Lewis – a replacement for the sidelined Ian St John – equalised.

Johnny Morrissey, allegedly sold without Shankly's permission three weeks prior to the derby, lined up for Everton. His transfer had caused quite a stir. Apparently, the Anfield manager had tendered his resignation at hearing of his board's decision. One can only imagine the Scotsman's chagrin as the outside-left restored Everton's lead on the hour mark, especially given the protestations that the effort had not crossed the line. 'At the time, I didn't think that it had,' claimed full-back Ronnie Moran some 25 years later. 'When I saw it the other day on the video, I still think it wasn't in.' The Toffees appeared to be cruising to another home success when Lewis beat Brian Labone in the air to set up Roger Hunt for the equaliser in the dying moments. Silenced by only drawing with their neighbours, Evertonians were more devastated at dropping a home point in the pursuit for the famous silverware.

The following Monday, Leslie Edwards summarised his observations: 'Hard, exciting, noisy, tense – but no classic. The Reds played above themselves.' A half-century on, Alex Young revealed just how tense things were that day: 'For many, it was a bruising encounter against Big Ron. Things happened in the tunnel that I prefer not to discuss, but sadly our friendship was never quite the same again.'

FIRST QUARTER REPORT: SO FAR SO GOOD

	P	W	D	L
Home	5	4	1	0
Away	5	3	0	2

So far, so good. In 2001, over a wet lunch at The Albany pub located in Old Hall Street, Brian Labone reflected on the club's standing after ten fixtures: 'We had started well, but given our two failures in London were far from indestructible. Nevertheless, our away form was much better than in the previous season. Back then, the objective was to win your games at home, draw them away and celebrate picking up the title with a total of 63 points. It was just a rule of thumb because Ipswich were champs with 56 points in 1962 and Tottenham with 66 points in 1961. Even after slipping up against the newly-promoted Reds, we had dropped just five points and were perceived as serious contenders throughout the land, even though the London media was reluctant to admit it.' That said, not all was fine and dandy behind the scenes, as Alex Parker acknowledged: 'We had good team spirit but there was some friction between Carey's men and the others. Personally, I thought of it as a divide between Celts and Anglos.' Gordon Watson elaborated: 'I spent my weekdays training the first-team squad. I enjoyed the banter, when things were running smoothly. Because Roy Vernon and Alex Young were ultra-competitive, Alex Parker loved to tease his captain: "You may be a Goodison favourite, but Alex is a Goodison god." Of course, both were the stars – Parker referred to them as the glory boys in a very good side – but, in my eyes, the most influential players in the early season had been Gabriel, Harris and Stevens. They were our unsung engine. Elsewhere, there was juicy gossip about the club signing different wingers and full-backs, which didn't please Billy Bingham or George Thomson. Another consequence of having access to Mr Moores's fortune is that younger lads were provided fewer opportunities. Those on the fringes – like Colin Green and Frank Wignall – became fed up. Both were capped by their countries during their post-Everton years.'

The race to be Everton's top marksman that campaign was well underway, but troubled by a predictable controversy – spot kicks. No one could have predicted that Everton would have been awarded five penalties in their first ten games – surely that good fortune happened only to their neighbours? Both candidates had been in fine form during the opening fixtures: Young had bagged five goals and Vernon had grabbed seven. However, the former preferred to record their efforts as: Young five goals and Vernon two real goals plus five penalties.

PART 2:
ONWARDS AND UPWARDS

FROM THE ELEVATED POSITION OF SECOND IN THE TABLE, HARRY Catterick selected an unchanged team for the arrival of West Brom and a lethal nemesis. Though stranded in the doldrums, the Midlanders fielded Derek Kevan – nicknamed 'The Tank' – who had an irritating habit of scoring against the Toffees. Only two years earlier, Kevan had notched five goals in a 6-2 hammering at The Hawthorns and had found the target about fifteen times in a dozen encounters. Ironically, Johnny Carey had attempted but failed to sign him for the club in 1959, and so had Catterick in 1961.

Fixture 11: Saturday, 29 September 1962
EVERTON 4 WEST BROMWICH ALBION 2
Morrissey 3, Young

Attendance: 45,471

Though the swirling wind made the conditions difficult for both goalkeepers, Everton started strongly and, for the second successive home game, Dennis Stevens had the ball in the net at the Stanley Park end, only for it to be ruled offside. After twenty minutes, they took the lead thanks to Johnny Morrissey and Lady Luck. Billy Bingham's corner was nodded on by Jimmy Gabriel to the left-winger, whose header was mishandled by keeper Tony Millington and pushed into the roof of the net. Ten minutes on and West Brom restored parity via another defensive error. Michael Charters described the clumsy incident: 'A fifty-yard kick by full-back Don Howe was dropping comfortably into the penalty area with Gordon West running out to collect it, but Brian Harris jumped in front of him in an attempt to head away and succeeded in glancing it into the empty net.' It was the first and possibly the sloppiest own-goal of the season.

The game changed when defender Stan Jones went down with no one near him. Much to the relief of the Goodison faithful, Kevan – West Brom's feared spearhead – was required to play at centre-half. Instantly, Everton took advantage of the extra man and moved into the lead. This time Alex Young chipped the ball from just outside the eighteen-yard box to Jimmy Gabriel, who headed across the goalmouth for Johnny Morrissey to add his second from close range. The Toffees increased their lead when Young's direct free-kick was deflected by a defender past the helpless Millington. Now in total control, Alex Young and Billy Bingham combined to allow Johnny Morrissey to complete his hat-trick with a glancing header in the 55th minute. Without further ado, the left-winger almost nabbed his fourth when put through by his skilful centre-forward. Despite the abundance of goal action, the contributions of Roy Vernon had been muted. Predictably, the West Midlanders adopted a more physical approach and nabbed a second goal. 'The Tank' robbed Alex Young and supplied Clive Clark who outpaced Mick Meagan before crossing for Alec Jackson to hit a rasping shot through Gordon West.

Notwithstanding his newspaper's bold headline 'Morrissey Grabs Three in Everton Joyride', Michael Charters ignored the claims of the irrepressible outside-left and picked Derek Kevan as man of the match: 'With the exception of Dennis Stevens, the Everton forwards had been disappointing.' He also observed that George Thomson had had one of his poorest games and was booed by the home crowd when he fouled winger Ken Foggo.

Alex Young was aware of his manager's admiration of West Brom's star man: 'Taffy and I realised that Derek Kevan was a potential replacement – make that a big strapping replacement – for one of us and were relieved when he was lured to Stamford Bridge by Tommy Docherty towards the end of that season. When things didn't work out for him at Chelsea, we were convinced that he would join us at the start of the 1963/64 campaign. Of course, he moved to Maine Road and racked up thirty or so goals for Man City in his first season in the Second Division.'

Though not pretty, the victory over West Brom bolstered Everton's standing just below their next adversaries, the mighty Wolves. Under the stewardship of Stan Cullis, a native of Ellesmere Port, the Black Country club had finished top three times, runners-up twice and in third place three times during the 1950s and was lauded as a powerhouse in the English game.

Fixture 12: Saturday, 6 October 1962
WOLVERHAMPTON WANDERERS 0 EVERTON 2
Bingham, Young
Attendance: 44,506

The match was a cracker. Despite missing captain Ron Flowers – who failed a late fitness test – Wolves exerted all-out pressure from the kick-off and Gordon West was required to make excellent saves from both Peter McPartland and Chris Crowe within the opening two minutes. Eventually, Jimmy Gabriel and Brian Harris took control of midfield and allowed the Vernon-Young alchemy to excel. Both forwards had great games. The Scotsman bamboozled his foes with his artistic touches, while the Welshman unsettled the defenders with his precise passes through the middle. Together, they made their opponents look almost pedestrian. The Toffees were unlucky not to score in the opening half. They went close on numerous occasions, with keeper Fred Davies saving from Johnny Morrissey and Jimmy Gabriel and full-back George Showell clearing Alex Young's header off the line. Billy Bingham also netted from a neat Vernon pass, but the goal was disallowed as the ball had gone out of play.

In the *Liverpool Echo*, Jack Rowe reported enthusiastically that the Merseysiders had dominated one of their main rivals for the title: 'For much of the first half, Everton had given unbeaten Wolverhampton a football lesson. That they were not in front was because the run of the ball had gone the way of the home side. There was no comparison between the sides as football exponents, with the Toffees playing the best stuff I had seen this season. In thrashing the leaders, Everton had, on this occasion at least, fulfilled all that they had promised.'

Concerned that the superiority might not be crowned with the success it deserved, there was no let-up as Everton sought to make their mastery count. Finally, the goals arrived. Harry Catterick's men went ahead on the hour when Johnny Morrissey beat Showell with a fine burst of speed before crossing for Billy Bingham to head home. The second, which arrived fifteen minutes before the end, was a beauty in conception and execution. Mick Meagan passed to his captain, who dribbled his way across midfield before slipping a wonderful ball for Alex Young to fire home.

Brian Labone acclaimed the team performance at Molineux and the return to the top of the table: 'It showed that we could be a top-notch side away from home. Every member of the team played well, especially the unsung Mick Meagan and much maligned George Thomson. Best of all, the victory elevated us to the place where we belonged, albeit by our superior goal-average. I was chuffed that the Sunday papers claimed that I had had a decent game against Peter McPartland – who could be a handful – and predicted that I would be selected to play for England against Northern Ireland.'

Fixture 13: Saturday, 13 October 1962

EVERTON 1 ASTON VILLA 1

Vernon (pen)

Attendance: 53,035

Next, the club welcomed the original architects of the Football League, Aston Villa. Under the stewardship of manager Joe Mercer – another native of Ellesmere Port whose playing career with Everton and England had been devastated by World War Two – the Birmingham club had returned to the top flight in 1960 and captured the inaugural the League Cup in 1961. It was the 138th time that the clubs had met – 133 occasions in the league, five in the FA Cup.

Although Alex Parker had missed eight fixtures with hamstring injuries, Everton had been fortunate in avoiding other injuries and had fielded the same XI except for fleeting outings by George Sharples in two games and Ray Veall in two games. As expected, the team was unchanged and near full-strength for the home game against Aston Villa.

Catterick's stars made an impressive start, moving like a well-oiled machine. Roy Vernon, Alex Young, Dennis Stevens and Jimmy Gabriel came close to beating Geoff Sidebottom in the opening twenty minutes. The Villa keeper was required to make one fine save after another. Eventually, Everton took a deserved lead via a Roy Vernon penalty – his sixth of the campaign – awarded for a foul by Gordon Lee – a future Goodison manager – on Dennis Stevens.

The Toffees had played well enough to have won the game by the interval. Alex Young had been awesome. 'The centre-forward had his admirers cooing with delight following one superb piece of football,' Michael Charters enthused. 'He cut inside three men and hit such a powerful shot that Sidebottom handled it as though it were red hot, dropping the ball which ran across the goalmouth.' Billy

Bingham, Jimmy Gabriel and Brian Harris had all made first-class contributions, but by comparison Roy Vernon had struggled against Vic Crowe – his international teammate – and was somewhat subdued and unhappy.

The Toffees continued to dominate throughout the second half, yet for all their superiority they had only one goal – and that a penalty – to show for their efforts. Although Joe Mercer's men had only competed in fits and starts, there was always the danger that they would snatch a goal as the game entered its closing stages. And in the 77th minute, Villa scored when the flight of Alan Baker's shot – only his side's third of the match – appeared to deceive Gordon West.

In the closing minutes, Villa kicked the ball – plus the odd opponent – anywhere to hold on to their gritty point. Some of their tackling was more than a little mean-spirited. Even so, Everton had plenty of chances to win. Roy Vernon had a goal disallowed for offside and Dennis Stevens missed a sitter before the end. There was a storm of booing as the teams left the pitch with pieces of unidentified fruit thrown at the Villa players and the referee.

'Every team must expect to drop a point at home occasionally,' opined Leslie Edwards in the *Echo*, 'but having dropped one to Liverpool last month, we were not expecting them to do the same thing against opponents denied of their star performers – Derek Dougan and Cammie Fraser.' Even with the dropped point, Everton stayed at the top of the pile.

With Billy Bingham, Brian Labone and Roy Vernon selected to represent their countries, the club's excursion to Nottingham on the following weekend was rescheduled to November. Amazingly, no member of their kilted legion was required by Scotland.

Before their next league fixture, Everton became the first Merseyside club to sample European competition. It had qualified to enter the Inter-Cities Fairs Cup and been drawn against Iraklis Salonika from Greece. For some unknown reason, their opponents withdrew from the competition and Everton were required to play Dunfermline Athletic. In the first leg of the first round, the Toffees earned a narrow 1-0 win in front of a crowd of 40,000 at Goodison. The goal was credited to Dennis Stevens. His back-header from an inswinging Bingham corner struck the underside of the bar and upon landing was ruled to have crossed the line. It was a scruffy goal. The negative defensive tactics adopted by the Scottish underdogs was criticised by Leslie Edwards: 'It was an ill-tempered, rough and ready battle in which feet and fists were raised. I've spilled more ink on this apology for a match than it was worth.'

Back to the pursuit of domestic silverware with the visit of the reigning champions. Harry Catterick was forced to make one change. George Thomson, who had been hurt against Dunfermline, was replaced by Mick Meagan. Ipswich Town, however, suffered a much greater loss. They were without Ted Phillips, hailed as the hardest kicker of a dead ball in the English game. His legendary partnership with Ray Crawford had earned them the Second and First Division titles in successive years. Surprisingly, fewer fans turned up for the match against Alf Ramsey's side than had done against a modest club from north of the border managed by Jock Stein.

Fixture 14: Saturday, 27 October 1962
EVERTON 3 IPSWICH TOWN 1
Morrissey 2, Vernon (pen)
Attendance: 39,695

Direct from the start, the hosts were as rampant as the visitors were lethargic. Faster and fitter, Everton took the lead via another penalty kick by Roy Vernon after 24 minutes. It was awarded for a double tackle by Larry Carberry and keeper Wilf Hall on the home captain. After another success, Leslie Edwards described Vernon's flawless technique from the penalty spot: 'The Welshman's unerring timing gives goalkeepers little chance to make up their minds where the chosen spot will be. He takes a nonchalant trot, moves fast only when a yard or so from the ball and fairly hammers it in.' Against Ipswich, he dispatched a low drive wide of the keeper's left hand.

Everton failed to take advantage of their dominance through frustrating finishing and unyielding goalkeeping. Strong in the air, especially at corners, Ipswich drew level through Doug Moran. The home side struggled to puncture the visitor's defence and were becoming desperate until Johnny Morrissey bagged a brace and nearly added a third within the space of sixty seconds. In the 74th minute, the winger struck a right-foot shot through a dozen legs to beat the unsighted Hall. No sooner had the game restarted when he sailed into the area to head another goal from Bingham's cross. Seconds thereafter, Alex Young set him up but his left-foot shot – for a perfect hat-trick – was thwarted by Hall.

Despite the win, which gave them an impressive total of 22 points from fourteen games, Harry Catterick's men slipped into second spot. Leslie Edwards advised his *Echo* readers: 'At present, Everton lack the ability to remain poised and balanced when things go against them. The mark of a great side is the propensity to change its tactics to suit the occasion.' It had not gone unnoticed that Vernon was the club's leading marksman, with an impressive tally of nine goals in fourteen league outings, but only two of them had come from open play, both of which had been in August. His recent performances had been uncharacteristically low-key bordering on lacklustre. 'I felt a little abandoned and needed his support against some big nasty defenders, especially away from home,' grumbled his partner in crime Young. 'I cautioned Taffy that he was dropping far too deep and playing as a schemer rather than a striker. I may have added that he was no John White. Again, he ignored me.'

Four days down the line, the Toffees were knocked out of Europe. The first half of the second leg at a full-throated East End Park was dominated by the fluent football of the Scottish side. George Miller levelled the aggregate score with a twenty-yard volley which Gordon West misjudged in probably the club's worst 45 minutes of the season. Dunfermline's second goal was more controversial. It came three minutes from time, when a speculative clearance caused confusion. Alex Parker appealed that Harry Melrose was offside but, unlike his opponent, the winger continued and pushed the ball past Gordon West. Amid protests, the referee consulted his linesman and awarded the goal, which allowed Dunfermline to progress 2-1 on aggregate and meet Valencia – the holders and eventual winners – in the second round. It had looked like Everton would take the tie to a play-off at a neutral ground, but Alex Young's last-minute effort was disallowed for an infringement by Johnny Morrissey. While the Toffees had attacked for most of the second half and Jimmy Gabriel might have scored on three occasions, the game will be remembered for the disturbing fact that neither Roy Vernon nor any other forward had a meaningful shot on target during the ninety minutes. Much to his annoyance, the Welshman had been shadowed and neutralised by Alex Smith all night long.

On 2 November 1962, Leslie Edwards broke the news that the Everton skipper had been dropped. He quoted the words of the manager: 'I have explained the position to Roy and have selected him at inside-left in the reserve side. I am playing Frank Wignall in his place at Maine Road.' Vernon's replacement –

a robust centre-forward – was the star of the Central League side.

The same *Echo* journalist speculated on Roy's relegation to the reserves: 'Undeniably, he is the best inside-left on the books. I do not doubt that Mr Catterick knows this as well as we do, therefore it follows that the player's dropping was not wholly due to the fact that he had scored only two goals other than penalties and had had a poor game in Scotland. The Welshman is not meeting his club's needs as a captain. There are many facets to captaincy. He must set an example to the remainder of the team – both in play and manners. He must encourage them to do their best. He must calm their moments of temper and suit his tactics to the special needs of the occasion. Vernon, as everyone knows, has a Celtic temperament, and doesn't take kindly to anyone dispossessing him. The fire in his play is part of his make-up. Could it be that Vernon after one week out of the side will have learned that remonstrations against decisions made in good faith are nothing more than pre-Christmas pantomime?'

During his visit to the Victoria, British Columbia, then the home of co-author David France in 2005, Alex Young reminisced: 'It happened almost fifty years ago but I still prefer not to divulge too much about it except that Taffy wasn't happy. He muttered something about him being good enough for his country but not for his club. The following Wednesday he represented Wales against Hungary in the European Nations Cup. Unfortunately, they lost by 3-1 in Budapest.'

Fixture 15: Saturday, 3 November 1962
MANCHESTER CITY 1 EVERTON 1
Wignall
Attendance: 40,336

Other changes when Everton faced Man City included Johnny Morrissey switching to the right-wing in place of the badly bruised Billy Bingham and Ray Veall returning at outside-left. While Harry Catterick's decision to drop his captain had shocked the football world, his team enthralled the large crowd at Maine Road. With Jimmy Gabriel and Brian Harris brilliant, Everton pressed for an opening goal. Dennis Stevens beat keeper Harry Dowd in the twelfth minute with a well-placed shot but what seemed like a perfectly good goal was disallowed. At the other end, City took the lead in the 34th minute through a fine effort from Peter Dobing.

After the break, Alex Parker and Mick Meagan advanced to support their forwards as Everton increased their grip on proceedings. Even though Frank Wignall had struggled to accept the opportunities presented to him, he kept trying and worried the opposition with his physical presence. His inclusion paid off in the 76th minute when he netted following a fine move involving Young and Veall. Throughout the closing minutes, Everton stormed forward with increased intensity and were unlucky not to secure both points. According to Michael Charters, 'Late on, Alex Young collected the ball on the edge of the penalty area, beat three defenders with his own version of the Twist then clipped a lovely shot fractions of an inch wide.'

The journalist summarised the clash at Maine Road: 'Mr Catterick must have been pleased with his forwards. There was more thrust about them than in recent away games. The main reason was the display of acting captain Alex Young. In defiance of the rugged tackling of Bill Leivers, he enjoyed his best outing since Molineux with his astute reading of the play, delicate touches, accurate passes and ceaseless foraging.'

Alex Parker had expected a shake-up sooner rather than later: 'Taffy wasn't happy about being dropped and made a scapegoat after the Dunfermline debacle. Frank Wignall – who was knocking them in for fun in the stiffs – took his place at Maine Road and scored. Controversially, he was replaced by Taffy for the next game. Frank was a robust and honest centre-forward – a more rugged version of Fred Pickering – who was dominant in the air and owned a powerful shot. He scored goals wherever he went. Capped by England in 1964, Frank bagged two goals in his two international appearances.'

As for Roy Vernon, he turned out for the reserves against Blackpool at Goodison. Coach Gordon Watson remarked: 'Our Second XI included several men with first-team experience like Albert Dunlop, George Thomson, Colin Green, George Heslop and George Sharples as well as a youngster named Colin Harvey. Even though we won comfortably by 4-2, Taffy was out of sorts and failed to find the onion bag. I think he sulked through the game.'

The manager, having made his point – that is, no one is immune from being dropped – restored the Everton skipper to the first team for the clash with Blackpool. Managed by Ron Suart, who would unearth Alan Ball and Emlyn Hughes, the visitors' defence included two existing England stars – namely Tony Waiters and Jimmy Armfield.

Fixture 16: Saturday, 10 November 1962
EVERTON 5 BLACKPOOL 0
Young 2, Bingham, Gabriel, Stevens
Attendance: 39,517

Although it took some minutes for both teams to adjust to the blustery conditions, the Tangerines appeared slow and listless compared to their hosts. While the Welshman didn't find the target, he did come close time and again. Early on, a smart header by Alex Young enabled him to dispatch a thunderbolt which unluckily struck the foot of the post. Time and again, Tony Waiters denied him with a series of spectacular stops. Following one astounding save, many of the Everton players applauded the Blackpool goalkeeper.

The Toffees continued to pin the Tangerines in their own half. As a result, Alex Young took the opportunity to entertain his enthusiastic admirers. One exquisite header from a first-class cross by Ray Veall went just wide of the angle with the crowd ready to acclaim a wonder strike. The goals soon flowed. First, Roy Vernon shrugged off the attentions of Bruce Crawford and Dave Durie to slide the ball via Dennis Stevens to an unmarked Billy Bingham. Though Waiters got his hand to the Ulsterman's shot, he could not prevent it crossing the line. Then Ray Veall sent a delicious centre for Alex Young to head a magnificent goal in the fortieth minute.

Blackpool showed a little more punch in the second half, quite literally. Barrie Martin and Jimmy Gabriel battled away, as did Bruce Crawford and Roy Vernon. Elsewhere there was no hint of slackening. Jimmy Gabriel nodded Ray Veall's cross to Alex Young, who turned the ball into the roof of the net to make it 3-0. Right-half Gabriel grabbed a fourth and the fast and furious forays continued until Dennis Stevens made it 5-0 a few minutes from time. On the left flank, both Mick Meagan and Ray Veall were impressive. The novice outside-left excelled against Jimmy Armfield. Even though he missed two or three good chances, the crowd rose to applaud him at the end.

Meanwhile, the sports pages of the national newspapers had been full of rumours linking an assortment of possible recruits to the Mersey Millionaires: 'If all the men Everton are interested in or about to sign were laid end-to-end, they would reach from Liverpool to Scotland,' wrote Leslie Edwards. 'First it was John

Fantham of Wednesday, then Ralph Brand of Rangers. Now it's Bobby Irvine, the Linfield goalkeeper and Duncan Mackay, the Celtic right-back. If you were an Everton first-teamer wouldn't you feel a bit peeved? I don't doubt that some of the named men have scarcely entered the head of Harry Catterick.'

Billy Bingham observed the impacts of transfer gossip on his teammates: 'It is a part and parcel of pro football. Personally, I was aware of the speculation regarding the club's interest in Mike Hellawell and John Connelly and had heard on the grapevine that the manager had made enquiries about the availability of Barrie Jones, Swansea's young right-winger who had been capped recently by Wales. All three had something I had misplaced – electric pace. Also, I'm sure Taffy knew about Harry's love affair with Johnny Fantham and interest in Ralph Brand, but he never talked about them.'

Regardless of the convincing victory over Blackpool, the Toffees remained in second place – one point behind Spurs, albeit with a game in hand. But given their title-winning form, the Merseysiders travelled to sixth-placed Nottingham Forest committed to returning to the pinnacle.

Fixture 17: Tuesday, 13 November 1962
NOTTINGHAM FOREST 3 EVERTON 4
Vernon 2, Gabriel, Veall
Attendance: 31,610

In the most exciting game of Everton's season so far, both sides produced a feast of fast, thrilling entertainment of the very highest calibre: 'This must have been one of the finest displays for seasons,' opined Michael Charters. 'They [Everton] recovered from the blow of being two goals down in the opening fifteen minutes to beat a side which had not lost at home since April.'

Initially, it was all one-way traffic towards Gordon West's goal. Wingers Trevor Hockey and Dick Le Flem were constant threats and there were more than a few goalmouth scrabbles before Forest scored their first through Colin Addison and their second via a penalty by Calvin Palmer. The spot kick was awarded when Len Julians beat Gordon West and Alex Parker handled the ball on the goal line. Though Palmer hit the upright with his first attempt, the referee ordered it to be retaken because Brian Labone had encroached into the area. He made no mistakes the second time around.

Down 2-0, Everton exhibited a new spirit by refusing to quit when things were going against them. Inspired by Alex Young and Roy Vernon, they took control throughout the remainder of the first half. Their dominance was duly rewarded. After twenty minutes Jimmy Gabriel passed to Alex Young, who took the ball up to keeper John Armstrong before unselfishly side-footing it to his striking partner to knock it across the line. The grateful captain added another by chasing a long ball from Alex Parker and neatly slipping it beyond Armstrong. Then, just before the interval, Vernon and Brian Harris linked up to enable Ray Veall to bag his first senior goal with a shot from a narrow angle.

It was one of those matches where you couldn't divert your eyes for a moment in case you missed some incident, and the home side levelled in the seventieth minute. Gordon West jumped to catch a cross from Le Flem but could not hold onto it after being bundled into by Julians. The ball fell to Johnny Quigley, who scored. Less than sixty seconds afterwards, Gabriel netted the winner with a brilliant header from a free-kick by Veall. The game ended with Forest bombarding the Everton penalty area for ten minutes in search of another equaliser.

Post-match, Young heaped praise on his side-kick: 'We played the kind of football which had been absent in too many of our away games. I'm delighted that Taffy, who had been out of luck with his shooting against Tony Waiters, rediscovered his best form at Nottingham and helped to lift us to our rightful place at the very top, with 27 hard-earned points from seventeen games.'

When talking to David France in 2000, Tom Eggleston disclosed: 'I knew we had a good team, but it was at the City Ground that I sensed for the first time that we had one capable of lifting silverware. That afternoon, the whole side showed the heart of a fighter and the determination of a champion after going 2-0 down. Jimmy Gabriel's winner did more than take us back to the top – it sent out a message to Spurs and others that the Toffees were contenders. Genuine contenders.'[2]

From the rarefied atmosphere at the summit, Harry Catterick's team looked forward to its eighteenth fixture against mid-table Blackburn Rovers. The hosts included two established England stars Ronnie Clayton and Bryan Douglas as well as two future Evertonians, namely Keith Newton and Fred Pickering. The visiting captain received a warm welcome on his second appearance at Ewood in Everton colours.

Fixture 18: Saturday, 17 November 1962
BLACKBURN ROVERS 3 EVERTON 2
Harris, Stevens
Attendance: 30,243

Following a bright start by Everton, the Rovers grasped control of the proceedings. With the centre of the pitch badly churned up, they raided down the flanks where Mike Ferguson and Mike Harrison had the better of Mick Meagan and Alex Parker. Prompted by Ronnie Clayton and Bryan Douglas, Blackburn looked the most likely to take the lead. Indeed, only the acrobatics of Gordon West kept his team in the game. He made one exceptionally courageous interception at the feet of Harrison to keep the game goalless going into the break.

After the rain had turned to sleet and then snow, Everton's forwards struggled to overcome the conditions and West was required to keep his teammates in the game – his series of amazing saves included one which thwarted a close-range thunderbolt from Fred Pickering. Not surprisingly, the East Lancashire club went ahead after 65 minutes when Douglas crossed for Ian Lawther to head home. Even though their preferred delicate passing approach had failed, Everton levelled via Brian Harris – or perhaps Alex Young – without delay. Following a foul by Douglas on Jimmy Gabriel, the right-half's free-kick floated into the penalty box where Matt Woods headed the ball down and Harris slammed it into the net from ten yards. Or did he? 'From the way that his teammates congratulated Alex Young, it may well have been that the ball flicked against the centre-forward,' Michael Charters reported. Either way, it was a goal against the run of play. Then, somewhat astonishingly, the Toffees took the lead. Alex Parker's free-kick, awarded for another foul by Woods on Young, was badly cleared by Mick McGrath to Dennis Stevens who smashed it past keeper Fred Else.

As the game got more physical, with numerous free-kicks awarded for rugged challenges by both sides, Blackburn regained control. With seven minutes to play, Harrison hit a low cross which was turned towards his own goal by Harris and Pickering dashed in to make it 2-2.

At that point and in such wintery conditions, Everton would have been satisfied with one point. But in the final minute, the Rovers were awarded a highly disputed penalty for a foul by Gabriel on Pickering. Coolly, Douglas took care of business from the spot. Michael Charters was dismayed by the decision: 'As the players came off the mud-strewn pitch, some of them began a derisive handclap at referee Frank Cowen. To me, it appeared that Fred Pickering had lost possession and fallen over Jimmy Gabriel. Apparently after the centre-forward had got the better of Brian Labone near the goal line, he kicked the ball too far forward and Jimmy Gabriel sliding in pushed it to Gordon West. Fred Pickering then did what many forwards do in such circumstances – flung himself headlong over the defender's outstretched leg.'

David France recounted the discomforts associated with the fixture at Blackburn: 'Braving the bitterly cold weather, I rode pillion on an older friend's motorcycle – a 150cc Ducati known as The Widow Maker. It was a terrifying experience. Everton were top of the league and confident – possibly overconfident – of victory but were outplayed in the heavy conditions. I had thought that Roy Vernon would dazzle against his old team – sadly he didn't. I remember that all of the action happened after snow had started to fall. In no time, the flurries had turned into a blizzard and defenders began to make errors at both ends. First, Blackburn took the lead with about twenty minutes left. Then – against the run of play – we responded with two goals of our own. I thought we would coast to victory. So, for that matter, did the travelling 10,000 Blues at the uncovered end of the ground who were singing "Jingle Bells" when Fred Pickering scored and then won a dodgy penalty. It was miserable ride home through the Lancashire slush.'

The unexpected defeat allowed Spurs to climb to the top via better goal-average. Charters was concerned about the impact of heavy conditions on royal blue displays: 'It may be that Everton facing heavy grounds will struggle to maintain their all-conquering form of the early part of the season.' The journalist added: 'By the way, I learned that Alex Young had scored by deflecting the ball with his head.' Nevertheless, Everton Football Club awarded the goal to Harris.

'Some men don't remember their goals,' the left-half joked. 'I can still picture most of mine. Of course, there weren't that many. My sole contribution during our most glorious season was at Ewood. Even though I may not have got the final touch, I still claim it. It was my reward for taking part in a dour contest in Arctic conditions. Shortly after Blackburn went ahead, I scored and Dennis Stevens added another. We thought we had done enough but paid the price for taking our collective feet off the pedal. This allowed Fred Pickering to score and then fall over his own feet to win a last-minute penalty which removed us from the pinnacle of the table. There is no fun in scoring if you throw away two points.'

During the week, Vernon turned out against an England side which included Brian Labone. Wales lost 4-0. In very cold weather, the game drew about 27,000 – the smallest crowd for an international at Wembley. On the half hour, Vernon had fluffed a good chance to equalise. It impaired his performance. Years later, the Last of the Corinthians attested: 'I played against Taffy numerous times when he was wearing the colours of Blackburn, Stoke and Wales. He was always a niggling sod.'

Fixture 19: Saturday, 24 November 1962

EVERTON 3 SHEFFIELD UNITED 0

Vernon 2, Stevens

Attendance: 42,017

With Tottenham playing at Burnley, Harry Catterick's side sought to return to the top rung of the greasy ladder with a victory over a hard-working Sheffield United side that had finished fifth – directly behind the Merseysiders – in 1962. The Everton forwards started brightly. After keeper Alan Hodgkinson had denied them with a couple of fine saves, Everton took the lead in the tenth minute when Roy Vernon scored a sensational individual goal.

It was not before time. Michael Charters detailed arguably the finest goal of the Welshman's illustrious career: 'Roy Vernon, positioned on the halfway line, took a pass from Mick Meagan, beat Gerry Summers with a body swerve, took the ball on thirty yards via a corkscrew run, repeated the body swerve to get round centre-half Joe Shaw and company, and lashed a left-foot shot from twenty yards with impudent abandon which sent Alan Hodgkinson the wrong way.'

The crowd rose to applaud his brilliance in anticipation of a flood of goals. In response, the home captain made another exhilarating run. This time he sped past a couple of defenders before crossing for Dennis Stevens to nod the ball home. Then, without warning, the visitors took control of the game. Time and again they pierced the home defence. Fortunately, Everton endured through a mix of poor finishing by Bill Russell and Keith Kettleborough and some great goalkeeping. Gordon West was required to make numerous saves including one sensational dive at full stretch to deny Kettleborough.

The Blades continued to influence the tempo, much to the displeasure of the Goodison faithful. However, shortly after the Toffees got back into the game, they made it 3-0. In the 75th minute, Alex Young – who had been almost invisible until then – ghosted around three defenders into the area and crossed to Billy Bingham, who headed the ball back for his skipper to unleash a fierce shot not the net.

The Everton centre-forward volunteered: 'I preferred playing against big lumps like Bill Foulkes, Maurice Norman, Peter Swan and, of course, Ron Yeats than Joe Shaw. The veteran stood 5ft 8in but was a giant of a footballer. His lack of height was rarely an issue, owing to his intelligent positioning, superb anticipation, shrewd reading of the action and timely interceptions. How can he have played 700 times for the Blades and not receive the England cap he deserved?'

From Old Hall Street, Michael Charters thought that the Merseysiders were a little fortunate and summarised the hard-fought contest: 'With all the best will in the world, I don't see Everton winning many similar games by 3-0. The picture conjured by the scoreboard is one of a match handsomely and comfortably won. This was far from true. Indeed, I would say with little fear of contradiction that they will never have to fight harder to win by such a margin.'

Lucky or not, Harry Catterick prepared his team – both physically and mentally – for the most challenging fixture of the season: The Pride of London versus The Mersey Millionaires. The matchday programme for the Sheffield United clash November cautioned: 'Next Saturday we are at White Hart Lane. Our recent record there is wretched. We have been beaten in each of our last six trips during which we have scored six goals and conceded no less than 27. Surely the time is ripe for a change in our fortunes.'

The sojourn to the nation's capital was hailed as the most demanding engagement so far. The Everton side had remained unchanged for five games since the reinstatement of Roy Vernon, while the North London outfit was chocked full of stars such as Danny Blanchflower, Jimmy Greaves and Cliff Jones. With John White out of commission, Bill Nicholson decided to move Dave Mackay to inside-right.

Fixture 20: Saturday, 1 December 1962
TOTTENHAM HOTSPUR 0 EVERTON 0
Attendance: 60,626

The Londoners were odds-on to win the eagerly-awaited fixture as well as the league title. Not surprisingly, the turnstiles at White Hart Lane were closed before the kick-off, leaving many home and away supporters outside.

While thrills were abundant as the home team sought an early advantage, Spurs missed the magic of John White, also known as 'The Ghost of White Hart Lane'. The absence of his ball control, passing and tenacious runs off the ball diluted their pass-and-move style of play. While gilt-edged goalscoring opportunities were limited, many of the chances that were engineered by Danny Blanchflower and Dave Mackay were blocked by Brian Labone or wasted by winger Cliff Jones.

Beyond doubt, Everton gave their finest team display of the season, even better than those at Nottingham and Wolverhampton. The goalless scoreline confirmed that the defence was equipped to provide the sound foundations on which to build the club's hopes and bright future. Tottenham's attack – renowned for its goalscoring prowess with 86 goals amassed in 1959/60, 115 in 1960/61 and another 88 in 1961/62 – was dampened as Everton's half-backs and forwards hurried back to reinforce their rearguard. Although they pressured continually, the nearest Spurs came to scoring was when Jimmy Greaves struck the bar with Gordon West beaten.

During the final twenty minutes, the Londoners threw everyone into attack in search of a goal. Yet somehow Labone, Gabriel and their fellow defenders snuffed out the threat of Greaves and mopped up the other advances. In fact, the visitors came closest when Roy Vernon and Billy Bingham counter-attacked at pace. Alex Young outwitted Maurice Norman to get his head to the outside-right's cross only to direct it into the welcoming arms of Bill Brown.

Young acknowledged that he and his teammates had enjoyed two slices of good fortune before a ball had been kicked: 'Spurs were without John White and played Dave Mackay in his position. I had grown up with John in Edinburgh. He was an exceptional schoolboy who had matured into the heartbeat of Tottenham's famous double-winning side. Also, I had been a teammate of Dave at Hearts where we had broken the Old Firm's grip on Scottish football. In my eyes, after the loss of Duncan Edwards, they were the two most influential men in the British game. Nonetheless, we fully deserved our point. The celebrations at the end confirmed that the travelling fans knew it more than an ordinary 0-0 draw.'

Michael Charters quantified the club's target: 'There was not a man in the Everton party who did not hail the point as a victory. Harry Catterick believes that with thirty more points from the remaining 22 games the title will be his. Only four times in the sixteen post-war seasons have the champions boasted a total of more than sixty points. At White Hart Lane, Everton's objective was to take a point. At Goodison, they will want two, and it is unrealistic to suggest that those two may be more easily earned than was the one?'

The Toffees approached the halfway stage in true championship-winning form, that is 1.5 points per game. In the eyes of Harry Catterick, his side was just ten home wins and ten away draws from silverware.

With thirty points required, the club's next game featured another club from the nation's capital, West Ham United. Managed by Ron Greenwood, the Hammers were languishing in sixteenth place and should have been modest competition.

Fixture 21: Saturday, 8 December 1962
EVERTON 1 WEST HAM UNITED 1
Stevens
Attendance: 38,701

Once again, Harry Catterick was able to select an unchanged team in which five members – West, Labone, Harris, Stevens and Young – had been ever-presents. The encounter, however, was an enormous disappointment. The Toffees opened the scoring in the fifth minute when Ray Veall's angled shot had been half-cleared and Dennis Stevens seized the opportunity to slam the ball home in for his 100th league strike, a very respectable tally for an unsung hero. The Hammers, having rarely moved out of their own half, levelled through Peter Brabrook fifteen minutes later. It was a painful experience for Harris. A thunderbolt from Johnny Byrne had slammed into the Everton man's face and the West Ham winger – who Everton had failed to attract during the summer – knocked the rebound past West.

Predictably, West Ham threw a blanket over the game. Pinned back by the wave upon wave of royal blue shirts, the Hammers could not keep the ball long enough to build any sustained pressure. Roared on by the partisan crowd, the Toffees were thwarted by the breathtaking goalkeeping of Jim Standen coupled with the resolute tackling of Jack Burkett, Joe Kirkup, Ken Brown and captain Bobby Moore. Though Everton seemed likely to go ahead again, they were profligate with their chances and tended to get into one another's way in the crowded penalty area. Veall and Roy Vernon were constant threats, whereas Alex

177

Young scarcely put a foot right and missed a sitter in the dying seconds.

Local journalist Leslie Edwards defended the number nine: 'If the game were played another half-dozen times on the same pitch by the same men, Everton would probably win them all. The crowd's frustration exploded in the final sixty seconds. Veall struck a shot which beat Standen but hit the foot of an upright. The ball rolled slowly to Young who in less tense moments might have side-footed it gently over the line. Seeing perhaps the glory of a winning goal, he elected to hammer it high over the target from three yards to the most agonising moan I've ever heard.

'The final agony of his nightmare awakened him to the realisation that some of the slow-handclapping and jeering which broke out as the players left the field may have been for him. My reading of the demonstration was that, frustrated by Young's miss, the crowd was not letting West Ham leave before telling them what they thought of their slavish defensive tactics – which made the contest virtually a game of stormtroopers against the West Ham barricades for ninety minutes. If spectators were angry with Young, then I'm sorry and surprised. For a man who has given such pleasure to followers of Everton week after week, to be even mildly barracked because he has had one of those days is almost cruel.'

The race between Young and Vernon was no longer neck-and-neck. After 21 games, the club captain had taken a four-goal lead and improved his average to an impressive 0.65 goals per game. Their tallies, using the Scotsman's formula, were Young nine goals and Vernon six goals plus seven penalties. Barring injuries, it was likely that both men would exceed twenty goals for the season.

SECOND QUARTER REPORT: A POSITIVE AND ENTHUSIASTIC LEADER

	P	W	D	L
Home	6	4	2	0
Away	6	2	2	1

It had been a solid second quarter, involving six wins and one defeat. Young summarised the club's performance to date: 'Taffy and I were upset by the loss at Ewood Park due to a disputed last-minute penalty and weren't thrilled by the points dropped in the home draws to Villa due an error by Gordon West and to West Ham due to an inexplicable miss by me. We had thrown away three points in those games. But our worst performance was at Dunfermline – it was a wake-up call for Taffy to find his shooting boots.'

Gordon Watson reminisced about improving an already near-impervious defence: 'While we didn't have the firepower of Spurs, the coaching staff were pleased that Alex had been so productive – sometimes spectacular in front of goal – and Taffy had rediscovered his predatory instincts. Therefore, we worked extra hard at improving our defending, especially the understanding between young Westie and those in front of him at corners and free-kicks, and our away tactics in which both wingers were expected to graft and Alex and Taffy were required to drop deep. We understood that the single points earned on the road were just as important as the victories at home.'

Not for the first time that season, Brian Labone praised his fellow defenders who, given his way with words, he described as undaunted and stout-hearted: 'By December we had found our rhythm and deserved our lofty position. Alex Parker, Mick Meagan and friends had been almost watertight, allowing just 23 goals in 21 games. Better still, we had tamed Jimmy Greaves and Tottenham when it mattered.'

Tommy Eggleston was more troubled by the weather forecasts for horizontal rain, blizzards and freezing ground temperatures: 'With heavy pitches and the odd quagmire on the horizon, I was concerned about both the height and the depth of our squad. By and large, we were a team of dwarfs who could get stuck in the mud. Also, while we had been lucky with injuries, I feared we would suffer if anything happened to Gabriel, Stevens or Vernon – such as them being sent-off and suspended.'

PART 3:
ON SCHEDULE FOR GLORY

BY MID-DECEMBER, WHILE HARMONY HAD YET TO BE FULLY restored, things had improved in the dressing room. 'Victories smooth frictions and squabbles,' Brian Labone affirmed. 'We were enjoying our football and were confident that wouldn't lose another game thanks to our unsung defenders. Even though we were playing two games every week, no one complained of being tired. We were at the very top and, I can assure you, were going to take some shifting.'

	P	W	D	L	F/A	Pts
Everton	21	13	5	3	47/23	31
Burnley	21	12	5	4	43/30	29
Tottenham	21	12	4	5	62/30	28
Leicester	21	10	7	4	40/27	27

With the club's league position making heartening reading, the second half of the season kicked off with a challenging clash with Burnley. Having thrashed them by 3-1 at Turf Moor in August with goals from Billy Bingham, Roy Vernon and Alex Young, Everton expected to win in a hard-fought contest.

Fixture 22: Saturday, 15 December 1962
EVERTON 3 BURNLEY 1
Stevens, Vernon, Young
Attendance: 48,443

Undeterred by the vicious winds, both teams served up a game of extraordinary football. The Toffees were the better side throughout the first half, their smooth football inspired by terrier-like tackling courtesy of Jimmy Gabriel and Dennis Stevens.

Everton made their opponents look almost pedestrian, and though Burnley packed their defence, the hosts took a deserved early lead. Mick Meagan's deep cross was headed out by John Talbut to Dennis Stevens, who slammed the ball home from fifteen yards. Four minutes thereafter, Roy Vernon added a second.

This time Alex Parker slotted a precise pass to him, and even though keeper Adam Blacklaw stopped his shot, the Everton skipper made no mistake with his second attempt. Just three minutes on, Vernon challenged Talbut to Stevens's cross, forcing the pivot to clear to Alex Young, who dispatched a bullet header – with Dean-like power – from twelve yards.

Michael Charters was revitalised by the display. 'This was Everton at their finest,' he reported. 'They had the match good as won inside 25 minutes with three great goals, the last of which by Alex Young sent 48,000 people half-crazed with delight. It was the most dramatic sequel to a goal I have seen for many seasons, possibly because the man who scored was the one who walked off the pitch the week before to jeers and derision.'

Despite being 3-0 ahead, the first 45 minutes had not been one-way traffic. Gordon West was required to make two important saves and Burnley had wasted three other half-decent scoring opportunities. In the second half, the contest developed into an end-to end affair. Burnley exploited their pace on the flanks and looked dangerous every time they crossed the halfway line. Even though Meagan had the better of John Connelly and Brian Labone had tamed Andy Lochhead, the visitors launched wave upon wave of attacks and pulled one back on the hour. It was a sloppy goal in which West got both hands to Jimmy McIlroy's volley but could not keep it out. As Harry Potts's side continued to dominate, the old stadium held its breath. In the closing minutes, West made a full-length dive – his best of the match – to deny Connelly. The young custodian explained his earlier error. 'I made a pig's ear of Jimmy Mac's shot. It had much to do with me being frozen to the ground following a long period of inaction. Well, that's my excuse.'

The crowd were euphoric at the final whistle. Their favourites had defeated one of their closest challengers for the second time and had vaulted into a three-point lead over Tottenham. Leslie Edwards was somewhat over-optimistic in his matchday summary: 'Who can prevent Everton? Injuries aside, it looks as though it's all over bar the celebrating.'

Brian Harris called to mind the contribution of another unsung teammate: 'Dennis Stevens had hit a purple streak of five goals in seven matches. If it had been Taffy, someone – possibly Taffy himself – would have erected a statue in his honour. It was the type of goalscoring form Dennis had shown alongside Nat Lofthouse at Bolton. Though I never told him, I pitied Dennis. I know that Labby and Westie shared my feelings. He had the thankless task of replacing Bobby

Collins, the one-time idol of Gwladys Street. Sadly, the fans on the terraces barely warmed to him even during his purple patch. Inexplicably, these otherwise knowledgeable fans failed to appreciate the key goals he contributed, the miles he ran, the tackles he made and the interceptions he timed perfectly to keep our engine room ticking over. I suppose that I didn't object too much because if they hadn't been booing him then they would have been taunting me or Mick Meagan.'

Labone, meanwhile, confessed his dislike of playing against Burnley's Lochhead: 'He was a first-rate forward, especially when alongside Ray Pointer. Big, strong and super aggressive in the air and on the ground, his comb-over rivalled those of Bobby Charlton and that other Burnley hero, Ralph Coates. At corners, his split-ends would get in my eyes. Westie and I liked to refer to him as "Andy Blockhead of the Ugly XI".'

Fixture 23: Saturday, 22 December 1962
SHEFFIELD WEDNESDAY 2 EVERTON 2
Young, Megson (og)
Attendance: 26,280

Harry Catterick had set a realistic target of 27 points from the final twenty games for his side to capture the title, and where better to start than his old stomping ground in Sheffield? The treacherous Hillsborough pitch – rock-hard and covered in frost – made the ball bounce unevenly, caused the players to lose their footing on countless occasions and led to lots of silly mistakes in an entertaining game. Even though Gordon West was called on to make saves from Bronco Layne and John Quinn shortly after the kick-off, Everton enjoyed a spell of dominance during which they hit the woodwork twice. First, a Billy Bingham free-kick deceived keeper Ron Springett, who managed to scramble the ball onto the bar. Next, Roy Vernon headed a Bingham cross against the post.

Despite these encouraging efforts, the Toffees struggled to implement their short-passing game and Wednesday looked the more purposeful side. Through their approach, which involved long balls and first-time shooting, they took the lead after twenty minutes when Tony Kay set up Quinn, a £100 bargain from Prescot Cables, who lashed the ball into the net. Subsequent raids by the goalscorer and Layne continued to stretch their opponents. Indeed, the visitors were in danger of being overwhelmed and West was required to make a series of important saves to keep the scoreline down to 1-0 at the interval.

Given the vigorous tackling of the Wednesday defenders, very little had been seen of The Dynamic Duo or any of the other forwards. However, the Toffees equalised possibly against the run of play in the 51st minute. It was a scrambled affair in which Brian Harris pumped a free-kick into the area where Bingham miskicked but deflected the ball to Dennis Stevens, who made no mistake. The home defenders protested in vain that Bingham had been offside. Everton Football Club recorded it as an own goal by Don Megson. With Wednesday rattled, the visitors pushed forward in search of another and almost took the lead. Veall's shot was halted by Springett and Roy Vernon directed the rebound towards the goal, only for the goalkeeper to demonstrate his remarkable reflexes.

As the game progressed, Layne's strength and aerial power made Brian Labone struggle. No question, he was the most difficult striker that the royal blue defence had encountered, and following several close shaves he eventually found the net. Unchallenged in the 66th minute, he jumped high to head home Eddie Holliday's corner. With the Merseysiders looking well beaten, their players lost their composure. The Yorkshire crowd became incensed as Alex Young tangled with Tom McAnearney, Stevens with Kay and Bingham with Megson. During a lull in these hostilities, Harris was booked. His crime? Kicking the ball away.

Then four minutes from time, the Toffees equalised. The move involved Jimmy Gabriel driving forward some forty yards before feeding Vernon. Although Springett saved the Welshman's shot, Young put the ball into the net and reduced Hillsborough to silence. Even though Bingham and Vernon almost sneaked goals in the last minute, the home team had been unlucky not to win. Nonetheless, Catterick's new club remained at the top with 34 points from 23 matches.

THE BIG FREEZE

What could stop them? Cue the Arctic weather of 1963 which boasted treacherous blizzards, gale force winds and heavy snowfalls. In one of the most ferociously cold winters on record, about six inches of snow fell in Liverpool city centre on Christmas Day and, with the freezing temperatures, lasted for months.

The football calendar was ravaged, so much so that Everton didn't play a league game for 52 days and didn't play on home turf for over ten weeks. The postponed fixtures were the homes games with Arsenal, Bolton and Fulham and the trips to

Anfield, Filbert Street, Highbury, Villa Park and The Hawthorns. The lack of matches wreaked havoc with the football pools, so Vernons, Zetters and Littlewoods introduced a Pools Panel to predict the outcomes of postponements. It comprised Ted Drake, Tom Finney, George Young, referee Arthur Ellis and Tommy Lawton.

The weather, however, didn't prevent the club from progressing through the third and fourth rounds of the FA Cup by winning their rescheduled games at Barnsley and Swindon. On 15 January, Everton conquered the Yorkshire club by 3-0 thanks to goals by Brian Harris, Dennis Stevens and Roy Vernon. The conditions were frigid. In fact, only twenty miles from Oakwell, Halifax Town had turned the Shay into a public ice rink. A fortnight on, they advanced past Swindon at the County Ground by 5-1 with Billy Bingham, Jimmy Gabriel and Johnny Morrissey adding to the brace from their captain.

With the league match at The Hawthorns called off, Harry Catterick fielded his first team in the Central League fixture with Derby County on 16 February. They won 4-0 with goals from Stevens, Gabriel, Morrissey and Alex Young in front of a crowd of 13,000. On Monday 4 March, the club beat Kilmarnock at home by 4-1 in friendly arranged to improve fitness. A goal from Young plus a penalty by you know who were augmented by a couple of strikes from new boy Alex Scott.

In fact, the club made two massive signings during the Big Freeze. In late December, Harry Catterick added Tony Kay from Sheffield Wednesday for £60,000, then the biggest transfer fee for a British footballer. The left-half divulged: 'I had read about Everton's interest in the Sunday papers. Then one morning, Vic Buckingham informed me that my old boss was waiting in the Hillsborough boardroom. Obviously, Harry wanted to strengthen his push for the crown. He got my attention with a staggering offer of double my wages plus a crowd bonus and a hefty signing bonus. And true to his word, after my first week in which we played two games I was paid £150. Of course, he knew all about my abilities as a team leader. In the longer-term, Harry wanted me to replace Taffy as team captain. But in the short-term, he asked me to sort out the defence, which was already the best in the land. Although Everton had the Scottish granite of Jimmy Gabriel, he wanted some Sheffield steel forged with a bit of the devil.'

Inevitably, Harris submitted a transfer request after learning of the deal. Back in 2002, ironically while in the company of his nemesis at the annual Hall of Fame celebrations, he let slip: 'I was unaware that the Yorkshireman had joined us until he showed up at training. I didn't feel let down by the boss – I felt betrayed. I had been an ever-present and mentioned in dispatches on several occasions. I could think of other positions that needed strengthening before mine. As for my transfer request, West Brom bid £25,000 but the transaction didn't proceed. For one reason or another, I struggled to get along with Roy. Things changed for the worse after I discovered that he had fingered me as a weak link. It may have been in response to a request from the Harry Catterick, but I understand that he recommended that the manager replace me with either Ronnie Clayton – his old pal at Blackburn – or Terry Hennessey – his new pal in the Wales international side. I wasn't pleased. After all I had battled fiercely with Mick Meagan for six or more years to secure the number six jersey and thought I deserved a decent run in the first team.

'Of course, it transpired that the boss ignored Roy Vernon's inputs and lured his own favourite from his old club, Tony Kay. Ironically, Roy, Tony and Mick had departed within a couple of seasons and, after much tongue-biting, I was on my way to FA Cup glory at Wembley.' He added: 'At times, I found Tony's self-confidence overbearing. He was a tremendous footballer who sadly wasted his talent and cost the club a massive transfer fee. Both the player and the club were harshly punished for an error of judgement elsewhere.'

Tommy Eggleston had his own thoughts about the new addition: 'Harry and I kept a list of the stars we would like to sign should they ever become available. Our targets included the likes of Denis Law, Ray Wilson and Gordon Banks. In our eyes there was only one candidate for the left-half position. Tony possessed the type of physical and mental toughness around which we could build a football dynasty like Herbert Chapman's Arsenal. Of course, he was a supremely talented footballer who read the game with the maturity of a 600-game veteran but, in my eyes, his level of fitness made him extra-special. As a trainer, I pushed my players hard – so hard that the weekend matches were pleasant relief from their weekday graft. Every now and then I worked them to exhaustion with sprints up and down the sand dunes at Ainsdale. Every one of them would be gasping for oxygen – except Tony. He would pound those dunes until the sand got tired.'

The second big signing was a right-winger. In mid-January, Catterick sought to sign Barrie Jones. He offered £45,000, which would have been a British record fee for a 21-year-old. However, Swansea were not prepared to deal. So, in early February, he redirected his focus towards a speedster hailed as one of the greatest wide-men in Scottish history. At the time of his boisterous induction into Gwladys Street's Hall of Fame, Alex Scott professed to co-author David France: 'After eight years in the first team, Rangers manager Scot Symon decided it was time for me to move on. Aye, that's the nature of the professional game. As a teenager, I had replaced Willie Waddell and it was time for eighteen-year-old Willie Henderson to replace me. Anyway, I was flattered by the interest of both Tottenham and Everton. Before I made up my mind, I talked to Alex Parker, who had played for Falkirk, my hometown club. He claimed that Goodison was the closest thing to Ibrox in England and added that Merseyside would be a home from home. There was George Thomson, Jimmy Gabriel and Alex Young as well as Ian St John, Ron Yeats and Willie Stevenson across Stanley Park. He added that while London was the UK's capital, Liverpool was the new centre of the universe.'[2]

So, for a mere outlay of £40,000, Catterick acquired the blue lightening he had been seeking for too many months. Scott recalled his first morning at Bellefield: 'Knowing that I had won four Scottish crowns at Rangers and a dozen caps for Scotland, Taffy Vernon shook my hand and said: "Welcome to the big time!"'[2]

To finance these initiatives, John Moores made a further loan of £100,000 and the club made it known that it was prepared to offload one of Thomson or Parker, one of Morrissey or Veall and either one of Webber or Wignall to raise funds. The biggest interest was shown in Wignall, who was averaging almost one goal per game in the reserves. However, Fulham's bid of £20,000 was rejected.

Severe weather had decimated the football calendar, and during the hiatus the Merseyside club had slipped into second place behind Tottenham, just above Leicester. When the thaw finally arrived in mid-February, a huge backlog of fixtures had to be dealt with. The club's first league outing in months was a tough one at Filbert Street.

Fixture 24: Tuesday, 12 February 1963

Postponed from 19 January 1963

LEICESTER CITY 3 EVERTON 1

Vernon

Attendance: 35,743

Without question, inactivity had affected Everton's form and rhythm when the programme resumed. It was a long, cold and sobering evening for Harry Catterick.

Even with the additions of Kay and Scott and the return of Morrissey, his side was outplayed and over-run by their rampant rivals. The Foxes – who had completed six games during Everton's enforced period of inactivity – adapted expertly to the peat-covered, yet bone-hard pitch and the Merseysiders were fortunate not to trail by more than a two-goal margin at the break. Fundamentally, the half-backs struggled to subdue Davie Gibson and Frank McLintock, whose accurate passes had allowed their forwards to sweep through the Everton rearguard seemingly at will. With Alex Parker and Mick Meagan struggling and Brian Labone less commanding than usual, the Leicester attackers – evidently much fitter – were dominant. They bombarded the goalmouth with crosses and were unlucky that Gordon West had one of his finest games. Still, Ken Keyworth netted a cracker after fifteen minutes and Mike Stringfellow added another six minutes on. There could have been many more.

By comparison, Everton laboured, and their short passes were infective in the less-than-ideal conditions. The Mersey Millionaires were impotent upfront, where Alex Young and Dennis Stevens were shackled by Ian King and Colin Appleton. And as for Alex Scott on his debut, he never got into his stride. Indeed, Roy Vernon was the only forward to worry the home fortifications. Unfortunately, he was required to spend too much time helping his overtaxed defenders.

Years later, Billy Bingham mulled over his playing days in the royal blue and white of Everton as well as the vaunted arrival of Flying Scotsman: 'My memory isn't what it used to be, but I do remember my transfer shortly after Mickey Lill had broken his leg. It was a dream to play in the same side as Collins, Young and Vernon and I like to think that I contributed my fair share of goals and what are now termed "assists". For me, turning out for Everton at Goodison Park comes second only to representing Northern Ireland at Windsor Park. Of course, football is a ruthless business. We were top of the heap heading towards glory when I was replaced by Alex Scott. Let's say that I wasn't too pleased.'

Clearly, Horace Yates admired the Leicester side: 'Wingers Howard Riley and Mike Stringfellow bubbled and fizzled like effervescent champagne. In the second half, the hosts demonstrated their dominance when Graham Cross hammered a third past Gordon West in the 63rd minute. Roy Vernon responded by nabbing a consolation goal. His fifteenth goal of the season ignited a modest fightback during the last twenty minutes. During that period, Jimmy Gabriel ran himself into the ground in an unremitting effort to rally his teammates, sadly to no avail. As for the other expensive recruit, Tony Kay worked hard and tackled his foes with intensity. Perhaps too much vigour because he was booed by the Filbert Street faithful every time he touched the ball.'

Far from being impressed, he added: 'The worst mauling I have seen this season came at the hands of a workmanlike, talented and efficient side.' The matchday programme published eleven days later February admitted: 'Our hopes took a blow. No excuses, Leicester are a fine team and deserved their success. The home side could have scored more than three goals.'

That week, the city of Liverpool became the cultural centre of the world when the Beatles topped the charts in the United Kingdom with 'Please Please Me'. Unfortunately, the Toffees no longer topped the table and Harry Catterick needed to re-establish his side's lofty ambitions. Unfortunately, the next visitors were unlikely to provide him any favours.

	P	W	D	L	F/A	Pts
Tottenham	25	15	5	5	75/34	35
Everton	**24**	**14**	**6**	**4**	**53/29**	**34**
Leicester	25	13	7	5	52/32	33
Burnley	23	13	5	5	48/33	31

When competitive league football returned for first time since mid-December, it became evident that Harry Catterick's lightweights would continue to struggle on soft sandy pitches. Certainly, they had lost their rhythm and their passing was not as fluid as that exhibited before Christmas.

Fixture 25: Saturday, 23 February 1963
EVERTON 0 WOLVERHAMPTON WANDERERS 0
Attendance: 62,616

While many of the men in the royal blue looked a shade rusty, Wolves were well-organised and disciplined. Their big defenders became increasingly influential as the game progressed. In particular, Ron Flowers excelled at breaking up attacks. He was aided by right-half John Kirkham, who shackled Roy Vernon, while full-backs George Showell and Bobby Thomson contained Derek Temple – who was deputising for the injured Alex Scott – and Johnny Morrissey.

Alex Young, unlike the rest of Everton's forward line, was in great form. His artistry mesmerised David Woodfield throughout the encounter. In addition to forcing three or four saves from Fred Davies, he created a dozen or more scoring chances for Dennis Stevens, Temple, Morrissey and Vernon. Michael Charters deliberated: 'Unfortunately, the skipper had one of those days when his jinking, wheeling, side-stepping, dribbles were gobbled up by the massively effective Wolves tackling.' The ball didn't run kindly for the other Toffees either and the closest they came to breaking the deadlock is when Tony Kay and Jimmy Gabriel combined to set up Young. The centre-forward's crisp shot seemed to have got past Davies but the Wolverhampton keeper flung himself across the goal to halt the ball and Showell cleared off the line.

On the rare occasions that Wolves advanced, they succeeded in exposing the home defenders as being short of match practice. In particular, Brian Labone was uncertain and caught dithering on more than one occasion. Although Gordon West was inactive for much of the game, he was required to produce two important saves to thwart Alan Hinton and Barry Stobart. Following a tackle with Kirkham, Gabriel limped through the proceedings. As a result, the middle of the park was bossed by Tony Kay whose energy, drive, reading of the game and astute use of ball allowed Everton to launch waves of attacks. The expensive acquisition didn't put a foot wrong.

In the final twenty minutes, the Toffees intensified their search for a winner. One excellent interchange between Vernon and Young gave the club captain a tremendous opportunity. Unfortunately, his instant shot grazed the post. Next the huge crowd thought that the home side had been awarded a penalty when Flowers brought down Morrissey, but the referee turned aside all appeals. Oddly, the club had been bestowed and converted seven penalties in their first fourteen league games but none during their last eleven fixtures.

Despite the valiant efforts of Kay and Young, the team's overall display was disappointing. It was the first time that Everton had failed to score at home that season. Though the club dropped into third place, Michael Charters remained optimistic: 'The defeat at Filbert Street – probably the best side in the land at the moment – and this home draw does not mean that vast cracks have appeared in the Everton armour. There is still a long way to go.'

Kay confessed that his first two league games didn't go as he had hoped: 'We were beaten – make that well beaten – at Leicester, who were lying third, and then drew at home to Wolves, who were also in the top six, in front of a massive yet frustrated crowd. Even though I did okay in the challenging conditions, I was gutted at the loss of three points. Mind you, I was not as upset as Harry Catterick and Tommy Eggleston.'

Fixture 26: Saturday, 9 March 1963
EVERTON 2 NOTTINGHAM FOREST 0
Parker, Young

Attendance: 45,068

Cue a visit from Forest, who appeared less intimidated by the conditions underfoot than their foes. The horizontal rains and strong swirling winds, coupled with the ground, heavy from the thaw, were not conducive to the type of football that Vernon and his colleagues liked to play. Forest defended from the start. Masterminded by manager Andy Beattie, their negative approach with a thick curtain of defenders involved centre-forward Peter Hindley – an eighteen-year-old making his debut – plus pivot Bob McKinlay, who spent the whole afternoon shadowing Alex Young in a poor, somewhat contentious, game with a satisfactory ending.

Young and Alex Parker netted in the victory that gave Everton 37 points from 26 outings. In the *Liverpool Echo*, Leslie Edwards mused: 'It is up to the sides faced by such defence in depth to find the answer to the problem. These negative tactics didn't work, and Forest forfeited two goals. In fact, it could have been five because Everton thumped the woodwork through Dennis Stevens twice and Young. Keeper Peter Grummitt made some stunning saves, but his mistakes contributed to both goals. First, he dropped Alex Parker's lob at the feet of Young in the twelfth minute. Then an hour later, he could not hold Parker's potent shot and the rebound was knocked over the line by Jimmy Gabriel [the club awarded the goal to Parker]. The right-half had been first rate throughout the match. Also, Mick Meagan – arguably the most consistent full-back on the club's books – demonstrated his intelligent use of the ball.'

While Tony Kay's power and skills caught the imagination of the royal blue faithful, Alex Scott amazed them with his blistering speed by running on to some judicious passes placed well ahead of him. During the following weekend, the club was eliminated from the FA Cup in a fifth-round tie at Upton Park via a hotly disputed penalty on the hour. The spot kick was awarded for a foul by Dennis Stevens on Bobby Moore. Most observers thought it was a free-kick to Everton.

The incident resulted in fights on the terraces. 'It was the worst decision I have ever seen,' Michael Charters claimed 'A draw would have been a fair outcome of the bruising struggle which masqueraded as a football match.'

Tony Onslow remembered the eight-minute penalty kick as if it was yesterday: 'After Dennis Stevens went toe-to-toe with Bobby Moore, the referee pointed to the spot – because it was Bobby Moore, the darling of the national media. Instantly, a shower of empty Guinness bottles – which had been sold from wooden sheds around Upton Park – rained down onto the pitch and a couple of Blues invaded the proceedings. It took Budgie Byrne eight minutes to take the kick. As cool as anything, he allowed us to concentrate on the league without distraction.'

Now that chairman John Moores's dream of a Spurs-like double was over for another season, the club focussed on winning the league title. Now trailing both Leicester and Tottenham, the pressure had got to the players, who were barely recognisable from the ones that had headed the table before Arctic conditions had enveloped the country. Improved results were required and where better to start than the reigning champions at Portman Road?

It turned out to be one of the key matches of the 1962/63 season. Michael Charters provided some insight: 'A talk by Harry Catterick in their hotel before the game coupled with a further confidence booster by John Moores in the dressing had much to do with the team finding its form for a first-class victory at Ipswich. The chairman reminded his players that they had been bought with the objective of playing attractive football. He told them to enjoy their football instead of worrying about results.'

Fixture 27: Tuesday, 19 March 1963

Postponed from 16 March 1963

IPSWICH TOWN 0 EVERTON 3

Young 2, Elsworthy (og)

Attendance: 19,712

It was an outstanding team performance in which Jimmy Gabriel and Tony Kay dictated the tempo of the game. In fact, every player moved the ball with speed and precision and in the eyes of Michael Charters 'reduced Ipswich to a struggling rabble long before the end'.

For once, the Toffees took control from the outset. After four minutes, Kay's powerful shot deceived Roy Bailey. The goalkeeper turned the ball onto the crossbar and, as the ball bounced down, Young flung himself full-length to head it into the net. The second goal was less spectacular. The Ipswich defenders had been unable to cope with the pace and power of Alex Scott. The outside-right hit a low centre into the goalmouth, which was turned into his own net by John Elsworthy. Then without delay, Roy Vernon fed Young who hit the target with a finely angled shot.

With great enthusiasm, Michael Charters penned: 'Everton might have doubled their lead for they were too fast and too good for opponents who were hurried into making mistake after mistake.' Brian Labone harked back to the fixture with guarded pride: 'Our defending was immaculate that day. More than anything, I remember the bookings. George Thomson, who had deputised for Mick Meagan, was distraught at being cautioned for the very first time in his career. His overreaction had much to do with his ongoing private troubles off the pitch. While his tackle on Roy Stephenson looked fair to me, Gabby had no complaints. After Dermot Curtis had fouled him, our number four retaliated in a biblical manner.'

Back to winning ways. The comfortable victory over Ipswich increased the pressure on the two leaders.

	P	W	D	L	F/A	Pts
Tottenham	29	19	5	5	86/39	43
Leicester	29	17	7	5	61/32	41
Everton	**27**	**16**	**7**	**4**	**58/29**	**39**
Wolverhampton	28	13	7	8	68/35	33

Fixture 28: Saturday, 23 March 1963

EVERTON 2 MANCHESTER CITY 1

Young, Morrissey

Attendance: 46,101

Four days later, Everton returned to their best form and thrashed Manchester City. The one-sidedness of the match was so extreme that City defended with all eleven of their players in their own half as the home side concentrated on improving their goal-average. Leslie Edwards summarised the contest: 'One of the most extraordinary matches ever seen – that's putting it mildly – is the most apt description of the contest in which Everton beat City by 2-1. With most of the action in the visitor's half, the game was an incessant battle between the royal blue forwards and the City defenders, whose covering of each other as well as keeper Harry Dowd was nothing short of heroic.'

Incredibly, Dave Wagstaffe shocked Goodison by giving City the lead after fifteen minutes with a cross that Gordon West should have reached. Jolted into action, Alex Young restored parity when he out-jumped both Bill Leivers and Dowd to Roy Vernon's cross to head a fabulous goal.

The contest became even more one-sided when Barrie Betts, City's influential captain, was stretchered from the field. Consequently, City faced tidal waves of fury, with Everton zoning in on Dowd's goal. After 62 minutes, Johnny Morrissey cut inside John Benson. His initial fierce shot was headed out by Leivers to the left-winger who – with great composure – volleyed the rebound home.

Roared on by the vociferous crowd, Catterick's side continued to monopolise possession. They out-thought and out-fought their opponents, so much so that Leslie Edwards acclaimed: 'In Gabriel and Kay, Everton have two of the most tenacious, hard-tackling half-backs in the game but whether they will always have a man in the middle as lenient as Mr Jennings of Stourbridge is open to more doubt. Dowd made dozens of saves – sometimes miraculously – whereas Stevens, Young and Vernon missed dozens of opportunities – sometimes miraculously.' Michael Charters singled out the Welshman: 'He seems to have lost his propensity for the big, well-aimed shot.'

The competition between Vernon and Young for the crown of 'Goodison Goal King' was turning in favour of the Scotsman. More important, both were exceeding the standard of one goal every two appearances. After 28 league games – two-thirds of the season – the status was Young fifteen goals and Vernon eight goals plus seven penalties.

Given that their opponents were down to ten men for most of the match, the games at Highbury and Hillsborough would provide a more reliable indication of whether the Toffees could maintain their challenge for the title. Rearranged games were coming every few days. The next one was in the nation's capital, where the Toffees had played four times without a win that season.

Fixture 29: Tuesday, 26 March 1963

Postponed from 29 December 1962

ARSENAL 4 EVERTON 3

Kay, Vernon, Young

Attendance:38,061

It turned out to be a seven-goal cracker in which the quality of football was a joy to watch. 'We will play much worse than we did tonight and win,' concluded Harry Catterick. 'It was a terrific game, a thrill from start to finish, but I feel that a draw would have been the ideal result.' The line-up remained unchanged except that Billy Bingham was drafted into the team to replace Alex Scott, who had a touch of flu. Unfortunately, the right flank of Alex Parker and Bingham was a sluggish weakness which Arsenal – managed by Billy Wright and aided by Les Shannon – exploited. So much so that the strongest defence in the First Division – who had previously let in just 30 goals in 28 league games – conceded four goals in one afternoon. Unfortunately, two goals were a direct result of the shortcomings of Gordon West.

Still, Gordon Watson retained his confidence in the nineteen-year-old novice: 'Westie was very young. The manager had been patient, but his mistakes were costing us sloppy goals and precious points. To avoid playing Albert Dunlop, his answer was the introduction of extra training sessions during which Alex Parker and I crossed balls to the youngster under the aerial challenges from our two biggest brutes, Frank Wignall and George Heslop. We didn't have a specialised coach, but Ron Lewin had kept goal for Gillingham and insisted on sharing his know-how with the most expensive goalkeeper in the world. My approach to repairing his confidence was different. I would put an arm around Westie and remind him that Gwladys Street loved him.'

Often, when one team advanced, the other responded. The timeline of the ebb and flow of the goal activity at Highbury:

5 minutes: Jimmy Gabriel crosses accurately for Tony Kay to bag his first goal for his new club with a well-struck drive: 0-1.

9 minutes: A terrible error of judgement by Gordon West allows inside-left Geoff Strong to level: 1-1.

28 minutes: Roy Vernon nets a beauty past Jack McClelland, leaving the home keeper motionless: 1-2.

34 minutes: Centre-forward Joe Baker scores against the run of play: 2-2.

46 minutes: Shortly after the resumption, Johnny MacLeod hammers home a cross from left-winger Alan Skirton: 3-2.

69 minutes: Alex Young shoulder-charges Laurie Brown off the ball to make it 3-3.

70 minutes: Skirton scores West mishandles MacLeod's corner 4-3.

With Young tormenting the home rearguard, the visitors storm forward in search of a fourth goal and both Johnny Morrissey and Jimmy Gabriel come close during the final fifteen minutes.

It wasn't to be enough. Evidently, Everton had a London bogey. They had now played five games in the nation's capital during the 1962/63 season without a win. In fact, they have experienced twelve defeats and three draws in their last sixteen games there. That solo triumph was against the Gunners in May 1962.

In the 60s and 70s, Everton managers were required to present team reports to the club's directors after every fixture. In one of the few to have survived, Harry Catterick summarised his observations at Highbury: 'Notwithstanding Bingham's very poor performance, this was one of our best forward displays. Only when our wing-halves were forced to cover for our slow full-backs did Arsenal start to dictate play. However, it was West's two mistakes that cost us the points we deserved.' Catterick's player ratings at Highbury were:

West   *Made several excellent saves but his two mistakes cost us two goals.* **5/10**

Parker   *Worst defender. Easily beaten for speed by his wingman and hesitant in the tackle.* **3/10**

Thomson   *Struggled for speed and was frequently outpaced by his wingman.* **5/10**

Gabriel   *Played well and gave good support to his forwards until he had to cover for Parker.* **8/10**

Labone   *Completely dominated the centre and used the ball well.* **8/10**

Kay   *Tackled and covered for Thomson and at times Parker. Scored a brilliant goal and gave excellent support to his forwards.* **9/10**

Bingham	*Worst performance. Lacked determination, speed and ability to beat even one man.* **3/10**
Stevens	*Did a sound steady job switching defence onto attack to good effect.* **7/10**
Young	*One of his best games. Good ball control. Worked and fought hard throughout. Took his goal well.* **8/10**
Vernon	*Scored an excellent goal and improved on recent games. Faded in last half-hour.* **7/10**
Morrissey	*Raided and beat his man repeatedly. Had several excellent shots saved.* **8/10**

As for the title race? Everton had fallen three points behind Tottenham with one match in hand. Harry Catterick and his men would have to pull out something special in the tougher games at the end of the campaign.

David France attended the match and remembered his father's flawed prediction: 'By age fourteen, I was hitchhiking to games but wasn't allowed to venture as far as London. Therefore, I was thrilled when my father took me to Highbury. Even though Evertonians were associated with the vandalism of trains, we saw nothing untoward that day. It was an exciting end-to-end match and we were unlucky not to get a point.

On the train home, we talked about strengthening the team. I proposed signing Ray Wilson and Gordon Banks. Ironically, Everton did recruit the world-class left-back in 1964 and agreed to sign the world-class shot-stopper. How Harry Catterick must have regretted the untimely leak to the press that nixed the acquisition? My father, who claimed to know much more about these things, proposed to move Alex Young – who had torn Arsenal apart – to outside-right and buy a big swashbuckling centre-forward, a new Tommy Lawton. He would say: "We'll win nowt with scrawny midgets like Vernon and Young."' The Toffees were struggling on heavy pitches but sought to bounce back at Sheffield. The Bramall Lane turf, which was practically void of grass, became less friendly thanks to the continuous drizzle. Also, the weather contributed to the modest gate – the lowest league crowd for an Everton match during the 1962/63 season – even below that recorded at Leyton Orient.

Fixture 30: Saturday, 30 March 1963

SHEFFIELD UNITED 2 EVERTON 1

Scott

Attendance: 21,839

The Blades started brightly. In their initial move – involving Brian Richardson, Derek Pace and Len Allchurch – they got their foes into a tangle. Gordon West appeared nervous and helpless. First, he was deceived by a deep cross from Billy Hodgson which rattled his crossbar. Next, he dropped a free-kick by Cec Coldwell. However, the goalkeeper improved and was able to block another effort from Hodgson. Pace thought he had scored when he chipped the rebound towards an empty net, but West recovered to punch the it to safety.

Subsequently, the contest deteriorated into a defensive scrap, with Joe Shaw and Brian Labone marshalling their respective troops effectively. With Roy Vernon sluggish and Alex Young completely innocuous, the forward-line could make no headway against the home offside trap. Their Sheffield counterparts had been significantly overhauled since their defeat at Goodison in November but were similarly ineffective until they took the lead after seventy minutes due to another goalkeeping blunder. This time, Gerry Summers pumped the ball high into the Yorkshire air. West came out to punch – possibly impeded by his own centre-half – and failed miserably. The ball dropped to Allchurch, who scored with ease. The home side added a second ten minutes later when Hodgson controlled a long pass from Summers, swerved around Alex Parker and hit his shot under the goalkeeper's advancing body. Finally, the visitors ventured forward, and Alex Scott reduced the arrears to 2-1 with three minutes remaining. It was a well-work move. From the right-winger's corner-kick, Dennis Stevens and Parker combined to enable Scott to beat Alan Hodgkinson.

The consolation goal failed to lift the gloom. Michael Charters summarised the excursion to Yorkshire: 'This was one of the most disappointing performances. The forwards must find greater penetration and thrust down the middle if they are to overhaul the leaders. Vernon was out of touch. Several times, Young made what seemed to be the lethal pass to him only for Joe Shaw to intercept.'

Tony Kay called to mind the visit to the city of his birth: 'That game in Sheffield was the turning point. We had lost three and drawn another of my first seven games and been knocked out of the FA Cup. But after the loss at Bramall Lane, we regrouped and went on an unbeaten run of twelve games until the end of the season. We grew in confidence and played some delightful football.'

Brian Labone was disappointed by the frequency of goalkeeping errors but refused to criticise his friend: 'As you know, the rule of thumb is win at home, draw away and we continued to slip below our points target. In my eyes, the points dropped at home to Liverpool, Villa, West Ham, Wolves had been just as damaging as the losses at Fulham, Orient, Blackburn, Leicester, Arsenal and, of course, Westie's performance at Sheffield United.'

Given Harry Catterick's overall target was sixty points, his team needed to earn nineteen points from the final twelve games – six at home, six away – in order to secure the glittering prize. Even though he made no changes to the line-up to face Villa, his side's performance was unrecognisable from that of disjointed outfit which had lost only two days earlier.

Fixture 31: Monday, 1 April 1963

ASTON VILLA 0 EVERTON 2

Gabriel, Young

Attendance: 31,377

His stars played like a side worthy of the 1962/63 crown. In addition to locking up the vital points, their first-class display sent out a warning to their rivals – the winter was over and Everton were back. Roy Vernon and Alex Young played with sizzling skill, dash and determination. If the scrawny inside-left excelled by recapturing his old form of fighting through tackles, making ground at speed and distributing the ball well, then his striking partner was even better. Harry Catterick was impressed by Young's contributions: 'One of the finest centre-forward exhibitions I have ever seen.' Michael Charters echoed the manager's glowing assessment: 'Alex Young gave a display of pure genius. He ran John Sleeuwenhoek ragged. He soared above him in the air, never failed to beat him on the ground and even had the home crowd applauding some of his exquisite touches.'

While the Toffees had the better of the early exchanges, the game was transformed following an injury to Alan Deakin which reduced Villa to ten men around the half-hour mark. This advantage allowed Jimmy Gabriel, Tony Kay and Dennis Stevens to support Young in dominating the proceedings. Despite their intensive pressure, the opening goal didn't arrive until the 48th minute via a superb move involving Scott, Roy Vernon and John Morrissey. The left-winger's perfect cross was headed down expertly by Young under John Gavan. The number nine was sensational as Everton sought to secure both points. His sublime skills provided numerous opportunities for Johnny Morrissey and others and he would have had a hat-trick but for brilliant goalkeeping. Though the visitors had the ball in the net in the 68th minute when Roy Vernon headed home following good work by Morrissey – yes, another headed goal – the linesman ruled the winger offside. Eventually, the Toffees clinched the points with a cracker in the last minute when the canny captain touched a free-kick to Gabriel who launched a missile.

Hopefully, Catterick's stars had rediscovered their best form and were ready to tackle the final eleven games of the campaign.

THIRD QUARTER REPORT: MUST TRY HARDER TO OVERCOME SETBACKS

	P	W	D	L
Home	4	3	1	0
Away	6	2	1	3

Unlike some of their rivals, Everton had floundered during the winter months. Through a handful of home draws and away defeats, Catterick's men had gathered only twelve points from ten games and forfeited their position at the top. In fact, they were trailing Tottenham by four points with a game in hand.

	P	W	D	L	F/A	Pts
Tottenham	32	20	7	5	91/42	47
Leicester	31	17	9	5	63/34	43
Everton	**31**	**18**	**7**	**6**	**66/36**	**43**
Burnley	30	15	8	7	57/41	38

The heavy pitches hadn't been friendly to their style of football. In addition, they had struggled with the more direct approach favoured by their more muscular foes. Brian Labone noted: 'Except for Westie, Gabby and me, we were a team of midgets. While we had been unstoppable on the manicured bowling greens of 1962, we were too easily dispossessed and struggled to deliver our short passing game on the grassless quagmires of 1963. Also, when it came to taking a more direct approach, we were limited to the aerial ability of Alex, supported by Gabby. Even though they could look after themselves, there was only so much that they could do against big strapping defenders, or yard-dogs, as I often referred to them.'

Alex Young praised the shrewd judgement of his manager and lauded the addition of Tony Kay: 'He was the man of the match in every game we didn't win. During the first half of the season, especially in the aftermath of the Goodison derby, I would complain to Labby that I was being kicked black and blue by defenders while he treated their forwards like gentlemen. That changed with the arrival of Tony. While I still got lumps kicked off me, it was reassuring to know that life was just as painful for opponents. Tony was an astute addition – one of the club's greatest ever signings. Impressed by the recruit, Young added: 'Tony was a confident footballer. He was an arrogant so and so. Because of his previous relationship with the boss, he was treated with some suspicion in the dressing room. Not everyone appreciated his swagger. In contrast, Taffy and I welcomed him like a long-lost brother because he would kick the enemy before it had time to kick us. More than our minder, he was a top-class footballer. One of the very best of his era.'

As for the race contest between the royal blue number nine and number ten? After 31 games, Alex Young had moved ahead. Young seventeen goals and Vernon nine goals plus seven penalties. The Scotsman had maintained his consistency at 0.55 goals per game, whereas Vernon had misplaced his shooting boots during the Arctic winter. Also, the awards of penalties had dried up.

PART 4:
LONG RUN-IN

WITH ONLY ELEVEN GAMES TO PLAY, COACH GORDON WATSON looked forward to an exciting run-in: 'I was confident that we would succeed as long as our key players stayed injury free, namely – in no particular order – Gabriel, Labone, Kay, Stevens, Young, Vernon. Thanks to Labby, we had exceptional fortifications. Also, we had the fittest and most industrious midfield in the land, and upfront we had two expert sharp-shooters who were guaranteed to contribute at least one goal per game between them. In secret and away from the prying eyes of the boss, Tommy Eggleston and I liked to study the remaining fixtures and predict the outcomes. Often, we concurred that we had a relatively easy run-in against moderate sides not involved in relegation battles. There were three potential banana skins – the Anfield Road derby, the visit of the Gunners and the long-awaited showdown with Spurs. The press and the fans continued to treat the latter as the title-decider, whereas we focused on the four matches to be played in the eight days between 13 and 20 April. Wins at Bloomfield Road, against Spurs at Goodison and against Birmingham at home and away and we would be in great shape.'

Fixture 32: Saturday, 6 April 1963

EVERTON 0 BLACKBURN ROVERS 0

Attendance: 39,790

The following weekend, Roy Vernon welcomed his former teammates in search of retribution for the infamous capitulation at Ewood Park in November. Facing a troublesome wind, Blackburn adopted ultra-defensive tactics which allowed their hosts to attack continuously. With their forwards supporting their resolute defenders, Matt Woods, Ronnie Clayton and Keith Newton appeared unruffled. Their well-rehearsed offside tactics were effective, especially in annoying the crowd. Then, after twelve minutes, Alex Young tangled with Woods before slipping the ball to his partner, who beat Fred Else with a crisp shot. The referee, however, ignored the advantage rule and disallowed what seemed to be a good goal. Instead, he awarded a free-kick for a foul by Woods on Young.

Even with Jimmy Gabriel and Tony Kay working diligently, Everton showed nothing like their best form. Johnny Morrissey, Dennis Stevens and others had attempts at goal to no avail. Even worse, Alex Scott had an absolute nightmare. Vernon, shadowed by his favourite newsagent Clayton, had been inconspicuous until he produced two accelerating raids down the middle to remind everyone of his true class. Michael Charters reflected on one slalom run through his former teammates: 'After Vernon swayed his way through half-a-dozen opponents, he tried to chip the ball into the far corner of the net but put too much strength in his shot.'

With the Toffees growing frustrated, Alex Parker advanced to join his forwards. The right-back beat the offside trap by dribbling the ball past Blackburn's defenders and hitting a thunderous shot – the best of the match – just over the crossbar. Nevertheless, the crowd remained anxious. Kay and John Bray then became involved in an exchange that looked more like a wrestling bout. When the referee awarded a foul against his teammate, Vernon showed petulance unbefitting of an Everton captain. Possibly still enraged, he proceeded to miss the clearest goalscoring chance of the afternoon. Young had swept down the left-wing and expertly cut inside Woods before passing to Vernon, who hit his shot against Else's lucky legs. A little later, his exasperation peaked when he put the ball into the net only for the referee to disallow his effort for a trip on – that's right – Clayton.

At full-time, there was a modest demonstration during which a few toilet rolls were thrown as the referee was escorted from the field. In the eyes of many, Mr James Carr of Sheffield had disallowed two good goals and two legitimate appeals for penalties. But the real cause of their collective frustration was the disappointing display that had resulted in another dropped home point.

A later matchday programme, dated 15 April, admitted: 'The goalless draw with Blackburn was probably the worst game seen this season. The crowd did not take too kindly to the referee's refusal to allow the two "goals" to stand. These decisions were a disappointment to Vernon personally, as it was his 250th league appearance, and, of course, it was against his former club.'

In the *Liverpool Echo*, Michael Charters concurred: 'Having seen Everton do so well at Aston Villa, I can on say that they are consistent in their inconsistency.

Despite their heavy pressure throughout second half, they didn't look like they would score if they had played an extra hour.' The disappointment left the Merseysiders three points behind both Tottenham and Leicester, but with a game in hand over the East Midlanders.

Fixture 33: Monday, 8 April 1963
Postponed from 9 February 1963
LIVERPOOL 0 EVERTON 0
Attendance: 56,060

Just two days on, Everton ventured across Stanley Park. The midweek fixture, which had previously been postponed on 9 February, was the club's first league appearance at its old home since January 1951. Mick Meagan was preferred to George Thomson at left-back. The Scotsman was displeased and submitted a transfer request, which was approved – the board of directors didn't need the distraction at this stage of the campaign. There was silverware to be captured.

There was not one dull moment in this memorable 88th senior derby. The capacity crowd was entertained to ninety minutes of pulsating action, though no goals. In the *Echo*, Leslie Edwards was effusive in his praise for both teams: 'A more impressive contest one could scarcely imagine. There wasn't a time when the ball was not flying about the dusty pitch with astonishing accuracy. The football was fast and furious, and no player could hold the ball for long.'

While there were no goals, there was lots of goalmouth action. This included keeper Tommy Lawrence saving from Roy Vernon and frustrating Dennis Stevens; his counterpart Gordon West thwarting Alf Arrowsmith; Kevin Lewis shooting wide and the Everton skipper bursting into the box and preparing to shoot, only to be brought down from behind by the home skipper. Inexplicably, no penalty was awarded against Ron Yeats by referee Leo Callaghan. Next, Alex Young evaded full-back Ronnie Moran and dispatched a powerful shot which Lawrence turned onto the woodwork; Roger Hunt shot high, then he shot wide and Young bamboozled Yeats but Lawrence blocked his shot. Probably, the greatest moment came in the final minutes when the so-called 'Flying Pig' not only got both of his hands to a fierce drive by Vernon but held the ball to stymie the onrushing foes.

The consensus was that 0-0 was a fair outcome. It meant that the blue side of the Mersey remained in third place with nine matches to go. Leslie Edwards mused: 'Ron Yeats's head must be bruised from his many solid contacts made with the ball in the air.' He continued: 'I never saw a derby which reflected more credit on the teams for sustained effort, great skill and blistering speed, or one which reflected less credit on the fans. Is it necessary for the factions to revile each other with "under-the-arm" chants?'

Roy Vernon's tally had suffered from Everton not being awarded a penalty at Anfield nor during the previous 18 matches and him netting once in nine recent outings. Therefore, his good friend and great rival had taken a narrow lead in their race. After 33 League games, the status was Young 17 goals and Vernon 16 goals – albeit nine goals and seven penalties.

Fixture 34: Saturday, 13 April 1963

BLACKPOOL 1 EVERTON 2

Young, Scott

Attendance: 27,842

Traditionally, English title races had been decided around Easter but, with so many fixtures rescheduled, this was not the case in 1963. In fact, the season was extended by four weeks from its original end point. On Easter Saturday, Everton ventured to Bloomfield Road, with Gordon West designated skipper for the afternoon against his former club, in search of both points.

Renowned for the occasional miracle, the young goalkeeper could do nothing about the heavy rain which caused men from both sides to experience difficulties in keeping their feet. Despite the conditions, Catterick's team went ahead after five minutes. Roy Gratrix lost possession during a challenge with Alex Scott and the winger – who had his best outing since moving from Glasgow – sprinted into the penalty area and drew keeper Tony Waiters from his goal-line before playing the ball squarely to Alex Young, who casually walked the ball into the net.

Thereafter, Blackpool took control of the midfield and did most of the pressing. They spurned several chances via Pat Quinn, Ray Parry and Ray Charnley. Indeed, the hosts almost drew level when Leslie Lea raced around Mick Meagan and centred to Bruce Crawford, who placed his shot agonisingly wide from six yards. Though the visitors were unconvincing and lacked cohesion, Tony Kay almost added a second when he latched on to Young's clever flick to power a long shot, which scraped the woodwork with Waiters well and truly stranded.

The increasingly tense affair boiled over following Roy Vernon's painful collision with John McPhee. Tempers had yet to calm when the Blackpool right-half retaliated by hacking down Young from behind after he had turned Gratrix with ease and was through on goal. The referee booked McPhee for the ugly foul and awarded a free-kick on the edge of the box. Blackpool, however, did not escape punishment. The Everton inside-left tapped the ball to one side for Scott to fire under the wall and inside the post.

The second half was lifeless. Jimmy Gabriel and Kay dropped deeper to protect the 2-0 lead and Blackpool's raids were soaked up by Brain Labone and his fellow defenders. Strangely, the save of the game was made by Alex Parker. Parry pulled the ball back from the byline to Crawford and with Gordon West nowhere, Parker threw himself at the goal-bound effort while standing on the line and was successful in keeping it out. In the final minute, the Tangerines finally broke Everton's resistance. Their goal came out of the blue. Again, West failed to make a clean punch at a lofted free-kick and the ball fell to Quinn, who returned it through Labone's legs into the net. Nevertheless, the Toffees had secured a vital away win and were still in third place, with 47 points from 34 games.

With the Merseysiders showing signs of tenseness, local sportswriter Jack Rowe contemplated: 'It was far from being a good match, especially in the second half when Everton, after taking a 2-0 lead by half-time, were intent on hanging on to what they had. We did not see the Toffees as we know they can play but if other teams regard it as their right to put up a defensive front there can be no criticism of a policy which was designed to make sure of these two points for Harry Catterick's side.'

Without question, West enjoyed the day: 'Imagine me, a young lad from Barnsley, captaining such a great club. Of course, it was a massive honour for me to lead out the side – especially at my old stomping ground of Bloomfield Road. Predictably, I lost the coin toss but, thanks to Nosey Parker, we won the game and picked up the two points.'

Next on the menu were fixtures on consecutive days against Birmingham City who – with two ex-Blues Jimmy Harris and Colin Green in the ranks – were struggling next to the bottom, just above Leyton Orient. With a shoulder injury to Labone at Bloomfield Road, the manager moved Gabriel to centre-half and brought in Brian Harris at right-half.

Fixture 35: Easter Monday, 15 April 1963

EVERTON 2 BIRMINGHAM CITY 2

Scott, Young

Attendance: 50,122

Despite languishing near the trapdoor, the visitors soon grasped control of the action. The members of their giant rearguard were masters of everything in the air. Upfront, Mike Hellawell left Mick Meagan in his wake time after time. Alongside fleet-footed Jimmy Harris, he terrified the home defenders who were fortunate to have so many offside decisions go against the Birmingham forwards.

Of course, the Toffees had their moments. Alex Scott was giving former Everton left-back Colin Green a torrid time and Alex Young was sparkling, albeit infrequently. The same could not be said of his partner: 'Vernon was having an undistinguished match and the crowd was not slow to notice it,' Leslie Edwards reported in the *Liverpool Echo*. Certainly, things weren't going Everton's way in front of goal. Alex Parker provided his captain with a point-blank opportunity, but Johnny Schofield saved courageously. Next the right-back cut the ball to Scott, who set up Johnny Morrissey, only for him to balloon it over the bar. Then, amazingly, the Toffees went in front via Young, whose spectacular diving header after 27 minutes left Schofield motionless. While the crowd demanded more goals, the visitor's well-organised defence – supported by the man of the match Terry Hennessey – had other ideas and Birmingham squared things up after Hellawell beat Meagan again and passed via Bertie Auld to Jimmy Bloomfield, who was so surprised that he almost missed the sitter.

The same journalist noted: 'Everton played progressively worse and worse and Birmingham better and better.' Even after Morrissey dropped back to help Meagan, the visitors continued to press, and Ken Leek grazed the bar with header. In truth, Everton had disintegrated and went behind on 69 minutes when Auld passed to Leek, who nodded the ball beyond Gordon West. Both goals were the sort that a regular pivot would have covered comfortably.

As a direct result, the game became increasingly combative. First, Jimmy Gabriel and Jimmy Harris clashed. Next, Schofield was on the receiving end of a double challenge from Morrissey and Gabriel after he had fumbled a shot from Scott. As Birmingham looked most likely to pick up both points, Everton worked harder and harder to avoid the indignity of a home defeat and death of their silverware ambitions. Their last Goodison defeat was at the hands of Manchester City on 6 September 1961, some 34 league games ago. With things not looking promising, Scott equalised. It was a simple goal. The right-winger outpaced Green over ten yards and struck from a fine angle. Without further ado, Gabriel joined the forward-line in a nail-biting conclusion during which Green blocked a Young header on the line and Gabriel himself nodded a header against the bar and while lying on the ground almost succeeded in shooting the rebound home.

Veteran sportswriter Leslie Edwards reported on the loss of a valuable point: 'Yesterday's encounter was always interesting, always entertaining, but home followers wanted more than that. They wanted the victory which would have enabled their side to go into battle with Tottenham on better than even terms. The Londoners' 7-2 home win over Liverpool proves that, far from being a spent force, they are back to their best.' That said, it appeared that Roy Vernon had misplaced his shooting boots once again. He had produced only one goal in the last twelve league games.

The two blue sides – one from near the peak, the other from the foot of the table – met again the following day.

Fixture 36: Tuesday, 16 April 1963
BIRMINGHAM CITY 0 EVERTON 1
Vernon
Attendance: 29,719

Harry Catterick made an important change to Monday's line-up. He discovered a round peg was a better fit for a round hole and gave George Heslop his first-team debut. The reserve team pivot did not disappoint. He was dominant in the air and near flawless on the ground. In addition, left-winger Johnny Morrissey dropped deep at the outset to help left-back Mick Meagan tame Mike Hellawell, whose blistering pace had caused so much panic at Goodison.

The performance at St Andrew's was like so many others in 1963: the defence was strong, the midfield was commanding, and the forwards played polished football with an alarming lack of finish. The Merseysiders didn't take control of the proceedings until an unfortunate injury to Johnny Watts, the Birmingham defender, which reduced their opponents to ten men. Ironically, his knee injury was the aftermath of his rugged tackle on Alex Young. It wasn't the first time that robust defenders had come off second best after tangling with a member of the Dynamic Duo. Consequently, Birmingham concentrated on defending and securing a vital point. In truth, Gordon West and Johnny Schofield had only one decent save to make each throughout the ninety minutes. The Everton keeper made a flying leap to stop a thirty-yard drive from Malcolm Beard, while his Birmingham counterpart flung himself across his goal to divert a half-volley from Roy Vernon.

As the battle intensified, there were several unsavoury confrontations. One involved another squabble between Jimmy Gabriel and Jimmy Harris, an encore from Easter Monday. The referee did not spot the initial wild kick by Harris but booked Gabriel for his blatant retaliation. Next, Ken Leek was booked for a vicious foul on Alex Scott. Even though Gabriel and Tony Kay pushed forward, the forwards were listless until ten minutes from time when Roy Vernon grabbed the vital goal. Kay crossed from the byline, and by chance rather than intention, the ball bounced off Terry Hennessey to his Wales teammate, who found the target from the edge of the eighteen-yard box.

Without question, this victory was hard earned. The visitors had made heavy weather of defeating a side who were trying to stay in the First Division and who had to play over a half with one less man. Yet without finding their pre-Christmas form, the Toffees were still a serious contender, now standing in joint second place, only one point behind leaders Leicester.

For most neutrals, the meeting between the Toffees and Spurs was hailed as 'The Clash of the Titans'. In the matchday programme dated 20 April, the editor extolled: 'When the decision was taken to make this fixture all-ticket entry, it was to have been the last home match. This is not now the case, but today's game loses none of its glamour. It is vital in the quest for the championship; the positions at the pinnacle of the table being what they are, the stage is set for a memorable match.'

Fixture 37: Saturday, 20 April 1963

EVERTON 1 TOTTENHAM HOTSPUR 0

Young

Attendance: 67,650

Everton were at full-strength, with Tony Kay assigned a roving commission and Jimmy Gabriel required to do one thing – shadow Jimmy Greaves, the First

Division's leading marksman. Despite being played on a heavy, grassless pitch with strong swirling winds, the contest lived up to its pre-match hype. Catterick's team produced some of the best football of the season. However, the proceedings started with a scare for the home supporters when the burly Bobby Smith outsmarted Brian Labone to create a scoring opportunity for Greaves. The inside-forward danced into the box only to mishit his shot inches wide.

By and by, Gabriel mastered Greaves, Kay commanded the midfield by breaking up attacks and feeding The Dynamic Duo, and the remainder of the action was all Everton. And with Goodison in full voice, Alex Young scored one of the most famous goals in the club's history. Leslie Edwards captured the moment: 'When the goal came after sixteen minutes, the applause literally shook the place. I'll swear that the press box moved inches up and down from the reverberations of the din. Vernon at outside-left clipped the ball high to make it hang in the wind and offer Young a meagre chance of heading for goal. Brown left his line but never leaped to challenge the centre-forward. With his remarkable propensity for jumping half his own height off the ground, Young soared over John Smith and edged the ball high over the line. If he never scores again, he will be remembered for this historic goal.' Many press reports claimed incorrectly that the Tottenham man out-jumped by Young was Tony Marchi. In fact, the defender was John Smith, the England Under-23 international. It should have been followed by many more. Young almost got a second when he chipped the ball towards the far post, with Bill Brown and Dave Mackay having to scramble it away for a corner. His striking-partner hit the woodwork on two occasions. Johnny Morrissey smacked the ball against the upright. It bounced out to Dennis Stevens, whose shot hit the other post before Ron Henry cleared off the line.

The relentless action continued throughout the match. Brown saved bravely from both Young and Vernon. The Welshman continued to make dangerous breaks down the middle, but his shooting failed to match his fire and directness and he squandered two chances within a minute. The final twenty minutes were agonising. With their key men tiring, Everton had one or two anxious incidents. Outplayed for so long, Spurs launched attacks during which Gordon West again misjudged a couple of crosses. It would have been an injustice if they had snatched an equaliser. The forwards had more goalscoring chances than in their previous six games. If they had taken the better ones, they could have won by five goals.

There were marvellous scenes at the final whistle as Harry Catterick's team returned to the summit with only five fixtures to go. David France recalled the winning goal: 'The Old Lady was packed and in full voice. To the soundtrack of the Boys' Pen singing "London Bridge is Falling Down", we murdered Tottenham and could have won by six or even eight goals. We were that dominant. Everyone there remembers the only goal of the game, when Alex Young rose above John Smith to meet Roy Vernon's cross and sent his header over Bill Brown. Back then, and for almost a half-century, I claimed that it was the greatest goal I had ever seen and assumed it would never be equalled. However, I saw a video recording of it some months ago and it didn't appear quite as astonishing as I had thought.'

As for the wager between the two teammates, the blonde bombshell had taken a strong lead, no matter how he looked at it. After 37 games, the status was Young twenty goals and Vernon seventeen goals, that is ten real goals plus seven penalties.

After such an impressive victory over Spurs, Goodison welcomed their North London neighbours and sought revenge, in a match rescheduled from Boxing Day, for the defeat in the seven-goal thriller in March.

Fixture 38: Wednesday, 24 April 1963
Postponed from Boxing Day, December 1962
EVERTON 1 ARSENAL 1
Vernon
Attendance: 56,034

Unfortunately, things didn't turn out as planned. But for a courageous performance by Gordon West, who played the final 45 minutes with a serious shoulder injury, the Toffees might have surrendered both points to Arsenal. Leslie Edwards detailed the accident in the *Echo*: 'It happened after nineteen minutes. George Eastham's free-kick was floating into the goalmouth when Alan Skirton and the goalkeeper collided, and Gordon West was thrown violently to the ground. The action paused for three minutes while he received treatment. After such a crunching fall, the miracle was that he was able to continue.'

The Gunners were physically bigger than their hosts. These extra inches meant that the home forwards were at a disadvantage whenever the ball was in the air. Accordingly, Catterick's men played the ball on the ground early on and their sharp and artistic approach swept Arsenal off the pitch. After seven minutes, Dennis Stevens knocked the ball to Roy Vernon who hit a waspish shot, right-footed without a moment's delay, for the first goal. The two inside-forwards missed other chances, the type that must be snapped up by potential top dogs.

Even so, Everton seemed destined for another gala performance. But after 39 minutes, John MacLeod out-paced Mick Meagan and squared the ball to Geoff Strong, who with his back to goal produced an acrobatic overhead shot to make it 1-1. Undeterred, the Toffees continued to create goalscoring chances with Vernon, Stevens, Alex Scott and Tony Kay going close before the enthralling contest turned into full-blooded combat, complete with reckless two-footed lunges. Billy McCullough and Stevens were booked for trading blows, while Kay's wonderful defensive finesse was aided by some strong tackling, some of which didn't connect with the ball and caused even the home supporters to gasp.

The Londoners came more into the game and tried to test the injured goalkeeper from long-range. In the closing minutes, full-back Jimmy Magill came close with two efforts that shaved the post with West motionless. Leslie Edwards concluded: 'Everton worked hard enough for both points. The demonstrations against the visitors and referee at the finish were mild and gave the impression that many supporters considered 1-1 to be a reasonable outcome. The club face the prospect of losing Gordon West for the final four games from which they must take seven points. The West Ham fixture is the crux. Defeat there would mean that they will not finish as champions.'

West was disappointed at the prospect of not being an ever-present: 'That night match was played on my twentieth birthday. I damaged my shoulder in a mid-air collision and because there were no subs in those days I had to continue. With Brian Harris out of the side, I think that Gabby or Labby would have taken over in goal because the rest were a bunch of short arses. I received a couple of pain-killing shots. It must have been strong stuff because I don't remember most of the match. Afterwards, Labby claimed that I hadn't moved around much, and Alex Parker added that I was the best goalie he had ever played behind. But I must have had a blinder because Arsenal failed to beat me.'

There is no doubt that West's courage had helped to secure the vital point and maintain Everton's place at the top. As, of course, did the captain's goal – only his second in nine outings – which brought him within two goals of his rival with four games to go.

Next up was a trip to Upton Park and hopefully the banishment of the infamous London bogey. The game against the Hammers, a team which boasted Bobby

Moore, Martin Peters and Geoff Hurst, was Everton's ninth game in the month of April and, more importantly, it was one that they couldn't lose.

Fixture 39: Saturday, 27 April 1963

WEST HAM UNITED 1 EVERTON 2

Temple, Vernon

Attendance: 28,391

To add more punch in front of goal, Harry Catterick replaced Johnny Morrissey with Derek Temple on the left-wing, and with Gordon West recovering from his shoulder injury, Albert Dunlop came in between the sticks. Thankfully, his side kept its composure upon its return to a venue of so much contention when the Toffees were eliminated from the FA Cup. Jack Rowe observed that the visitors were booed whenever they touched the ball: 'Tony Kay kept his head and refused to be drawn into retaliating when fouled. In the end, those in the crowd who had been vociferous in their reception of him were applauding his first-class display.'

Without doubt, his teammates were up for the challenge. After Bobby Moore barged into Dennis Stevens, Jimmy Gabriel implemented his favoured free-kick routine in which he touched the ball to his skipper. Although Vernon shot low and hard under the wall of defenders, keeper Jim Standen was able to fingertip the ball away for a corner. This was followed by a free-flowing move in which almost every member of the line-up was involved, though the interplay concluded with Dennis Stevens hammering his shot straight at the goalkeeper. Then, totally against the run of play, the hosts took the lead. Peter Brabrook outpaced Alex Parker and his low cross was turned into his own net by Mick Meagan under pressure from right-winger Alan Sealey.

West Ham escaped when Vernon intercepted a back-pass from Jack Burkett to Standen but had his shot blocked. From another free-kick Gabriel and Vernon tried their usual routine, but this time the Scotsman missed the target by some distance. The Everton captain equalised in the 32nd minute when Alex Young collected a through ball from Kay and skilfully flicked it for Vernon to control and beat Standen from eight yards. Some ten minutes afterwards, they took the lead via Temple. Again, Kay started the move by passing the ball to Young, who back-heeled it into the path of Alex Scott. His shot was too hard for Standen to hold and the left-winger slipped the rebound into the net.

Troubled by badly blistered feet, Young was limping and spending most of his time on the right-wing. Even so, he was able to display his magic by skipping round three defenders in the box. In contrast, Vernon did a tremendous job of grafting and foraging in the second half when Everton concentrated more on protecting their lead. West Ham provided little in response. When they did, Brian Labone and Kay combined to mop up any danger. Kay, the man of the match, was forceful in everything he did and set the standard for the rest of his team.

Towards the end, West Ham pushed forward in increasing numbers only to be halted by Dunlop. The veteran goalkeeper excelled at catching crosses and blocking shots. Looking more reliable than West, his best saves were reserved for Martin Peters, who lashed a volley from the edge of the eighteen-yard box which he turned over masterfully, and Ken Brown, whose firm header from Sealey's corner was saved magnificently. Local journalist Jack Rowe summarised his Everton's performance: 'Catterick's team has had many fine performances in its chase for the title, but I rate the one at West Ham as one of the most outstanding, not solely because of the outcome but because of the way it was achieved. They looked like champions.'

West had watched the action from the stands: 'Putting it politely, I was miffed because I had enjoyed a run of fifty uninterrupted appearances in the first team but realised that I was going to miss the final four matches. After cheering the win over Bobby Moore and his mates, I was convinced that we were going to be crowned champions. Tony Kay had been a shrewd signing and had become extremely influential. While Gabby and Stevo had been enforcers and John Morrissey was a fearless warrior on the wing, the recruitment of Tony Kay brought Dave Mackay-like granite to the side. He presence allowed "The Goodison Darlings" of Vernon and Young more opportunities to do their magic during an era in which two-footed tackles from behind were part and parcel of the game. The fellow Yorkshireman wasn't my favourite teammate, but I admired him and his worldly ways. Perhaps because I was a little afraid of him, I predicted that he would assume the captaincy and lead us to four or five seasons of glittering success.'

	P	W	D	L	F/A	Pts
Everton	39	22	11	6	75/41	55
Tottenham	38	22	8	8	106/55	52
Leicester	38	20	12	6	75/43	52
Burnley	38	19	10	9	71/53	48

Gordon Watson hailed the newly-found camaraderie and recalled his fond memories of the train journey home from London: 'Jimmy Gabriel, Taffy Vernon and strangely Albert Dunlop were conducting a choir consisting of their teammates and supporters in a rousing chorus of "Bless 'Em All – The Long and the Short and the Tall". Their faces were beaming with the imminent expectation of glory. I looked at them with pride. By and large, they were expensive signings – the best money could buy – who had gelled into a wonderful football side. Many associate their success with Mr Moores's money, but I put it down to the players' dedication and commitment during training at Bellefield. They had earned their glory the hard way.'

Having opened a three-point gap, few Evertonians feared about the destination of the title as long as their side performed like it had at Upton Park. With their fate in their own hands with three victories required from the remaining three games, Harry Catterick selected an unchanged side for the home fixture against Bolton, who were languishing in nineteenth position.

Fixture 40: Saturday, 4 May 1963

Postponed from 2 December 1963

EVERTON 1 BOLTON WANDERERS 0

Vernon

Attendance: 52,047

The clash proved to be an anti-climax, albeit one with a favourable result, as the Toffees scraped a 1-0 win. Michael Charters pondered the team's inconsistency: 'The Everton team, unrecognisable from the classy outfit who trimmed Mighty Spurs down to size only a fortnight earlier, floundered and fumbled their way to a 1-0 victory over a side with no pretensions to being anything more than workmanlike. Prospective champions should have been capable of paralysing a team of Bolton's calibre.'

The Trotters were content to adopt defensive tactics from the start and the Toffees struggled to penetrate their barricades and battlements. Far too many moves lacked purpose and went Kay-Vernon-Young-Vernon-Kay, by which time the defenders had organised their forces. Except for the moves involving Alex Scott, the build-up was too laborious and too susceptible to Bolton's offside trap, with none of the sweeping attacks produced against Tottenham in evidence. At the other end, the home defence seemed capable of frustrating anything Bolton could produce.

The opening half was extremely dull, with the Toffees showing neither the initiative nor enterprise to beat very ordinary adversaries. The highlight was a splendid run by Scott, who took the ball some forty yards before forcing Eddie Hopkinson to make a full-length save. The first real shot of the match came from Dennis Stevens, who tried a twenty-yarder which kissed the post. In fact, the visitors came closest to scoring when Peter Deakin dribbled the ball along the goal-line and lobbed it over Albert Dunlop, only for Jimmy Gabriel to save the day.

Nerves caused mistakes galore as well as some wretched shooting. Stevens, who had fired blanks since mid-December, had a nightmare against his former club. A storm of booing broke out as the inside-right shot wide from one of his half-dozen chances. Gwladys Street's whipping boy missed another sitter after a clever body swerve from Alex Young had pulled the opponent's defence out of position. Then, from a Scott corner, he headed wide after the centre-forward had nodded the ball down to him.

Everton looked more dangerous when quicker through balls from Young and Tony Kay opened up the defence. Finally, they took the lead in 71 minutes. Stevens won the ball and passed to Gabriel who, swept the ball upfield. Both Young and Bryan Edwards went up for the ball which deflected to Vernon, who placed it beyond keeper Hopkinson. Just in time, the Blue Dragon – always the man for the big occasion – had rediscovered his form. His goal took him level with his blonde rival. After forty games, their totals were Young twenty goals and Vernon twenty goals (thirteen goals plus seven penalties).

Michael Charters shared the crowd's relief: 'When his shot hit the back of the net, it was as though a pin had burst a giant balloon and the pent-up frustration of so many thousands exploded into a massive roar.' The Trotters fought back and caused some moments of indecision on the home defence. At one corner, all but Vernon came back, and it was Young who headed clear from the six-yard line.

Charters summarised the status of title race: 'The championship is now, as expected, between Everton and Tottenham. Leicester, their eyes understandably gazing towards Wembley, lost on Saturday and with three more away matches to play can bid farewell to their hopes of the double, leaving the leading two to battle it out for the greatest prize of all. When the Toffees have completed their fixtures against Fulham next Saturday, Spurs will still have two more away matches to play, plus the final of the European Cup Winners' Cup.'

With only two games to go, Gordon West admitted: 'The worst part of being injured was having to forfeit my green jersey to Albert Dunlop, who had bullied me since my arrival. Almost five decades have passed but my impressions of him haven't changed – he was such a horrible man. Of course, to his credit he allowed only two goals in the final games of the season. The home match against Bolton should have been a pushover, but it was the toughest of the four. Though struggling in the relegation zone alongside Man United, Man City and others, Bolton made us fight – literally – for the points. Dunlop did well and kept a clean sheet against such bruising combatants. When I congratulated him in the dressing room, he ignored me.'

Fixture 41: Tuesday, 7 May 1963

Postponed from 16 February 1963

WEST BROMWICH ALBION 0 EVERTON 4

Young 2, Vernon (pen), Williams (og)

Attendance: 25,280

Everton's fate was still in their own hands. If the Toffees triumphed at The Hawthorns and defeated Fulham at home, they would be finish top no matter what Tottenham did in their remaining games. Therefore, an army of Evertonians ventured to West Brom prepared for battle and much more. However, they never ever expected their heroes to play such an important game against ten men for eighty minutes as well as benefit from a penalty award, an own goal and a farcical mix-up by two defenders to lead to a tap-in.

An unchanged team – with Albert Dunlop in goal and Derek Temple wide-left – set about their task determined to clinch two vital points. The visitors had the better of the early exchanges even before an injury to Ron Bradley. The left-half fractured his elbow and retired from the match after nine minutes. His exit provided the Mersey Millionaires with an enormous advantage.

The first goal arrived in the 37th minute. Michael Charters detailed the farcical proceedings: 'Alex Young was penalised for offside in the West Brom box and stood aside waiting for the resulting free-kick to be taken by Graham Williams. Keeper Ray Potter appealed that the number nine was encroaching and had not retreated ten yards. The referee waved play on and Williams passed the ball casually to his goalkeeper. Before Potter could react, Young had intercepted the ball and walked it into the net. Many of his teammates were amazed by his initiative.' Alex Parker laughed at the impudence of his fellow Scotsman: 'From the far end of the pitch, I couldn't believe my eyes. Even though Alex Young and Alex Scott were celebrating, I was as convinced as the opposing players that the goal would be disallowed. I turned around to look at Albert Dunlop and he mouthed "Champions! First Division champions!" They were the nicest words he ever said to me.'

Young added a second – and the goal of the match – in the 58th minute. The build-up was far more elegant. Temple sped down the wing, pushed the ball around right-back Don Howe, leapt over his outstretched leg and retrieved the ball at the byline before chipping it to the blonde Scotsman, who beat Potter comfortably. Thereafter, the Everton forwards tormented their foes. As a raiding winger, Scott gave his finest performance in a royal blue shirt. Young revelled in another artistic outing. As for Roy Vernon, he never had a better game. The way in which he brought his two wingers into the action was as effective as it was attractive.

The Toffees had two good appeals for penalties turned down when Howe dragged Dennis Stevens to the ground and then handled the ball in his own area. Eventually, when a spot kick was awarded in the 69th minute, after Stan Jones had flattened Scott, you know who maintained his 100 percent record and converted his eighth penalty of the campaign with aplomb.

Even though West Brom had suffered the misfortune of playing one man short, there is no doubting that Everton displayed the type of football usually associated with worthy champions. Albion's bad luck continued when left-back Williams put through his own goal just before full-time. Parker claimed that the football gods were smiling on him and his teammates: 'I couldn't believe our luck. We played five times against teams reduced to ten men through injuries. All were influential foes – Tom McAnearney of Wednesday, Stan Jones of Albion, Johnny Watts of Birmingham, Barrie Betts of City and finally Ron Bradley at Albion. Also, we won all five matches – many quite comfortably.'

Horace Yates acknowledged that Catterick's galaxy of stars was within sight of silverware and praised the travelling support at The Hawthorns: 'Not only was there an enormous following but they made sure that people noticed their presence with roars which swept around and around the ground – seemingly without end.'

	P	W	D	L	F/A	Pts
Everton	41	24	11	6	80/41	59
Tottenham	39	23	8	8	110/57	54
Leicester	39	20	12	7	76/45	52
Burnley	40	20	10	10	72/54	50

Brian Labone noted that the game was much easier than anticipated: 'The West Brom game was an odd one. For starters the travelling fans outnumbered and out-shouted their hosts. Their vocal support was relentless and occasionally spine-tingling. Although the Albion didn't appear to give up, they went down to ten men, gifted a daft goal, an own goal and a soft penalty. It was a hollow win, if you know what I mean?'

Alex Young added to the conspiracy theory: 'At the time I was delighted by the ease of our victory, but over the years I've been troubled that such an important match was the least demanding contest I had ever played in. At one point Taffy asked who was marking me and I had to reply: "Don't know. Not seen him all night!" Possibly, we were the beneficiaries of good fortune. I didn't complain as we headed towards the club's first piece of silverware in almost a quarter-century.' Young's two goals had taken his tally to 22 goals in 41 appearances. Vernon's spot kick had taken his total to 21 goals, of which eight were penalties, in forty games.

Parker was confident that the trophy had the name of Everton Football Club on it: 'Let's say we won at a canter. Unlike some of my Scottish pals, the title was a really big deal for me. Alex Young had won a full set of medals with Hearts and Alex Scott had done the same with Rangers. I felt confident that nothing would stop me picking up an English league medal. Certainly not Fulham at home. Some people can smell fear, I could detect the aroma of success.'

Young had retaken the lead in the unofficial race for the epithet of 'Goodison Goal King'. He admitted: 'I reminded Taffy that the he had converted eight penalties and only thirteen proper goals against my tally of 22 proper goals. I added that had I been given the chance to take spot kicks, the totals would be thirty for me and a paltry thirteen for him. Unimpressed, he complained that I had played in one more league game, so, I countered that his non-participation wasn't through injury but because he had been dropped. I teased him that I planned to take my wife Nancy out for a slap-up meal and buy some gifts for my wee children. He warned me not to count my fivers until after the Fulham game. And we all know what happened on that afternoon.'

The challenge of Tottenham had fallen away when they lost three of their six matches in April. In truth, the fixture congestion had been unkind to them. Even though the season had been extended, Spurs were required to play four games in eight days at one point. Therefore, prior to the finale, all Evertonians were aware that victory over Fulham would guarantee glory. Harry Catterick's men were five points ahead of Spurs, who had two games in hand. A victory would ensure realise John Moores' objective.

Fixture 42: Saturday, 11 May 1963
Postponed from 12 January 1963

EVERTON 4 FULHAM 1
Vernon 3, Scott
Attendance: 60,578

With Gwladys Street in full voice, the pre-match noise was tumultuous. It got even louder after five minutes thanks to Roy Vernon. Alex Parker put the ball through to the Welshman on the edge of the area. He drew Tony Macedo in and then danced around him before netting from a narrow angle. Better still, just three minutes on, he added another. The inside-left chased a long clearance from Alex Parker but an unnerved Alan Mullery got to it first and overhit his back-pass to keeper Macedo. The ball rebounded from him to Vernon who netted unopposed. The captain was invincible. The crowd was euphoric.

Although Fulham's slow and sideways passing had got them nowhere, they shocked their hosts after twenty minutes when Johnny Haynes crossed accurately for Johnny Key to volley past Albert Dunlop. In a flash, the Toffees responded. Dennis Stevens put the ball into the net from Alex Young's threaded pass, but the referee awarded a free-kick some ten yards outside the box for a foul by Bobby Keetch on the Scotsman. Everything turned out well because the champions-elect added their third from the free-kick. Taken by Vernon, the ball hit the wall of defenders and rebounded to Alex Scott, who found the target thanks to a healthy deflection.

Catterick's side had put on a first-class display. Vernon had been phenomenal. Stevens had enjoyed a magnificent game after his nightmare against Bolton. Also, Young had tormented his marker with his unparalleled artistry. It could have been more. Courtesy of the unselfish centre-forward, shots from Scott and Vernon appeared goal-bound but whistled past the post.

The cacophonous crowd had enjoyed a feast of football and, in a carnival spirit, chanted 'Ev-er-ton, Ev-er-ton, Ev-er-ton,' and the home captain put the icing on the cake when he completed his hat-trick in the 85th minute. Dunlop's long clearance was headed by Young to Vernon who again evaded Mullery, drew Macedo and struck from another acute angle to make it 4-1. All of his goals had been similar in construction and execution.

At the final whistle, the delirious fans cheered themselves hoarse. For David France, it was one of his most memorable afternoons at Goodison: 'The club would announce the results of all First Division fixtures shortly after full-time and before the lap of honour someone used the tannoy system to proclaim: "Let's see who the runners-up will be!" The crowd roared with laughter as he shared the news that Spurs had lost at Maine Road by 1-0 and Leicester had suffered a similar fate at Burnden Park by 2-0. It was royal blue heaven. I was surrounded by one big happy Everton family. We were immersed in an ocean of ecstasy – the sort of bliss that only football can provide. Little did I appreciate that we would experience this title-winning exhilaration on only three other occasions during the next 57 years and counting.'

The Everton players strolled through a lap of honour and, even though a ring of policemen prevented a pitch invasion, were pursued by photographers and about twenty schoolboys. From the press box, Michael Charters noted: 'If the Pier Head pigeons were disturbed by the noise, I would not be surprised. It was ear-shaking approval for the team and management who had amassed 20 of the last 24 points at stake.'

Then the crowd turned their attention to the Main Stand calling: 'We want Moores! We want Moores! We want Moores!' The hatless chairman – who had lost his headwear when celebrating the second goal – acknowledged their applause. In due course, he was joined by Roy Vernon with cigarette and champagne in hand and Tony Kay with cigar in mouth. It was a great moment in the club's long history. Without doubt, there was a mutual feeling of appreciation between the players and the fans.

As expected, Moores praised his manager and predicted that the team would be even better next season. He proclaimed that while winning the title was one of his great ambitions, he would have been content to have finished in the top three. The chairman added that if someone became available who the management thought would be an asset, they would move quickly for him.

As for their rivals in the title race? For the record, Leicester City surprisingly lost by 3-1 to Manchester United, who had narrowly avoided relegation, in the FA Cup final at Wembley. Tottenham Hotspur fared much better. They crushed Atlético Madrid 5-1 in the European Cup Winners' Cup final in Rotterdam to become the first British club to win a major European trophy.

The triumph was extra-special for the four Merseyside-born men in the squad – Brian Labone, Brian Harris, Derek Temple and Johnny Morrissey. For the Last of the Corinthians, it was the first of many medals earned during a career that involved 534 league and cup games for his one and only club. He reviewed his role in the final fixture: 'To be honest, I had little to do and cruised through the proceedings. Then near the end, I realised that my dream was about to come true. I would be remembered as a member of an Everton team – my boyhood club and my only club – to win the championship. Yes, I was about to go down in history alongside legendary centre-halves like TG Jones and Johnny Holt. I became quite emotional as my chest swelled with pride and got grit in my eyes. We finished with a formidable defensive record of 42 goals conceded in 42 games and an impressive away record of eleven wins and four draws. We were a very good side and worthy champions.'

There were no tears of joy for Brian Harris who did not attend the Fulham finale: 'Football can be cruel. I had been a first-team regular and played in over half of the matches but wasn't at the title-clinching game. Along with Billy Bingham, John Morrissey and George Thomson, I was required to turn out for the reserves in a meaningless Central League match at Gigg Lane which, by the way, we won 2-1. I was more than a little disappointed that four men with about 100 appearances between them should not be invited to enjoy the climax to the campaign. I thought that the boss could have rested us and played some of the up and coming youngsters so that we could have joined in the post-match celebrations. But that's the merciless nature of professional football.'

	P	W	D	L	F/A	Pts
Everton	42	25	11	6	84/42	61
Tottenham	42	23	9	10	111/62	55
Burnley	42	22	10	10	78/57	54
Leicester	42	20	12	10	79/53	52
Wolverhampton	42	20	10	12	93/65	50

The senior author affirmed the post-match euphoria: "Still in royal blue heaven, I floated along Scotland Road to Central Station. Every passing stranger – Blues and Reds alike – enquired about the final score. By the time I reached my destination, I had been transformed into a messenger of good tidings. At the station, my progress to the Widnes train was halted by an elderly gentleman. He asked: "How did we get on?" I answered: "The champions won 4-1." He asked: "Who scored?" I answered: "Scott got one and Vernon got a hat-trick." Then he smiled: "You know, Vernon will never be as good as John Willie Parker.""

FOURTH QUARTER REPORT: A JOB WELL DONE

	P	W	D	L
Home	6	3	3	0
Away	5	4	1	0

PART 5:
CHEQUE BOOK CHAMPIONS

EVERTON'S ACCOMPLISHMENT WAS TREATED WITH GRUDGING respect beyond the boundaries of Merseyside. Many labelled them 'The Cheque Book Champions'. Indeed, the club had invested £350,000 – an enormous amount in 1962 – to woo Roy Vernon, Alex Young, Tony Kay, Alex Scott, Jimmy Gabriel, Alex Parker, Gordon West and other top-class footballers. But in hindsight, John Moores was merely an ambitious trailblazer as other English clubs with billionaire backers would adopt his approach to dominate the honours and the media.

Leslie Edwards claimed that the club was at the beginning of an era which would make some of its illustrious history seem pale by comparison: 'I congratulate Roy Vernon and his team on a magnificent sprint down the finishing straight. I congratulate chairman John Moores, who has sometimes had as many kicks as the pence he's invested in his famous club and Messrs Harry Catterick and Tom Eggleston for being expert backroom boys who have done their job quietly and efficiently and never with the bull associated with teams at or near the summit. I have been critical in some matches and I daresay I shall be again, but I do acknowledge their remarkable work, their recovery when things appeared to be going against them and their belief up top that only the best will do for the Everton fan. Money still cannot buy success. It is money and knowledge which makes great teams. The signings of both Kay and Scott have been justified where it matters – on the field.'

In total, Catterick called on a squad of twenty players, with five of them appearing five or less times. As expected, The Dynamic Duo were the glory boys, however others – especially those raiding down the flanks – made meaningful contributions. The wingers chipped in with goals (Morrissey 7, Bingham 5, Scott 4, Veall 1 and Temple 1), other forwards 8 (Stevens 7 and Wignall 1), half-backs 7 (Gabriel 5, Harris 1 and Kay 1) and defenders 2 (Parker 2).

In 2008, Alex Parker attended an event entitled 'An Afternoon with The Golden Vision' hosted by Billy Butler at Radio Merseyside and gushed about the special encounter with Fulham: 'After the final whistle went, we enjoyed a lap of honour then went down into the dressing room for a glass or two of champagne. We could hear the crowd calling for us, so we went out onto the directors' balcony. The cheers were deafening. Eventually, I made my way home. Later, the lads got together at a nightclub to watch a recording of the game on television. For me, winning a championship medal in front of such loyal and knowledgeable fans was a truly memorable experience.'[6]

The right-back praised Moores, the architect of the club's revival from the relegation zone to the top of the table: 'Besides capturing the Scottish Cup with Falkirk in a previous life, I hadn't won a sausage. When I arrived in the summer of 1958, our modest first team included Wally Fielding, Dave Hickson, John King and Tommy Jones with some exciting boys on the books such as Dunlop, Meagan, Labone, Temple and Brian Harris. Four of these youngsters appeared against Fulham and shared my delight at capturing the First Division crown. But perhaps not as much as Sir John Moores. He was elated. After five years of steadfast commitment, enormous investment and hard work, he had achieved the first of his ambitious objectives.'

When interviewed by David France in 2001, Alex Scott re-visited his first five months at Everton: 'The club hadn't tasted success since the war, but I sensed that it was on the horizon. Goodison and Bellefield were like home-from-home. Alex Parker, George Thomson and Alex Young were hungry to repeat the triumphs they had enjoyed in Scotland. As for the final game, it remains a blur. I remember scoring – via a kind deflection – but little else. I was used to winning silverware draped in blue ribbons. During my Ibrox career, we captured four Scottish titles, one Scottish Cup and two Scottish League Cups. Footballers never get tired of lifting silverware. So for me, capturing the English title was just as thrilling as my first Scottish title triumph in 1956. Of course, we went on to capture the FA Cup at Wembley but there should have been more trophies draped in those blue ribbons.'[2]

With no little pride, Alex Young looked back on the key games during the season: 'The fans talk about our home win over Spurs, but I think that the one at Upton Park was the turning point. After recovering from so much slipping and sliding during the brutal winter, we were disappointed to lose at both Highbury and Bramall Lane and relax our grip on the title. Thankfully, we rediscovered our form to leave my old pal Dave Mackay and his teammates trailing in our wake with a final total of 61 points – a club record. Spurs were a quality side, but we finished six points ahead of them with an unblemished home record. I had won my first

Scottish League title as a pup alongside Dave at Hearts. We had battered the likes of Celtic and Rangers in a one-horse race. In fact, we dropped only six points and amassed 132 goals and conceded only 29 to make a goal difference of 103. Perhaps because I was older, I appreciated the one with Everton even more.'[2]

Even though he had made only five first-team appearances, Derek Temple waxed lyrical about the campaign: 'Taffy's quickness of mind and movement plus his thunderbolt shot made him some player. As a right footed inside-left, however, he would instinctively cut inside rather than involve his left-winger. Like every prolific striker, Taffy was a selfish bugger. Though I shared the number eleven shirt with Roy Veall and John Morrissey, I had the good fortune to deputise for the latter during the run-in. With Spurs distracted by a European final, the Foxes pre-occupied with an FA Cup final and Taffy basking in a terrific vein of form – six goals in the final four games – we enjoyed a smooth conclusion to the season. I like to think that I did my bit by netting the winner at Upton Park. I don't remember much about it except for Jim Standen – a county cricketer – spilling a shot into my path. We were worthy champions. For a boyhood Blue like me, it was a thrill to join Taffy and the lads during the lap of honour. The fans were so passionate. For once, I didn't mind them calling me "Shirley".'

Tony Kay highlighted the contributions of the unsung heroes: 'While the class and fabulous skills of Vernon and Young hogged the spotlight and the adoration of the crowd, we were very strong across the midfield. For me, it was the graft of Gabriel, Stevens and Morrissey, who were not lauded lavishly by press but were willing to run until they dropped, that clinched the title. They were warriors covered in blood – not always their own.'

Brian Labone promoted those of his fellow defenders: 'Spurs amassed 111 League goals but finished runners up in 1963. Why? Well, football is full of wise sayings, some true and some obsolete. One of the most enduring is "Defence wins championship titles." Although we racked up 84 goals with The Dynamic Duo contributing 46 of them, we were successful because we allowed only 42 league goals, an average of one goal conceded per game. My fellow defenders West, Parker, Thomson, Meagan and Gabriel should take a deep bow. While Taffy and Alex captured the headlines, the unsung heroes were Mick Meagan and Jimmy Gabriel. Not surprisingly, our defenders secured the title again in 1970. While the Holy Trinity of Kendall, Harvey and Ball hogged the glory, my fellow defenders allowed only 34 league goals. This time, West, Wright, Brown and Hurst should take an even deeper bow. I don't care what pundits say – goals may be sexy but impervious defences win championship titles.'

ALLEGATIONS OF WRONGDOING

THERE WAS TO BE AN UNEXPECTED TWIST. IN THE 4 SEPTEMBER 1964 edition of The People newspaper, Albert Dunlop made a ludicrous accusation that some teammates – including Vernon and Young – were drug-addled cheats and the title triumph owed much to the use of Drinamyl and Benzedrine. The goalkeeper claimed: 'They were distributed in the dressing rooms during training and an hour before matches. We didn't have to take them, but most the players did. We would take up to four pills before big matches. Soon some players could not do without the drugs.' The club's directors issued a statement that denied any complicity in the drug use but did admit some mild stimulants had been used entirely as a matter of personal choice and medically, we are told, these pills, in the quantities taken, could not possibly have had any harmful effect on any player.' In due course, Messrs Vernon, Young and Parker gave instructions for writs to be issued against The People in October 1964, regarding a false statement made in that newspaper.

Gordon Watson was appalled by these claims: 'Dunlop was the most disliked man at the club. While his loutish behaviour worsened after the arrival of Gordon West, he liked to draw attention to himself by threatening to sell his story to the tabloids, and shortly after his departure to Wrexham, The People newspaper claimed that we captured the title because he and his teammates took drugs. He claimed that amphetamines were distributed in the dressing rooms before all matches. To my amazement, the club acknowledged that some mild stimulants had been used by the players as a matter of personal choice. This was news to me. The only stimulants I saw were a strong mug of tea, a sip of whisky, a drag of nicotine, a chug of glucose, an injection of cortisone and a kick up the backside. I understand that purple hearts enhance alertness and a general feeling of well-being. Personally, I would have thought that pulling on an Everton jersey had the same effect. Perhaps I was naïve and didn't know what was going on around me. I hope so because I believe that we were crowned champions because we were a team of expensively assembled, well-organised, supremely talented footballers who ran their socks off for the royal blue cause.'[2]

He added: 'My own career was influenced indirectly by performance enhancers and I enjoyed a long run of outings after a 7-0 humiliation at Molineux. Led by Major Frank Buckley, Wolves used monkey testicle tissue to improve the stamina of their stars. After they crushed Leicester by 10-1, the Football League carried out an investigation and declared that players could take glands but only on a voluntary basis. In truth, I'm a bit disappointed by Dunlop's words. I had expected him to conjure up a more sensational headline: Taffy Vernon Smokes Monkey Glands in the Goodison Tunnel!'[2]

After Dunlop's claims had been dismissed and almost forgotten, Alex Parker hailed his captain's contributions, especially his composure from twelve yards: 'Roy could be a bit of a hot-head during games but was a cucumber cool penalty taker. He was without nerves. Possibly, it had something to do with the nicotine in his blood. Although we had several men who were accomplished from twelve yards, no one got a sniff of a chance. There was George Thomson – the penalty specialist at Hearts during their productive league and cup campaigns, Alex Scott – who had a hard and accurate shot with his right foot, plus Gordon West – who had a kick like a horse and secretly fancied himself as a buccaneering striker. And, of course, yours truly. Because Dave Hickson didn't like to take them and Tommy Jones was injured, I converted my one and only effort against Villa in early 1959 but didn't get another look in. Penalties were Taffy's domain. He practiced his technique every day even when Bobby Collins had been designated the match day duty. Also, Alex Young never got to take one. In the 60s, he would work on penalties now and then in training with Brian Harris, who was a decent emergency goalie. I don't think Brian saved many but Alex being Alex wasn't happy unless he had sent the bamboozled goalkeeper the wrong way. Alex complained that he had been allowed to take only one direct free-kick during his time at Everton, from which he scored. Set-pieces were the preserve of Taffy and Gabby.'

GOODISON GOAL KING 1963

ALEX SCOTT HAILED THE GOALSCORING PARTNERSHIP OF VERNON and Young: 'They were an impressive double act – Labby referred to them as the Pinky and Perky of marksmen. I'm not sure which was which, but they bagged 46 goals between them that season. It's odd that some claim Alex was inconsistent. Far from it. While he was no Jimmy Greaves, who mustered forty goals for

Tottenham, Alex had only one lean patch which lasted a half-dozen games. That's something that even prolific goalscorers like Greaves experience at one time or another. Of course, Taffy stole the headlines with his fantastic hat-trick against Fulham. Before that match, he had chalked up only thirteen goals from open play, about half the number he had got the previous season.'[2]

As for the conclusion of the royal blue wager, Taffy conjured up eight strikes in the final seven matches – including his famous hat-trick on the final day of the season – and finished as the team's leading marksman with 24 league goals. His playmate bagged 22. A review of the goals credited to the Dynamic Duo shows that, possibly due to the departure of Bobby Collins, Vernon had failed to find the lethal goalscoring form exhibited in previous campaigns. Alex Parker was alarmed that his pal had started so slowly: 'Taffy kept his place by netting a penalty kick almost every game. I think we had seven or eight in the ten games – which is a strange statistic because we had only one in the next thirty games and two during the previous twenty games. His goals from the spot masked his Sahara-type dry spell in which he found the net only twice from open play during the first three months and caused him to be rested at the start of November. He had a similar drought after the Big Freeze in early 1963 and was lucky not to have been dropped again after his listless performance against Birmingham at Easter. Of course, he rediscovered his shooting boots and averaged a goal a game during the final six or seven games.'

There was no transfer of monies between them. Instead they both made generous gifts to unsung heroes: Gordon Watson, Ron Lewin and the other coaching staff. Why? Well one week after the famous achievement, the club awarded bonuses to the manager, secretary, coaches, groundsman and other staff. Taffy was shocked to discover via the Bellefield grapevine that the boss would receive £2,000 and his sidekick £500, while Watson and Lewin would receive only £50 each.

Alex Young explained: 'Gordon had been inspirational. There wasn't a more dedicated Evertonian at the club – not even Labby. He showed us how to pass on snow-covered surfaces, nursed our wounds, bandaged my blistered feet, improved our confidence when things weren't going to plan. His wife even darned our woollen socks. We thought that the bonuses offered to Gordon and Ron were derisory. Taffy was even more irritated. In his position as club captain, unofficial shop-steward and royal blue pain in the arse, he complained to secretary Bill

Dickinson that Gordon should receive a league winner's medal to go along with the one he had won as a player in 1939. I don't think that the coach/trainer got one but I do know that Mr Dickinson did.'

That summer, the newly enthroned 'Goodison Goal King' was interviewed by Jerry Dawson. Rarely shy to speak his mind, Roy Vernon offered only short and direct responses to questions about his and Everton's season:

Q: What was your reaction when the whistle blew for the end of the game with Fulham?

RV: I was delighted – for everyone's sake. The pressure had been on since Easter when we knew we had a good chance of the title, and we all felt it was in our grasp when we scored two goals in the first eleven minutes of the game.

Q: Which would you have preferred to have won – the league or the FA Cup?

RV: A From a personal view, the FA Cup – it has more glamour attached to it. But from a club perspective, it's the league and its associated entry into the European Cup.

Q: What do you think has been the biggest factor in your winning the Championship?

RV: No argument: team spirit. Not that we always agree – we don't – but our differences are thrashed out at meetings. They really are discussions with everyone chipping in.

Q: As leading scorer, which [goals] do you feel were: Your most important? Best? Jammiest?

RV: The goal against Bolton in May, which gave us two points when all seemed set for a draw, was very important. One of my best goals was against Sheffield United in November when, luckily, I sent two men running the wrong way after picking up the ball in midfield. My 'jammiest' was the one against Birmingham at Easter. Tony Kay centred, a defender mis-headed and the ball dropped at my feet. I took a swipe towards the goalkeeper's right, but as he dived, the ball skidded off my feet and rolled into the opposite corner.

Q: Did the captaincy make it a more difficult season for you?

RV: It didn't worry me a scrap. The manager and trainers lay down policy and tactics, and the boys have enough intelligence to carry out their duties without prompting from me.

Q: Do you think Everton have won the title chiefly on their home record?

RV: Definitely not. We played very well away, and set a club record for eleven away victories.

Q: Everton have been criticised by some London journalists for their tactics and the behaviour of their supporters. Has the side deliberately played roughly?

RV: I strongly refute the rough tag. We play hard, yes – soccer is a man's game. We may have a hard team, but we go in fairly. And our supporters are the best in the land.

Q: Are your supporters as black as they have been painted?

RV: At Goodison, the club has no trouble with the supporters. It can't control the few – and they are a few – who misbehave outside our or any other ground. It was once reported that cushions had been thrown into the directors' box – it was one cushion, thrown by a man holding a complimentary ticket.

Q: There was a lot of controversy last season about referees. Did you find them to tough?

RV: Some of the newer referees were a bit extreme due to inexperience. But the old hands can still handle a game with a word here and there, and without major demonstrations. I feel that standards could be raised by employing full-time refs. We suffered a little from what we thought were harsh or wrong decisions.

Q: Do you think all players in a team should be paid the same amount?

RV: I believe that the present system in which every player negotiates his own terms. I'm satisfied with my own arrangements. If anyone in the team gets more, good luck to him. Also, I think all contracts should be honoured, by players as well as by clubs.

At the start of the next campaign, John Moores reinforced his ambitions in matchday programme, dated 17 August 1963: 'It gives me great pleasure to welcome you all to Goodison Park for a new season of football which we hope will be at least as memorable as the last one. Our success enables us to participate in two extra competitions – the FA Charity Shield and the European Cup. This afternoon's match could hardly be more attractive and in the European Cup we have been paired with Internazionale, one of the stronger teams in Europe. Whatever happens, you can be sure that Everton want first and foremost to play good football. We must defeat our opponents by skill with the ball. Last time our players showed they could do. We have done it in Britain, now let us do it in Europe as well.'

FOND MEMORIES OF TAFFY

LIKE ROY VERNON, MANY OTHER KEY MEMBERS OF THE 1962/63 title-winning side have passed away. However, during his pioneering work associated with Gwladys Street's Hall of Fame and the Everton Former Players' Foundation between 1998 and 2010, David France took the initiative to cross-examine many of them to gather their memories about the 1962/63 campaign and, of course, about skipper Roy Vernon.

First up was Brian Labone (1940-2006) who led the club to an FA Cup victory in 1966 and the league championship in 1970: 'You've heard the clichés: colourful, tempestuous and headstrong. Chain smoker, gambler and bit of a lad. Well, most of them are true, but Taffy was an extra-special striker. Quick, cunning, incisive, the ruthless assassin had honed his knack for being in the right place at the right time. Therefore, it was no surprise to me that he was our top goalscorer year after year and hailed as one of our most lethal predators of the post-war era. And yes, he liked to challenge authority. After greyhound racing, it was his favourite hobby. While Johnny Carey tolerated his rebellious temperament, Harry Catterick didn't. The manager was a disciplinarian who expected his sidekicks – Tommy Eggleston and Gordon Watson – to keep the superstar quiet. As a captain, Taffy wasn't a consensus builder or an inspirational leader and only the boss knew why the Welshman had been appointed, but he guided us to the title. However, like many of my teammates, I appreciated the peace and quiet after he moved on to Stoke.'[2]

Labone admitted: 'There was a special bond between Taffy and the Jocks. I referred to them as the Celtic Clique. It was something Harry Catterick discouraged. Like him, I thought it wasn't good for team morale. The Dynamic Duo enjoyed a flutter. Alex preferred the horses, whereas Taffy would bet on anything. At the dog track, he would place bets on which greyhound would win and which would finish last. I sensed that there was a battle to be top-dog, but it's a good job that the boss and his lieutenants were kept in the dark. Mr Catterick needed only the slightest excuse to banish both of them to the Central League.'

Gordon West (1943-2012) added: 'Labby told me about their rivalry after the championship confetti had blown away. It couldn't have been a serious bet because Alex was so generous in teeing up so many opportunities for Taffy, especially during the skipper's dry spells – and there were a few of them. While the Scotsman lacked the selfishness of a Jimmy Greaves, the Welshman didn't.'[2]

Like most custodians, the one-time world's most expensive goalkeeper was impressed by his captain's prowess from the penalty spot: 'Pure and simple, Taffy possessed a wicked shot. With minimum back-lift, his thunderbolts would sting my palms during training. All Evertonians know that he was "The Deadeye Kid", with his venomous spot kicks a few inches off the ground and a few inches inside the goalpost. At Bellefield, he would alternate left then right then left again. On occasions, he would show off and point to the spot where he planned to put the ball. Very rarely did I save one. Even then, I suspected that he allowed me to do so in order that I didn't become too disheartened. He must be one of the finest penalty kings in the history of the game.'

Few defenders forget their first encounters with the Welshman, and Alex Parker (1935-2010) wasn't one of them: 'My first exposure to Taffy was during the Scotland-Wales clash at Hampden in 1957. The visitors had some top-class footballers and I had my hands full containing a turbo-charged outside-left named Cliff Jones. Partnering him was the thinnest man I had ever seen play international football. Honestly, my initial impression of the twenty-year-old inside-left was that he needed to eat more porridge and wouldn't last five minutes in the Scottish League. Then shortly after we had taken the lead through Bobby Collins, I played a short pass out wide to Alex Scott and Taffy made a sly stamp on my ankle after the goal had gone, which deserved some kilted retribution. Bobby Evans, Tommy Docherty and, of course, Bobby Collins sought vengeance, but none of them could get close to him. He was too fast, too illusive, too thin. Subsequently, both of us were lured to Goodison by the desire of John Moores to pay top wages and for his teams to play cultured football. We became great pals, so much so that I liked to remind him about his deliberate stamping of my ankle in Glasgow with his left boot and that I had yet to see him kick a football with it. Nowadays, comparisons are made with Denis Law – who could be a bit naughty also – and Jimmy Greaves. From my experiences, I would rate the Scotsman as the better footballer, the Englishman as the better goalscorer and, without any hesitation, the Welshman as the best smoker of the three.'

The international right-back noted the big influence that Scots have had on Merseyside football: 'During my playing days at Everton, there was George Thomson, Sandy Brown, Alex Scott, Bobby Collins, Jimmy Gabriel, Alex Young, Eddie O'Hara, Tommy Ring... and Taffy Vernon. Of course, Taffy was a proud Welshman but, as an honorary Scotsman, liked to join our social gatherings with

Willie Stevenson, Ron Yeats and Ian St John from Anfield. It took him some time to understand our dialects, fondness for a wee dram of single malt and nostalgia for the poetry of Rabbie Burns, but Taffy matured into a typical friendly Scotsman – you know the type that will call an ambulance before thumping you.'

Next, the unsung heroes of the team. Dennis Stevens (1933-2012) noted: 'We all did our bit, but Taffy and Alex played a crucial part in our title win. Together, they formed a devastating partnership. It's one of many Everton mysteries why their combination was broken up to accommodate Fred Pickering. Of course, another is why they sold Bobby Collins and bought me.'

Winger Derek Temple, who would progress to bathe in Wembley glory in 1966, made a handful of appearances during the run-in: 'I'm sure the rest of his teammates have said the same thing. Taffy was a great player. His finishing was second to none, especially during the final and perhaps most crucial games of the season. He had the utmost confidence in his own ability, especially smashing the ball into the net. The fans used to claim that he was as thin as a rake and elusive as a Welsh unicorn and whenever Taffy entered the penalty area he would turn sideways so that defenders couldn't see him.'

Never missing an opportunity to supplement his wages, Roy impressed some – if not all – of his teammates. Tony Kay noted: 'I liked Taffy. He was worldly and something of an entrepreneur who liked a bit of wheeling and dealing together with a bit of betting on the horses and greyhounds. One of his infamous ventures involved Rufford Jack, who let's say was a bit of a spiv. It involved the sale of tea salvaged from a shipwreck. I better not say any more.' Roy Parnell concurred: 'Everyone – even the younger lads like me – received a Wembley final ticket. Shortly after we got them, Roy would be waiting outside our dressing room to buy them off us. He paid almost twice the face value.'

Closer to home, Colin Green, his young teammate at Everton, spoke of his frightening pace: 'When we played together for Wales, he was unbelievable – the quickest thing over eight or nine yards you have ever seen – quick as lightning. But after twelve yards he was goosed. If he did 100 yards, you'd have needed a calendar, not a stopwatch, to time him.' Cliff Jones, the flying winger at Tottenham Hotspur and another of Roy's international teammates, concurred: 'I much preferred playing with him than against him. He was deceptively quick, had an edge to him and got his share of goals. He was a bit of a lad and someone who mixed well. We always called him Taffy Vernon – and that was the Welsh lads.'

This leads us to Gordon Watson. An overlooked and often forgotten character in the club's history, the soft-spoken Geordie played alongside Dean and Sagar, captured the league championship with Lawton, coached the likes of Young and Vernon and oversaw the development of Harvey and Royle. Again, the senior author chatted regularly with his old pal before his passing in 2001. Their interactions resulted in the production of Gwladys Street's Blue Book, which log his memories of the first men at the 'School of Science' to be crowned league champions since his own playing days in the late 30s.

From his home and his hospital bed, Watson paid tribute to Roy Vernon: 'Older Evertonians love to talk about the goals and magic of Roy Vernon and Alex Young. Why? That's easy. I've never seen such a partnership and that includes Dixie and Nat Cunliffe, Dave and John Willie Parker, Big Joe and Jimmy Husband, Graeme and Gary Lineker. They were so easy on the eye.'

'Having spent sixty-odd years – in one capacity or another – at Everton Football Club, I've seen my fair share of mavericks and odd fish. There have been some belters. Often prone to recklessness, some strived to replicate the euphoria associated with professional football on their nights out. Billy Cook loved a drink or two, Jock Dodds liked an argument or two and Tommy Eglington welcomed the craic. And when it came to nicotine, Taffy Vernon and Harry Cooke were untouchable. Both used a dying fag to light the next one. Seriously, they created an ICI-like smog in the treatment room.'

'When you spend morning and afternoons training and coaching young footballers, you become family and get to know their inner struggles. For example, Taffy was disappointed by the decision to replace Johnny Carey with Harry Catterick and I was charged by Tommy Eggleston, Harry's right-hand man, with helping him adjust to the new and more rigorous training methods and much more. The latter included keeping him out of trouble by encouraging him to think twice before opening his mouth. Both were challenging tasks. As a player, I was impressed by his great technique, superb balance, fearless courage and more than a bit of the devil. He could be unplayable on matchdays but possibly the least enthusiastic participant in training. When it came to sweating in a tracksuit, he was up there with dry-as-a-bone Nobby Fielding and perspiration-free George Thomson.'

'Taffy struggled to adapt to the stricter code of conduct, especially the timekeeping element. Everyone had to sign in at Bellefield. No exceptions. At

10:00am sharp, I had the unenviable task of drawing a red line, under which the latecomers had to sign. No exceptions. They were all treated like naughty schoolboys. Nevertheless, we got along. I think he was impressed by my tales of playing alongside Dixie.'

'While the problem is much bigger nowadays, some stars in the 60s were seduced by the few extra quid in their pockets and the excess spare time on their hands. For his part, Harry Catterick maintained a list of men who he thought lacked stability and needed watching. This leads me to another unenviable task. My relationship with Taffy was damaged after he spotted me patrolling Manchester Street near the Royal Tiger and Yates's Wine Lodge looking for cars with familiar license plates on Friday nights.

I've been teetotal all of my life and therefore had never entered either establishment. I understand, however, that journalists, actors and musicians patronised the nightclub and budding alcoholics frequented the pub. While the younger footballers liked to let their hair down on Tuesday and Thursday nights, because they could sweat out the toxins during training the following morning, they were banned from drinking on Fridays. I hated being a snitch and was so embarrassed that I preferred not to mention his transgressions to the manager. Still, he never trusted me again.'

'When it comes to the 1963 crown, I remain convinced that we captured the trophy thanks to some impressive defending as much as the goalscoring of Vernon and Young. We forfeited only one goal per game and, in doing so, turned previous losses into hard-earned draws and previous draws into narrow victories. Therefore, I suggest that no little praise should go to unheralded defenders such as Gordon West – still a teenager – Alex Parker, Mick Meagan and Brian Labone as well as the midfield shield of Gabriel, Kay and Stevens. The latter deserves significant praise. Unsung Dennis had a Rolls Royce engine like that of his cousin Duncan Edwards and worked tirelessly in every game. In addition to tackling opponents and intercepting passes to protect his defenders, he found the energy to support the glamour duo in the box. Alex would condition his praise: "Dennis is Mr Perpetual Motion but is no Bobby Collins," whereas Roy was far more generous. He appreciated the fact that Dennis would dispense retribution to anyone who even thought about kicking the Welshman.'

'Besides being a free-spirit and a real handful, Taffy was an exceptional footballer. He reminded me of a hard-headed whippet with the sting of a bad-tempered wasp. It's sad that he never got to make an appearance at the Hall of Fame dinners and hear how much Evertonians loved him. I'm sure that he would have enjoyed the hero worship and adulation.'

Finally, there remains the words of the other half of the Dynamic Duo – Alex Young. The senior author interviewed his dear friend on many occasions between 1996 and his death in 2017. Their collaborations resulted in the production of the biography titled Alex Young – The Golden Vision and the documentary, namely Alex the Great.

With a smile on his face, Alex cast his mind back to his times with Roy Vernon both on and off the pitch: 'Our paths first crossed when I played for Scotland at Ninian Park in 1960. Indeed, Taffy scored Wales's second goal in a 2-0 triumph. My first impression of him? He reminded me of a malnourished Denis Law except that he was one-footed and impotent in the air. I liked the fact that he shared Law's combative spirit. Without question, he could take care of himself on the pitch. About a month later, I bumped into him again during my first visit to the home dressing room at Goodison. I had yet to agree terms, but Mr Carey wanted me to relish the atmosphere under Everton's massive floodlights.'

'It was crammed with old pals from Scotland – Alex Parker, Bobby Collins, Jimmy Gabriel and Tommy Ring (on crutches) – a couple of other big money signings – Billy Bingham and Mickey Lill (also on crutches) – as well as a gang of Scousers – Albert Dunlop, Tommy Jones, Brian Harris and Derek Temple. But I gravitated towards an immaculately dressed man seated quietly by the door. Taffy confided that had been sent off a few weeks earlier and was serving his suspension on the naughty bench. While young centre-forwards such as Jimmy Harris and Frank Wignall viewed my presence with suspicion, he greeted me like a long-lost brother and, in an almost religious ceremony, offered me a cigarette. This ritual of the sharing of tobacco was the start of a great friendship.'

'Surprisingly, we didn't gel at first. During one sequence of fifteen league games, he netted only twice. Even worse, I had fired all blanks. Troubled that we were, failing to realise our potential, we worked extra hard at improving our understanding of each other's strengths and blending our talents. More specifically, we concentrated on exploiting his electrifying acceleration over five to fifteen yards and his fierce shot. As an inside-left who was all right foot, he had the knack of making perfect contact with the football. Together we practiced cushioning balls towards his lethal right boot and clipping balls into space for him to run on to. Also, I taught him to dribble around goalies, something he may dispute. By the end of that season, our interactions became telepathic and our partnership became one of – if not – the most productive in the club's long history. Taffy had scored 26, I had added fourteen and Everton recovered to finish fourth.'

'We continued to score goals for fun and pushed each other to earn the title of the club's top scorer. The record books show that he won with his 24 league goals to my 22 [in the title-winning campaign], but I've often joked that his ten goals from the penalty spot shouldn't count. Whenever my dear pal bragged about his superior tally, I liked to remind him: "I made plenty of chances for you but can't remember any provided by you. You're a greedy so-and-so!"'

'Incredibly, the 1962/63 title was our only silverware together. I believe things would have been different if the champions of England hadn't met the champions of Italy in the qualifying round of the European Cup. The games against Inter Milan in 1963 had significant impacts on the club and its international profile. If only Taffy's effort hadn't been disallowed in the home game? If only we hadn't lost the services of Tony Kay for the final seven games of the 1963/64 season? If only we had delayed the signing of the prolific Fred Pickering to the start of the new season? If only? If only? As events transpired, we tumbled from the summit after coming a cropper at The Hawthorns and picked up only three points from our final five games [at the end of the 1964/65 campaign].'

'Compared to the rest of us, Taffy was worldly-wise and savvy – not unlike Alan Ball – and wasn't shy in presenting his case for more money. He loved his pounds, shillings and pence and ensured that he was the highest paid player because, after every new arrival, he complained to Harry Catterick about his "pitiful pay" and inadequate bonuses for goals and gates. Eventually, friction developed between the captain, manager Catterick and chairman Moores and he was discarded. During my career, I was saddened to see Dave Mackay leave Hearts and Bobby Collins leave Everton, but I was traumatised by Taffy's exit to Stoke. Even though his predatory powers were on the wane, I didn't know how we would replace his impressive technique, uncommon turn of speed and razor-sharp instincts.'

'I'm disheartened that my old pal has been almost forgotten. Taffy was a genuine star whose glittering goals captured glittering silverware. Besides being one of only eight Everton captains to have lifted the famous league trophy and averaging a goal every two games (much higher than the stats of Dave Hickson, Alan Ball, Duncan Ferguson and, of course, yours truly), he remains the only

Evertonian qualified to smoke in the showers without drenching his precious Senior Service cigarettes. Once he was accused falsely of smoking when entering the pitch, but in those days we had little ammonia capsules to liven you up before the game. You stick it up your nose and it got your attention. That said, Taffy did stub his fags out in the special ash trays installed halfway down the tunnel. Only kidding.'

For captain Roy Vernon, his teammates and all Everton supporters, the 1962/63 season had been a glorious experience. Alex Young concluded by addressing the magnetism of Mr Moores's cheque book: 'Little John had assembled a galaxy of stars. Like my soulmate Roy Vernon, I was proud to be one of them. But our success was down to a team effort. Vernon and Young didn't win the league, Everton Football Club did. The media made a big deal about us competing for the European Cup, but I would have preferred the club to have concentrated on creating a football dynasty by winning the league title again and again and again.'[2]

APPENDIX B

Recollections of Royston

'Lifting the league trophy is one of the greatest moments of my life. It was extra special to be following in the footsteps of Roy Vernon, a fellow Flintshire lad and Wales international, who had led my club to the title a couple of decades earlier.'

Kevin Ratcliffe

Neville Smith

Slight build, confident demeanour, whippet-like pace and a lethal right foot, Roy would lurk around the eighteen-yard box then strike with the precision of a mob hitman. He was the cleanest striker of a ball I have ever seen and the ideal partner for Alex Young. We loved to celebrate their goals by singing: 'Bless 'em all, bless 'em all – the long and the short and the tall. Bless Wee Alex and Royston too, bless all the boys who are wearing royal blue.' Joe Royle claims that Alex Young's divine skills made people fall over. From what I saw, Roy Vernon's sharp elbows did the same thing.

Tony Kelly

I have never seen anyone like him. His party-trick was dribbling round the goalie – you don't see British footballers do that nowadays. In addition, he had a shot like a thunderbolt. Like all good footballers, he was a snide with an edge to his game, someone who knows when to leave his foot in – a bit of a dirty bastard.

Gavin Buckland

As both team captain and potent goalscorer, Roy Vernon was possibly Everton's most important player in the first half of the 60s. His standing, however, has been eclipsed by contemporaries such as Alex Young. Consequently, Vernon's vital contributions during the 1962/63 season have been overshadowed by the drama of the FA Cup triumph and the dominance of the Holy Trinity towards the dusk of that decade. Because his early death in 1993 predates the nostalgia boom – especially the raucous Hall of Fame celebrations – there have been few opportunities to elevate his profile with younger fans and the charismatic Welshman remains one of the club's finest post-war players.

Paul Kelly

We were awarded lots of them [penalties] in the early 60s as rugged defenders attempted to tame the trickery of Alex Young. It seemed ironic that the Scotsman would get kicked black and blue and his mate would get the glory of netting from twelve yards. All his penalties were powerful daisy cutters and over time he adopted the arrogance of pointing to the spot where he intended to hammer the ball. The record books show, but I don't remember, that he missed one at Tottenham when he scuffed his effort.

Jimmy O'Neill (Everton)

The FA Cup loss at Third Division Bradford City in early 1960 was the turning point in the club's fortunes. Mr Moores was so angry that he burst into the dressing room and expressed his disappointment. His rollicking didn't go down well with Bobby Collins and they had a public exchange of opinions, something that the wee Scotsman regretted immediately and the billionaire never forgot. Within a month Mr Moores had written giant cheques to sign Tommy Ring, Mickey Lill and Taffy Vernon. Straight away, the Welshman established a productive relationship with Bobby Collins and Jimmy Harris and their goals ensured our safety. During that ten-game spell, Taffy nabbed a goal a game and his partners added a good half-dozen each. Overnight, gates almost doubled to 65,000. In the pre-match dressing room, Taffy would ask: 'Boys, can you hear the turnstiles clicking? It's bonus time.'

Len Capeling

Royston was the perfect footballer. Balance, pace, flair, ability to deceive goalkeepers with a shimmy and knack of putting the ball into the net – he had the lot. He scored over 100 goals in his league games for Everton – always taken with a swagger – and I probably saw ninety of them. On his day he was unstoppable. In my head, I can visualize him about to score against Fulham in 1963. He looks like a ballet star.

Jack Simmons MBE

People forget that I played football for Great Harwood in the Lancashire Combination as well as professional cricket in the Lancashire Cricket League. My memory isn't so good but think I trained with Roy at Wood Street, but don't remember playing alongside him in league or cup games. After I joined Lancashire County CC in 1969, I wasn't allowed to play competitive football. It had to do with the fact that, a few years earlier, I had broken my leg on three different occasions during one ten-month period at the Showground. Of course, I met Roy on several occasions there. In addition to talking football, he liked to gamble. Again, I can't remember whether he was a card shark or not, but Roy was one of the finest footballers of his generation.

Aiden Maher

I had watched Royston before I joined the club as an apprentice. He was as skinny as a rat but deceptively strong and not easy to knock off the ball. Like Bobby Collins and Alan Ball, he was very passionate and took great pride in playing for Everton Football Club. The nice thing about Roy and his teammates was their interest in the development of the younger lads. Some would come to reserve games and, the following day, advise us that we should have done this or that. It was very helpful.

Peter Fisher

Royston was the greatest player in our post-war history and a man for the big occasion. He possessed the rare skill and confidence of scoring goals from any angle, along with the ability to pirouette round goalies. When he on the pitch alongside Alex Young, we feared nobody.

Lord John Grantchester

Roy and Alex were favourites of my grandfather, Sir John Moores. Living with my parents in Kingston-On-Thames, I only got to visit Liverpool in school holidays. Once there, I was always keen to visit Goodison with him, which meant all three generations going together. They were memorable outings as my grandfather loved to share his time with fans and hear their opinions. One Saturday, quite probably at the start of the 1962/63 season, he borrowed my autograph book and disappeared like an excited schoolboy into the team's changing room. He returned with a huge smile on his face. It was no wider than the one across mine after I saw the autographs of Alex Young on one page facing that of Roy Vernon on another. I was thrilled to bits but perhaps not as happy as him.

Chris Williams (born in Hans Road)

By 1960, I knew I was watching something special in Royston. In those days skilful players had to get their retaliation in first. Consequently, he was arrogant, bad-tempered and inclined to put it about, but his skill, touch, pace, shot and passing ability were awesome. On his day he was the best and he knew it. Like all great sportsmen, the greats can do it when it matters. His partnership with Alex Young was greater than the sum of its parts. Two greatly gifted artisans at their peak, confident in their own and each other's ability.

George Orr

What a player. With his ability to release rocket-like shots with laser precision, Vernon could have scored goals for any team, in any league, in any era. As hard as nails, he was rarely knocked off the ball even by opponents three stone heavier than him. With a knack of finding Alex Young instinctively, I suspected that he could have been Britain's first blindfolded professional footballer. Sadly, in the eyes of some – especially Harry Catterick – Roy was a disruptive rebel and was offloaded without ceremony.

Chris Williams (born in Winslow Street)

When supporters of my vintage get together, we usually get misty-eyed over Roy Vernon and Alex Young. The Golden Vision has a lounge at Goodison, had a testimonial (as have other luminaries from our history) but whither Roy Vernon? Where's his recognition? I suppose because of Ken Loach's film The Golden Vision, the light around Alex would always be brighter. He is an Everton icon and rightly so. But Roy – in my view – was bigger, better and more effective. Probably our most bad-tempered player ever, he was as tough as old boots and a fully paid-up member of the awkward squad, but he did everything with style. That was part of his appeal. I feel lucky that I witnessed his magic. Evertonians should recognise Royston – my hero – in some tangible way.

Ronny Goodlass

Vernon should always be mentioned when talking about great strikers. As a nine-year-old season-ticket holder in the Upper Bullens Road Stand, I went to the match with my dad and Granddad. It was a special time to be an Evertonian. The partnership between Vernon and Young was one made in football heaven. I don't think I was alone in thinking that Roy wasn't the most athletic-looking footballer, but despite his wiry physique, he had the knack of unsettling the biggest defenders and not giving them a moment's peace. Perhaps it had something to do with the fact that he was as tough as nails. Looking back, I think he brought joy to the life of this young Evertonian every time he pulled on the number ten shirt.

Billy Johnson

In the early 60s, I was arrested, along with my teenage friend John Flynn, for playing football in the street. We were by Prince Rupert School on Mill Road. I discovered at the cop shop that the lads had been warned to stop before I joined in. When we went to court, Roy Vernon was there for a traffic offence – leaving his car overnight in Lime Street Station. He defended himself but lost. The magistrate was probably a Red. We were fined ten shillings. We chatted to Roy and he laughed out loud when we told him why we were there.

John Duffy

My treasured memory is of meeting him and shaking his hand. It was 1963 and I was a ten-year-old playing football for St Joan of Arc in Bootle. Our school team had won our league and were gathered in the church hall excited that our football teacher had invited someone famous to present our medals. Then in walked Roy Vernon. A true gentleman.

Trevor Lynes

Vernon, along with Collins and Young, were a phenomenal trio of crowd-pleasers. Roy edged out Alex as my favourite because he thrived on the physical side of Merseyside derbies. He was very similar to Ian Rush as a predator and, on his day, was unstoppable. Certainly, he has provided me more excitement and pleasure than any other number ten.

Albert Perkins

Nowadays, there aren't professional footballers or characters like him. I recall one warm-up when he deliberately kicked the ball into the crowd near me and as he reached for the ball grabbed a ciggie from a supporter's mouth, took a drag and returned it.

David Brown

Some fifty years after his last appearance at the Victoria Ground, Roy Vernon remains one of my favourites. While he struggled to reach the heights of his Everton days and niggling injuries disrupted his appearances, there were many occasions when he looked top class. My best memories include a brilliant solo effort at home to Man Utd in 1966 – he dribbled past several defenders and the goalkeeper before rolling the ball across the line; a superbly taken goal against Cardiff in a 1968 FA Cup tie – he showed exquisite close control before drilling his shot into the corner; a star-turn in Dennis Viollet's testimonial game in 1967, and his last game against Wednesday in 1969 when he totally dominated the game.

Harry Berry

A frail lad when he arrived at Blackburn as an amateur, it was crystal clear that he could play. Roy was quick, good on the ball and when he hit the ball, even those old heavy balls, it flew. He got around the field, put in the tackles and never backed down when anyone tried to intimidate him. Slowly you realised that his lack of size was not a handicap. I understand that he was not an easy man to handle off the field. The Christmas before he left for Everton, he was the instigator of a players' protest against the privileges that the club was giving to Ronnie Clayton. It was a pity because on the field he was a complete footballer.

Ken Rogers

Roy was a class act in Everton's great Welsh tradition, one of the top inside-forwards of his era who could glide through games and win them with that trusty right foot. He scored over 100 goals for Everton and I was a young teenager standing on the Gwladys Street terrace at that time, supremely proud as we swept to the 1963 title. Perhaps we were too enthralled, even all consumed, with the legend of the Golden Vision to truly appreciate the delicate skills and cutting edge of Roy Vernon, who wasn't one of those drawn to Merseyside after his great days were behind him. Perhaps this was why other names claimed and retained our focus. Roy moved on and we were soon lauding these new super heroes whose names roll off the tongue. Nevertheless, he was a key building block in our 'School of Soccer Science' and someone we should never forget.

Fred Cumpstey

In Roy Vernon and Bryan Douglas, Rovers spawned the two most naturally gifted and influential footballers in the club's history. In any era of football, their stock would be of the highest level. Both ended their careers as inside-forwards having initially found success as wingers, but that is where the comparison ends. Roy had the slightest of frames – a passing breeze could have blown him over – and didn't resemble anyone's idea of a footballer, but with his slick black hair and his oiled thighs he was a master craftsman.

Aided by Eddie Quigley, he developed the talent of being the cleanest striker of a football I've ever seen. Roy could spray passes all over the pitch and land them on a tanner. He possessed a thunderbolt of a shot and that great quality of the exceptional player: an acute football brain. He could see an opportunity two or three moves before it opened. He had supreme confidence in his own ability, but perhaps was frustrated by those around him who didn't possess one ounce of his ability. His passing, short or long, was often subtle but always sublime. His work rate on and off the ball was magnificent. Set against all of that he has been described as temperamental and petulant, but most likely that was what shaped him.

Frank Keegan

As a nine-year-old, I was captivated by Alex Young's apparent ability to glide over any sort of surface. But it was his striking partner who became my hero. Pencil thin, Vernon seemed, like Young, physically incapable of matching up to, never mind bettering, giant defenders. But better them they did. Whilst Young was rapier thrusts, his partner was the dagger straight to the heart. He scored many great goals. One of my top picks was against Bolton at Goodison in 1963. A cameraman captured it with a sequence of stills, with the final frame showing the goalie on his knees along with an army of defenders who he had slalomed past to nab the only goal of the game and keep us on the road to the title.

Rick Tarleton

When, in the early hours of the morning, I find myself wide awake, I usually drift to thoughts of things blue and the winter of 1962/63, the coldest I can remember, when Everton ruled supreme. My Everton was that of Young and Vernon. Enough has been written of 'The Golden Ghost', rechristened 'The Golden Vision' for the seminal play. He is rightly celebrated as a footballer of the highest class. But it's Royston Vernon on whom I wish to focus. More than the captain of that magnificent team and more than a prolific goalscorer, he often dropped back into midfield to feed his wide men with superbly weighted passes. No one ever felt Vernon was soft; he was, to put it bluntly, a dirty player, one who thrived in the heated atmosphere of the Merseyside derbies of the mid-60s. If Young looked golden, Vernon looked distinctly seedy – more at home in a betting shop. However, he reigned supreme at Goodison. He had a bag of trademark tricks including running up to a defender, pointing to the left-hand corner flag and rapidly accelerating away to the right. It seemed to work time after time. Yet, when Evertonians talk of their greatest players, Vernon's name is rarely mentioned. How has one of the finest to wear the royal blue and white of Everton slipped below the radar?

Derek Thomas

As a striker Roy Vernon was in the Ian Rush – Gary Lineker mold, using his speed of brain and foot to get in behind defenders. But he was much more than a tap-in merchant. Roy could hit them from distance too. And when he hit them, they stayed hit. When required, the Welshman could be a true inside-forward sitting deeper, tackling opponents and picking passes all day long. The trouble was that Roy knew his own mind and spoke it too. Also he loved a late night out, which didn't help matters. While Catterick turned a blind eye when Roy was firing on all cylinders, the manager didn't need any extra excuse to get rid when his form dropped.

Chris Sawyer

Roy Vernon disliked being closely marked from behind. Because he was usually up against a robust centre-half – and therefore not in a fair fight, Roy had a habit of back-heeling them in the shins, which could disrupt their game.

Jay Harris

Roy was such an amazing footballer that I revered him more than The Golden Vision. Sacrilege, I know. My abiding memory is the way he would weave around defenders and then the goalkeeper before planting the ball in the net. Of course, he was a bit of a lad. It wasn't just the smoking that was an issue for him. I remember one incident when he was stranded on the beach near Crosby from the night before and missed the team coach. I think that was the beginning of the end as far as Harry Catterick was concerned.

David Prentice

Vernon was a footballer I only saw in black and white photographs, flickering black and white video clips, black and white newspaper articles but those images, clips and cuttings all told the story of a kaleidoscopically colourful character – an uncompromising individual who did things his way. Whether that was smoking pre- and post-match – and even at half-time – standing up to Harry Catterick's omnipotence or playing the game the way he felt it should be played, Vernon was unshakeable in his resolve. A black and white footballer to me, but a royal blue legend to all who witnessed him.

CAREER DETAILS

Statistics: Clubs

BLACKBURN ROVERS

	League		Cups		Europe		Total	
	App	Goals	App	Goals	App	Goals	App	Goals
1955/56	12	1	1	0	-	-	13	1
1956/67	31	11	1	0	-	-	32	11
1957/58	37	15	6	0	-	-	43	15
1958/59	36	16	2	1	-	-	38	17
1959/60	15	6	3	2	-	-	18	8
Total	**131**	**49**	**13**	**3**	**-**	**-**	**144**	**52**

EVERTON

	League		Cups		Europe		Total	
	App	Goals	App	Goals	App	Goals	App	Goals
1959/60	12	9	0	0	-	-	12	9
1960/61	39	21	5	1	-	-	44	22
1961/62	37	26	3	2	-	-	40	28
1962/63	41	24	3	3	2	0	46	27
1963/64	31	18	6	3	2	0	39	21
1964/65	16	3	0	0	3	1	19	4
Total	**176**	**101**	**17**	**9**	**7**	**1**	**200**	**111**

STOKE CITY

	League		Cups		Europe		Total	
	App	Goals	App	Goals	App	Goals	App	Goals
1964/65	10	5	0	0	-	-	10	5
1965/66	31	10	5	1	-	-	36	11
1966/67	20	4	1	0	-	-	21	4
1967/68	19	2	4	1	-	-	23	3
1968/69	5+3	1	2	0	-	-	7+3	1
1969/70	0	0	0	0	-	-	0	0
Total	85+3	22	12	3	-	-	97+3	24

HALIFAX TOWN - ON LOAN

	League		Cups		Europe		Total	
	App	Goals	App	Goals	App	Goals	App	Goals
1969/70	4	0	0	0	-	-	4	0
Total	4	0	0	0	-	-	4	0

ENGLISH CLUBS TOTAL

	League		Cups		Europe		Total	
	App	Goals	App	Goals	App	Goals	App	Goals
Total	396+3	172	42	14	7	1	445+3	187

OTHER CLUBS

Mostyn YMCA (1952-54)	not available
Cleveland Stokers (1967)	11 appearance, 2 goals
Cape Town (1970)	not available
Great Harwood	not available

Statistics: Wales

WITH BLACKBURN ROVERS: 9 APPEARANCES, 1 GOAL

Date	Fixture	Result	Goals	Competition
10 Apr 1957	Northern Ireland v Wales	0-0		British Home Championship
1 May 1957	Wales v Czechoslovakia	1-0	(1 goal)	World Cup qualifier
19 May 1957	East Germany v Wales	2-1		World Cup qualifier
26 May 1957	Czechoslovakia v Wales	2-0		World Cup qualifier
25 Sep 1957	Wales v East Germany	4-1		World Cup qualifier
19 Oct 1957	Wales v England	0-4		British Home Championship
13 Nov 1957	Scotland v Wales	1-1		British Home Championship
15 Jun 1958	Sweden v Wales	0-0		World Cup finals
18 Oct 1958	Wales v Scotland	0-3		British Home Championship

WITH EVERTON: 13 APPEARANCES, 1 GOAL

Date	Fixture	Result	Goals	Competition
6 Apr 1960	Wales v Northern Ireland	3-2		British Home Championship
28 Sep 1960	Republic of Ireland v Wales	2-3		Friendly
22 Oct 1960	Wales v Scotland	2-0	(1 goal)	British Home Championship
23 Nov 1960	England v Wales	5-1		British Home Championship
11 Apr 1962	Wales v Northern Ireland	4-0	-	British Home Championship
12 May 1962	Brazil v Wales	3-1		Friendly
16 May 1962	Brazil v Wales	3-1		Friendly
22 May 1962	Mexico v Wales	2-1		Friendly
20 Oct 1962	Wales v Scotland	2-3		British Home Championship
7 Nov 1962	Hungary v Wales	3-1		European Championship
21 Nov 1962	England v Wales	4-0		British Home Championship
12 Oct 1963	Wales v England	0-4		British Home Championship
20 Nov 1963	Scotland v Wales	2-1		British Home Championship

WITH STOKE CITY: 10 APPEARANCES, 6 GOALS

Date	Fixture	Result	Goals	Competition
17 Mar 1965	Wales v Greece	4-1	(1 goal)	World Cup qualifier
31 Mar 1965	Northern Ireland v Wales	0-5	(2 goals)	British Home Championship
1 May 1965	Italy v Wales	4-1		Friendly
2 Oct 1965	Wales v England	0-0		British Home Championship
27 Oct 1965	Wales v USSR	2-1	(1 goal)	World Cup qualifier
24 Nov 1965	Scotland v Wales	4-1		British Home Championship
1 Dec 1965	Wales v Denmark	4-2	(2 goals)	World Cup qualifier
30 Mar 1966	Wales v Northern Ireland	1-4		British Home Championship
12 Apr 1967	Northern Ireland v Wales	0-0		European Championship qualifier
21 Oct 1967	Wales v England	0-3		European Championship qualifier

Wales International Totals: 32 appearances, 8 goals

Acknowledgements

THIS BOOK COULD NOT HAVE BEEN POSSIBLE WITHOUT THE HELP and cooperation of many people.

Sincere thanks to the Sawyer family: Paula, Sian, Ceri and Joan.

Sincere gratitude to Elizabeth France for her indefatigable patience.

Thanks to Norma Vernon and her children, who have been helpful in sharing recollections and granting access to family documents and photographs and to Gary Edwards for his research into his uncle's early years.

The authors would like to acknowledge Billy Smith, who has dedicated decades researching and transcribing newspaper archives for his website, bluecorrespondent.co.uk, and Steve Johnson, who has spent a lifetime compiling comprehensive statistics related to all competitive games involving Everton. His website – evertonresults.com – was used to verify match and player details. Also they are indebted to the trustees of The Everton Collection and the staff at the Liverpool Record Office for providing access to the world's finest and most complete collection of memorabilia and an unrivalled source of information about Roy Vernon and his teammates.

Many thanks to Bill Kenwright, who very kindly provided an insightful foreword to the book. Also they express their appreciation to John Roberts who toiled through an early manuscript and made many useful suggestions, their colleagues at the EFC Heritage Society – the trailblazing group which documents and celebrates the history of Everton – who came to their aid on numerous occasions and Fred Cumpstey, who was an invaluable source of information and first-hand recollections of Roy Vernon's time at Blackburn Rovers.

This book would not have been published without the Kickstarter campaign organised by deCoubertin Books in mid-2019. Both authors are indebted to

Lyndon Lloyd and Michael Kenrick at ToffeeWeb for their generous promotion of the initiative and, and of course, to the 187 backers whose generous pledges surpassed the campaign goal.

Many others provided contributions and encouragement. They include: Dave Abrahams, Bill Atkins, Ian Ball, Mick Bernard, Harry Berry, Mike Berry, David Brown, Harry Burrows, Len Capeling, Barry Cass, Roy Cavanagh, Robert Clarke, Tommy Clayton, Peter Coates, Brendan Connolly, Terry Conroy, Charles Culshaw, Phil Cunliffe, David Currie, Eric Curwen, Bryan Douglas, John Duffy, Alan Durban, George Eastham, Janet Edwards, Mike Ellis, Ken Farrington, Peter Fisher, Rob Gill, Richie Gillham, Gerry Glover, Lord John Grantchester, Colin Green, Darren Griffiths, Jay Harris, Jimmy Harris, Colin Harvey, Ian Herbert, Bernie Horne, Bert Hulse, Jimmy Husband, Mike Jackman, Pete Jackson, Hyder Jawad, Gwyn Jenkins, Lorna Jenner, James Johnson, Cliff Jones, Howard Jones, Matt Jones, Mel Jones, Ray Jones, Sylvia Jones, Tony Kay, Frank Keegan, Paul Kelly, John Leonard, Graham Lewis, Andy MacLeod. Aiden Maher, John Mahoney, John McFarlane Sr, Michael McGrath, Peter McPartland, Bill McQueen, Mick Meagan, Johnny Meynell, Bill Minshull, John Moore, John Morrissey, John Murray, Geoff Nulty, Mel Nurse, Tony Onslow, George Orr, Dave Parker, Simon Paul, Dave Pearson, Mike Pejic, Alf Perkins, Rob Philpott, Ethel Powell, Dave Prentice, Thomas Regan, Ken Rogers, Mike Royden, Joe Royle, Billy Russell, Paul Salt, Chris Sawyer, George Sharples, Geoff Shaw, Bryan Shenton, Terry Simpson, Alex Smith, Denis Smith, Willie Stevenson, Ian St John, Stephen Stokes, Fred Street, Howard Talbot, Becky Tallentire, Derek Temple, Derek Thomas, Ray Veall, Alex Wallace, Dave Whelan, Terry White, Frank Wignall, Chris Williams (Hans Road), Chris Williams (Winslow Street), Graham Williams (West Bromwich Albion), John Wiltshire, Dennis Yaeger, Nancy Young and Steve Zocek. Sadly, some contributors passed away before the book's publication. These include Tony Kelly, Fred Pickering, Graham Williams (Everton) and John Worsdale.

Finally, the authors would like to express their unbounded gratitude to James Corbett, Jack Gordon Brown and Megan Pollard at deCoubertin Books and to Thomas Regan for his cover design, Amanda Lewis for her expert photo restorations and Leslie Priestley for his skilled typesetting.

Bibliography

Books

Alex Young, The Golden Vision, *David France* (Skript Publishing, 2008)

A-Z of Stoke City, *Tony Matthews* (Breedon Books, 1997)

Blackburn Rovers: An A-Z, *Dean Hayes* (Palatine Books, 1993)

Blackburn Rovers: An Illustrated History, *Mike Jackman*
(Breedon Books, 1995)

Blackburn Rovers: The Complete Record, *Mike Jackman*
(Breedon Books, 2009)

Brian Harris, The Authorised Biography, *Chris Westcott*
(Tempus Publishing, 2003)

Colin Harvey's Everton Secrets, *John Keith/Colin Harvey* (Sport Media, 2005)

Dr Everton's Magnificent Obsession, *David France and David Prentice*
(Sport Media, 2008)

Everton Crazy, Sixty Seasons, Two Million Miles, *David France* (GSHOF, 2016)

Everton Greats, Where are They Now?, *Jon Berman and Malcolm Dome*
(Mainstream Publishing, 1997)

Everton in the Sixties: A Golden Era, *George Orr* (Blue Blood, 1997)

Everton Player by Player, *Ivan Ponting* (Hamlyn, 1998)

Everton Proud, *David France* (GSHOF, 2017)

Everton: The Official Centenary History, *John Roberts* (Mayflower, 1978)

Everton: The Official Complete Record, *Steve Johnson*
(deCoubertin Books, 2016)

Everton: The School of Science, *James Corbett* (deCoubertin Books, 2010)

Faith of our Families, *James Corbett* (deCoubertin Books, 2018)

Goals at Goodison, *Alex Young* (Pelham Books 1968)

Goodison Glory, *Ken Rodgers* (Breedon Books, 2000)

Gwladys Street's Hall of Fame, *David France* (Skript Publishing, 1999)

Gwladys Street's Blue Book, *David France & David Prentice*
(Skript Publishing, 2002)

Harry Catterick, The Untold Story of a Football Great, *Rob Sawyer*
(deCoubertin Books, 2014)

Money Can't Buy Us Love, G*avin Buckland* (deCoubertin Books, 2019)

Real Footballers' Wives: The First Ladies of Everton, *Becky Tallentire*
(Mainstream Publishing, 2012)

Ronnie Clayton: A Slave to Soccer, *Ronnie Clayton* (Stanley Paul, 1960)

Still Talking Blue, *Becky Tallentire* (Mainstream Media, 2001)

Talking Blue, *Becky Tallentire* (Breedon Books, 2004)

The Encyclopaedia of Stoke City: 1868-1994, *Tony Matthews with Peter Wyatt*
(Stoke City 1994)

The Everton Encyclopedia, *James Corbett* (deCoubertin Books, 2012)

The Legends of Stoke City, *Tony Matthews* (Breedon Books, 2008)

The Official Everton Autobiography, *compiled by James Cleary*
(Sport Media, 2012)

The People's Club, *David Prentice* (Sport Media, 2007)

The Pride of North Wales Football, *Mark Currie and Gareth Bicknell*
(Sport Media, 2009)

Three Sides of the Mersey, *Rogan Taylor and Andrew Ward with John Williams*
(Robson Books, 1993)

Toffee Pages, The Post-War Years, *David France* (Skript Publishing, 1997)

Tony Waddington: Director of a Working Man's Ballet, *John Leonard* (Pitch
Publishing, 2018)

When Pelé Broke Our Hearts, *Mario Risoli* (Ashley Drake Publishing, 1998)

Who's Who of Welsh International Soccer Players,
Gareth M. Davies and Ian Garland (Bridge Books, 1991)

You Don't Remember Me Do You? The Autobiography of Terry Conroy,
Terry Conroy (Pitch Publishing 2015)

Newspapers and Periodicals
Blackburn Rovers matchday programme

Blackburn Times

Daily Express

Daily Mail

Daily Mirror

Daily Post (North Wales edition)

Everton Football Club matchday programme

Lancashire Evening Telegraph

Liverpool Daily Post

Liverpool Echo/Liverpool Echo and Evening Express

Liverpool Football Echo

Stoke City Football Club matchday programme

The Sentinel/Evening Sentinel

The People

The Herald

The Evertonian magazine

Online
Blue Blood fanzine

bluecorrespondent.co.uk

Clarets Mad fanzine

evertoncollection.org.uk

evertonresults.com

greatharwoodtown.co.uk

news-herald.com

nsno.co.uk

ToffeeWeb.com

Welsh Football Data Archive (www.wfda.co.uk)

When Skies Are Grey fanzine

Radio
BBC Radio Lancashire (Great Harwood feature – April 2019)

Suggested other reading

If you enjoyed this book and wish to delve further into the context of Roy Vernon's football career, the following may be of interest:

To learn more about the experiences of Norma Vernon and other Everton footballer's wives over the decades, Real Footballers' Wives – The First Ladies of Everton by Becky Tallentire (self-published e-book available on Amazon) is highly recommended.

Manager Johnny Carey's tenure at Ewood Park is covered in Mike Jackman's Blackburn Rovers: An Illustrated History (Breedon Books, 2006) and Gentleman John: The Biography of Johnny Carey, Manchester United and Ireland Legend by Roy Cavanagh and Carl Abbott (publisher unknown, 2018).

For an insight into how Everton operated under Harry Catterick and John Moores in the 1960's, Gavin Buckland's book Money Can't Buy Us Love (deCoubertin Books, 2019), offers an unparalleled level of detail.

Also, to understand how manager Tony Waddington revived Stoke City's fortunes in the 1960s with a band of seasoned professionals – culminating in the 1972 League Cup triumph – seek out Tony Waddington – Director of a Working Man's Ballet by John Leonard (Pitch Publishing, 2018).

Roll of Honour

This book was made possible by the many backers who committed funds to the successful Kickstarter campaign held in July 2019. Kickstarter.com exists to help bring such creative projects to life.

Hyder Jawád	Frank Leyland Powell	Andrew Davies
Kenneth Giles	John Dela	Dave Lewis
Dave Barker	Geoff Harrison	Fred Cumpstey
Mike Comber	Danny Reynolds	Steve Green
Alan Dunn	Gurvinder Singh Sandher	Paul MacDonald
Steve Mahon	Paul McMorine	Ben Moore
Elizabeth France	Joan Sawyer	Colin Lord
Maria Jaques	Darren Arnold	Ian Cant
Neil Poole	Ed Dagnall	Richard M Clist
Chris Marks	Robert Pendleton	John Williams
Mark Atherton	Kevin Markey	Geoff Pearl
Jonathan Meynell	Jamie Roche	Steven Jones
Steve Henshall	Pete Owen	John Auld
Kevin Wood	Steve McBride	Andy Weir
Vincent Taylor	Mark Allsop	John Guy
Dave Rusk	Marie O'Connor	David Deas
Mick Summers	Jack Thornton	Andy Clarke
Gordon Dale	Sue Brown	Keith Parsons
John Hughes	John Hardie	Duncan Lewis
Martin Conroy	Hugh Hamlin	Craig McDonald
Tony Horne	Rich Ferrie	David Benn
Ron Symington	Bernard Ormrod	Richard Humphrey

Pete MacKereth

Frank Thomas

George Bond

Gary Gavan

Ian Robert Lewis

Chris Williams

Eifion Williams

Jim Sloan

Paul Turton

Lisa Edwards

David Giles

Mike Kempson

Jenny Ehrhardt

Tommy Malone

Chris Moody

John Waddington

James Bryan

Janet Edwards

Anthony W Diggle

Chris Cowton

Bill Todd

Jason Murray

Steve Rogers

Neil Bennett

Gerard Cannon

Phil Martin

Dennis Lamb

The Entwistle Family

Tom the Toffee

Joe Harrison

Matthew & Joshua Myers

Michael Rogers

Andrew Roberts

Derek Jackson

Jimmy Walker

Gary Edwards

Will Schlotzhauer

David Briscoe

Matthew Brazier

James Yoxall

Lyndon Lloyd

Chris Owens

Joseph B McGuinness

Rev. Euron Hughes

Anthony William Doran

Steve McAlister

Patrick Cushion

Harold Somers

Phil Parker

Lily Remy Vanderwerff

Michael Ward

Gary Daniel James Jones

Michael Hardman

Frank Malone

Bryan Maddocks

Dennis Stevens

Brian Peter

Mike Styles

Jim Townson

Brendan Connolly

Martin Bainbridge

Paul & Katie Owens

Vin McFarlane

David Dickin

Billy Ross

John Clarke

Andrew Cope

Ian Murray

Paul Fowler

Bernard Walker

Trevor Edwards

Bill Cooper

Stephen Dutton

Eddie Patterson

Ian Stewart

Ian MacDonald

Anthony Fletcher

John Blain

Mark Campbell

Alex Whyles

Alan Rex Barrett

Chris Ainsworth

www.decoubertin.co.uk